The Family Handyman

Home Improvement

2007

The Family Handyman

Home Improvement

2007

by The Editors of *The Family Handyman* magazine

THE FAMILY HANDYMAN HOME IMPROVEMENT 2007
(See page 288 for complete staff listing.)
Executive Editor: Spike Carlsen
Managing Editor: Mary Flanagan
Contributing Designers: Teresa Marrone, Bruce Bohnenstingl
Contributing Copy Editors: Donna Bierbach, Peggy Parker
Indexing: Stephanie Reymann
Marketing Director: Kristen Kochan

Editor in Chief: Ken Collier
President, U.S. Publishing: Bonnie Kintzer Bachar
Group Director, Home & Garden Group: Kerry Bianchi

ISBN 0–7621–0853-3

Address any comments about *The Family Handyman Home Improvement 2007* to:
Editor, Home Improvement 2007
2915 Commers Drive, Suite 700
Eagan, MN 55121

To order additional copies of *The Family Handyman Home Improvement 2007,* call 1-800-344-2560.

For more Reader's Digest products and information, visit our Web site at www.rd.com.
For more about *The Family Handyman* magazine, visit www.familyhandyman.com.

Printed in the United States of America.
1 3 5 7 9 10 8 6 4 2

INTRODUCTION

Fifteen years ago we used to give my brother-in-law, Ray, a hard time about his do-it-yourself prowess. The only tools he had were two battered screwdrivers, a 3-ft. measuring tape he'd gotten as a promotional item and a worn-out hammer stashed in the back of the junk drawer. As for lumber, he had a single 2x2 standing in the corner of his garage.

We got a lot of mileage out of kidding Ray about his 2x2—but then something happened. He painted a bedroom and added a few brushes and rollers to his tool stash. He hung some pictures and acquired a small level and a stud finder. On his 35th birthday I gave him a subscription to *The Family Handyman* magazine. Then, one momentous day, he decided to not only install a towel bar, but to buy a drill—his first power tool. Slowly but surely, Ray added

tools to his new toolbox, lumber to his new lumber rack and confidence to his new home improvement mindset.

Today, Ray is a bona fide do-it-yourselfer. He has a workbench cluttered with tools and his 2x2 has lots of company. When something breaks, he no longer picks up the phone. Now he picks up his toolbox and magazine back issues. He's built shelves for the family room, and he's talking about building a deck.

Learning how to improve, maintain and repair your home is like learning how to do anything else. You learn from your successes and mistakes. You have good days and bad. But one thing is certain; you'll learn faster and better when you have the right instructions and information. That's what you'll find in this book. Dig in.

—The crew at *The Family Handyman* magazine

Contents

INTERIOR PROJECTS, REPAIRS & REMODELING

ELECTRICAL & HI-TECH

PLUMBING, HEATING & APPLIANCES

WOODWORKING & FURNITURE

EXTERIOR MAINTENANCE & REPAIRS

OUTDOOR STRUCTURES & LANDSCAPING

AUTO & GARAGE

SAFETY FIRST–ALWAYS!

Tackling home improvement projects and repairs can be endlessly rewarding. But, as most of us know, with the rewards come risks. DIYers use chainsaws, climb ladders and tear into walls that can contain big and hazardous surprises.

The good news is, armed with the right knowledge, tools and procedures, homeowners can minimize risk. As you go about your home improvement projects and repairs, stay alert for these hazards:

Aluminum wiring

Aluminum wiring, installed in about 7 million homes between 1965 and 1973, requires special techniques and materials to make safe connections. This wiring is dull gray, not the dull orange characteristic of copper. Hire a licensed electrician certified to work with it. For more information visit www.inspect-ny.com/aluminum.htm.

Asbestos

Texture sprayed on ceilings before 1978, adhesives and tiles for vinyl and asphalt floors before 1980, and vermiculite insulation (with gray granules) all may contain asbestos. Other building materials, made between 1940 and 1980, could also contain asbestos. If you suspect that materials you're removing or working around contain asbestos, contact your health department or visit www.epa.gov/asbestos for information.

Backdrafting

As you make your home more energy-efficient and airtight, existing ducts and chimneys can't always successfully vent combustion gases, including potentially deadly carbon monoxide (CO). Install a UL-listed CO detector.

Buried utilities

Call your local utility companies to have them mark underground gas, electrical, water and telephone lines before digging. Or call the North American One-Call Referral System at (888) 258-0808.

Five-gallon buckets

Since 1984 more than 200 children have drowned in 5-gallon buckets. Store empty buckets upside down and store those containing liquids with the cover securely snapped.

Lead paint

If your home was built before 1979, it may contain lead paint, which is a serious health hazard, especially for children six and under. Take precautions when you scrape or remove it. Contact your public health department for detailed safety information or call (800) 424-LEAD to receive an information pamphlet.

Spontaneous combustion

Rags saturated with oil finishes like Danish oil and linseed oil, and oil-based paints and stains can spontaneously combust if left bunched up. Always dry them outdoors, spread out loosely. When the oil has thoroughly dried, you can safely throw them in the trash.

Mini-blind and other window covering cords

Since 1991, more than 160 children have died of strangulation from window covering cords. Most accidents occur when infants in cribs near windows become entangled in looped cords or when toddlers looking out windows or climbing furniture lose their footing and becoming wrapped up in cords. Recalls, regulations, new products and new designs have lessened the dangers, but older existing window covering cords still pose a threat, and some experts maintain that no corded window treatment—old or new—is completely safe. In addition, some older vinyl blinds present a lead poisoning threat. For more information visit www.windowblindskillchildren.org or the Consumer Product Safety Commission at www.cpsc.gov. or (800) 638-2772.

1 Interior Projects, Repairs & Remodeling

IN THIS CHAPTER

HomeCare & Repair

TIPS, FIXES & GEAR FOR A TROUBLE-FREE HOME

10 TIPS FROM VACUUM PROS TO CLEAN CARPET THOROUGHLY & FAST

You might think there's nothing more to vacuuming wall-to-wall carpet than running the machine across it. But folks who spend hours each day behind a vacuum know better. To stay in business, they have to do the job both effectively and efficiently. Here are some of their techniques for fast, thorough vacuuming:

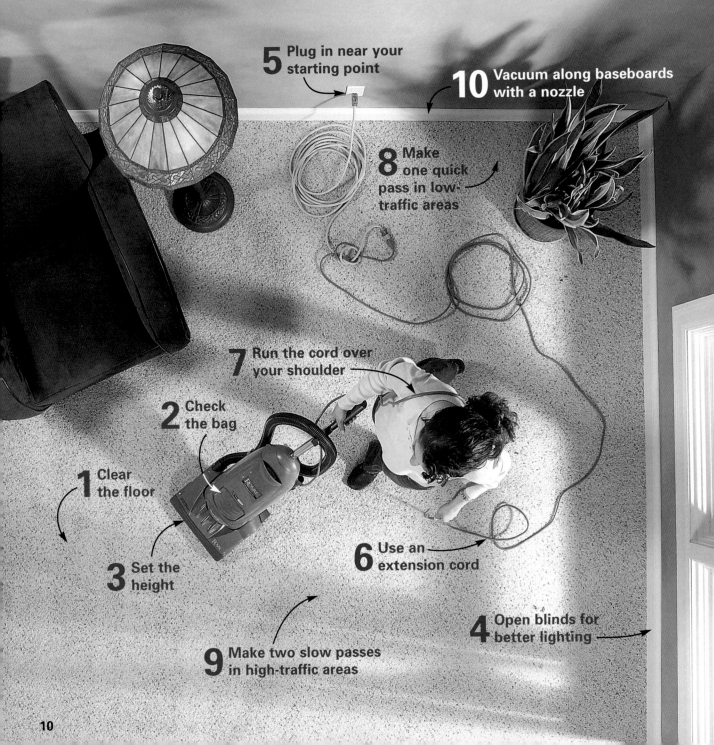

5 Plug in near your starting point

10 Vacuum along baseboards with a nozzle

8 Make one quick pass in low-traffic areas

7 Run the cord over your shoulder

2 Check the bag

1 Clear the floor

3 Set the height

6 Use an extension cord

4 Open blinds for better lighting

9 Make two slow passes in high-traffic areas

1. **Clear the floor first.** Picking up toys and other obstacles before you vacuum is faster than picking them up or shoving them around while you vacuum.

2. **Check the bag or filter.** A dirty filter or a bag that's more than three-quarters full can cut suction power by more than 50 percent.

3. **Set the height to match the carpet.** A too-high setting is ineffective; too low is bad for the carpet and the vacuum. To set the ideal height, raise the vacuum to its highest setting, turn it on and lower it until you can feel the vacuum trying to tug itself forward.

4. **Open blinds and switch on all the lights.** Ample light lets you see which areas are clean and which spots need a second pass.

5. **Plug in near your starting point,** not near the middle or end of the job. That way, the cord is always behind you instead of a constant obstacle in your path.

6. **Extend your range with an extension cord.** Stopping to plug into another outlet wastes time. Use a 14-gauge-wire cord; lighter cords (16- and 18-gauge) can lower the voltage supply and shorten the life of your vacuum.

7. **Run the cord over your shoulder** and around your back and hold it in your free hand. Do this, and you'll never run over the cord.

8. **Make one quick pass** over areas that get no foot traffic. In these spots, the vacuum only has to pick up surface dust.

9. **Go over traffic paths at least twice.** Two slow passes removes ground-in soil more effectively than several fast passes.

10. **Vacuum along baseboards** with a nozzle attachment every second or third time you vacuum.

REINFORCE A SAGGING DRAWER BOTTOM

You don't have to replace a sagging drawer bottom. A typical drawer has a cavity beneath it that's just deep enough so you can strengthen the bottom with a piece of plywood. First make sure the drawer box is square by using a large framing square or by taking diagonal corner-to-corner measurements (equal diagonal measurements mean the box is square). If the box isn't square, square it up, clamp it and drive brad nails through the bottom (**Photo 1**). Two brads placed near the middle of each side usually provide enough strength to hold the box square. The back of the drawer shown here was bulging outward, so the clamps drew it in while we drove in the brads.

Stiffen the old drawer bottom with any 1/4-in. plywood. A full 4 x 8-ft. sheet costs about $10. Many home centers also sell half or quarter sheets.

Measure between the drawer sides, front and back, and cut the plywood 1/4 in. smaller than the opening (1/8 in. on each side). Then glue the new panel in place (**Photo 2**). If the underside of the bottom is unfinished, use wood glue. If it has a finish, you can sand the finish or use construction adhesive. Set books or other weights on the panel. Wood glue forms a strong bond in about 15 minutes. If you use construction adhesive, leave the weights in place overnight.

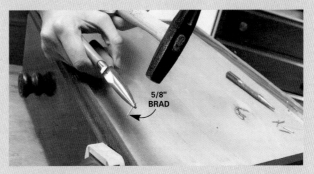

1 SQUARE the drawer box and drive 5/8-in. brad nails at an angle through the drawer bottom and into the drawer sides.

2 GLUE a plywood panel to the underside of the drawer bottom and place weights on it until the glue sets.

HomeCare&Repair

FLOOR-FRIENDLY FEET FOR FURNITURE

Most manufacturers put small metal buttons on furniture legs. Metal feet slide easily across factory and warehouse floors, but they can damage any type of hard flooring in your house (even ceramic tile). On carpet, a spilled drink can even lead to rust stains. So whenever you get a new piece of furniture, run to your local home center or hardware store, where you'll find a variety of furniture feet for less than $5.

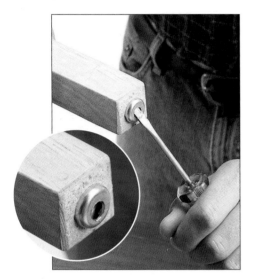

1 REMOVE metal buttons on furniture legs. If a button is sunk deep into the wood and you can't pry it out, drill a 1/4-in. hole and lever it out with a small screwdriver.

2 STICK self-adhesive pads to the legs or drive in nail-type feet. On hardwood legs, drill a pilot hole slightly smaller than the nail shank.

Pads

Glides

Felt or cloth pads are gentle on floors, but they don't slide as easily as plastic feet.

Plastic glides slide smoothly across hard flooring, but don't use plastic or rubber on wood flooring—chemicals in plastics can stain wood finishes.

SCRAPE AWAY CEILING TEXTURE FOR A NEATER PAINT JOB

A neat, straight paint line at the top of a wall is tough to achieve next to a bumpy ceiling. So before you paint, drag a narrow flat-head screwdriver lightly along the ceiling. You'll get a clean paint line and no one will ever notice that the bumps are missing.

BETTER ANCHORS FIX LOOSE TOWEL BARS—FOREVER

When towel bars come loose, it's usually because they weren't well fastened in the first place. The small, wimpy wall anchors included with most towel bar sets just don't have enough holding power. But with sturdy new anchors, you can remount towel bars so they'll never come loose again. Don't put off this fix. The longer you wait, the more likely you are to scar the wall or mar the bar's finish. You can also use these techniques to remount towel rings, toilet paper holders and hooks too. Everything you need is available at home centers and hardware stores.

First, remove the loose end posts (**top photo**). If one post is rock solid, leave it in place (chances are it's fastened to a wall stud). You'll need a hex wrench or mini screwdriver to loosen the setscrew. There's a slight chance that the existing anchors are adequate but the screws have loosened. So try to tighten the screws that hold the mounting plates in place. If they tighten up securely, just remount the posts and the bar. If they don't tighten firmly, remove the screws and the mounting plates. To remove the old anchors, pry them out with a screwdriver or poke them in and let them fall inside the wall. The next step depends on what kind of wall you have.

For fast, solid mounting on drywall, use E-Z Toggles (a pack of two costs $3). These clever anchors are self-drilling and have a T-clamp that folds out when you push the screw into the shaft. On tile, 1/4-in. tubular plastic anchors hold firmly, whether there's drywall or cement backer board behind the tile. Be sure to buy tube-shaped anchors as shown here ($2), not tapered anchors, which don't hold as well.

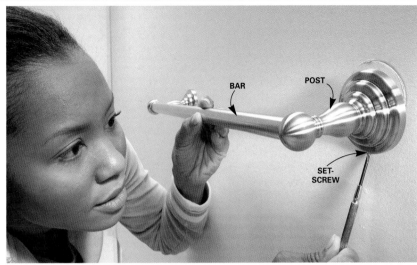

Loosen the setscrew that fastens the post to the mounting plate. Remove the post and the bar. Then unscrew the mounting plate from the wall and remove the old anchors.

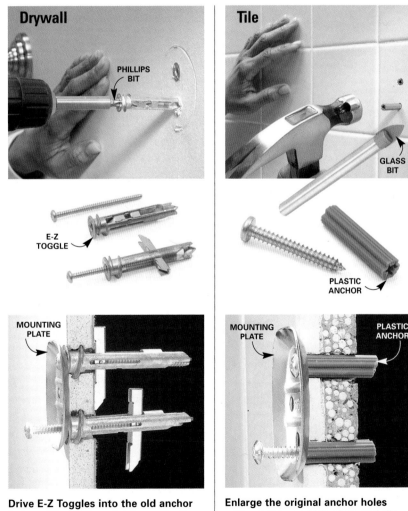

Drywall

Drive E-Z Toggles into the old anchor holes with a drill containing a No. 2 Phillips bit. Refasten the mounting plate with the long toggle screws. Then re-install the post and the bar.

Tile

Enlarge the original anchor holes with a 1/4-in. carbide glass-and-tile bit ($5). Tap in 1/4-in. plastic anchors and fasten the mounting plate with screws.

HomeCare&Repair

A NEATER WAY TO USE BLEACH ON GROUT

In a damp area like a shower, there's no permanent cure for mildew growing on grout. But bleach, along with light scrubbing, is a good way to clean it off and kill it off—at least temporarily. The trouble with applying bleach to a large area is that nasty fumes fill the air. Plus you risk damage to other nearby surfaces (bleach can harm many metals and plastics with prolonged contact). A bleach pen, on the other hand, lets you apply bleach only where you need it. And since the bleach is in a gel form, it grips vertical surfaces—that gives it time to penetrate and kill mildew in the grout's pores. You'll find bleach pens ($4) alongside fabric detergents at discount and grocery stores. If you have colored grout, test for discoloration on a small spot.

CLEAN YOUR BAGLESS VACUUM FILTER, OR ELSE...

"Bagless vacuums are good for business," according to one vacuum repairman. The problem isn't design or manufacturing but user negligence. Vacuum owners empty the dirt canister but often don't clean the filters. Plugged filters lead to an overworked motor. And sooner or later, the motor burns out. Motor replacement costs at least $100.

People avoid cleaning filters because it's a messy job. The typical method is to tap the filter against the inside of a trash can until most of the dust falls off. But this raises a thick cloud of dust and doesn't get the filter completely clean. Here's a faster, neater, more thorough approach: Take the vacuum out to the garage and clean the pleated filter with a shop vacuum. Some pleated filters have a special coating that you can damage, so be gentle with the shop vacuum nozzle. Clean prefilter screens and post-filters the same way.

FILTER

20-MINUTE TUNE-UP RESTORES A VACUUM'S PICKUP POWER

If your upright vacuum isn't sucking up dirt the way it used to, don't assume you need a new one. Vacuums, like cars, need replacement parts and a little maintenance from time to time. But unlike cars, vacuums are fairly simple machines, and you can make the most common repairs yourself.

The first step in maintaining a vacuum is to open it up and expose the roller brush. If you don't know how to do this, it's well worth taking a few minutes to learn. On most vacuums all you have to do is remove a cover plate on the underside (Photo 1). This plate is held in place by screws or latches. On some vacuums exposing the roller is more difficult. You may have to remove the shroud on top of the vacuum, for example. If you can't see how to get at the roller simply by looking at the vacuum and you don't have the owner's manual, you may be able to find a diagram online. Some manufacturers and parts suppliers offer online diagrams of common models (www.vacshopusa.com is a good place to start). Before you go online, find the model number; it may be on the underside of the vacuum or inside the filter bag compartment.

Slice away all the hair and thread that's wrapped around the roller (Photo 2). Then remove the roller so you can replace the belt. The roller may be held in place by screws, clips or end caps that slip out of the housing (Photo 3). Most people never replace belts unless the roller stops turning or they smell burning rubber. But rollers lose power as belts wear, so most manufacturers recommend frequent belt replacement (ranging from six months to three years). Some vacuums have a label that provides the replacement belt number. Belts typically cost $2 to $5.

Before you install the new belt, set the roller back into place and spin it by hand. It should turn freely. If not, the bearings inside or the fittings at the ends are probably worn out. The solution is to replace the entire roller ($15 to $40). Also replace the roller if the bristles are badly worn. Finally, check the suction port for clogs (Photo 4). If the port is connected to the hose, pull off the hose and push a broomstick through it to force out any clogs.

1 UNPLUG the vacuum, turn it upside down and remove the cover plate on the underside of the vacuum to expose the roller.

2 USE a sharp utility knife to slice through hair, yarn and thread that are wrapped around the roller. Then pull it all off the brushes.

3 REMOVE the roller and replace the belt that drives it. If the bristles on the roller are badly worn or the roller doesn't turn freely, replace the roller, too.

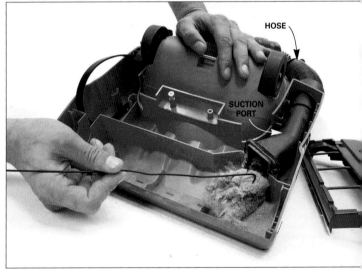

4 PULL clogs out of the suction port with a wire hook made from a coat hanger. Also remove and clear the hose connected to the port.

Tip

Finding vacuum parts

If your vacuum was produced by a major manufacturer, you won't have any trouble finding replacement parts. But first, you'll need your vacuum's model number. The label may be hidden on the underside of the vacuum or even in the dust bag compartment. To get parts locally, check the yellow pages under "Vacuum Cleaners, Supplies and Parts." There are also dozens of online suppliers. Just go to any search engine and type in the brand of your vacuum followed by "replacement parts."

3-STEP
WALL TEXTURE & COLOR

*Get the look of plaster and an infusion of color—
all in one day!*

by **David Radtke**

Handcrafted plaster walls have a classic beauty that perfectly flat drywall can never achieve. Picture the walls in an old Italian villa or a 1920s American bungalow with wide, ornate trim. Now you can easily create the look yourself using one of several new products that are texture and color all in one.

The three-step product we chose for this project is called Manda Mudd. It comes in three standard 1-gal. paint cans (enough for an average 350 sq. ft. of wall space). Most rooms can be completed in less than a day. Cleanup is easy

with soap and water. So if you consider yourself an average do-it-yourselfer in the painting zone, you'll be able to tackle this forgiving process after reading this article and following the step-by-step photos.

Many other color/texture techniques require you to choose your own color combinations and glazes, leaving the end result a bit iffy. This product removes the guesswork by creating the color combinations for you. Each of the 42 color sets available (with more to come) consists of three complementary colors. The first coat is the base color and the next two applications add texture as well as color to the wall, resulting in a rich three-dimensional effect. In

fact you can use this product over existing wall texture or hard-to-remove wallpaper (see "Problem Walls," p. 19).

Go to the Buyer's Guide on p. 19 for information on where to find this product and get color samples. Figure on spending about $115 for the three-step product and another $35 for the application kit and the video that comes with it. You can save money by forgoing the application kit and using a plastic dustpan and a grout float (a tool used to spread tile grout). You'll also need 1-1/2-in. masking tape and self-adhesive masking paper to cover the baseboard and the tops of doors and windows.

Prep your walls and practice

Begin the project by filling any nail holes and repairing damaged drywall or plaster. (See "Prep for Painting," p. 25.) If the room has been occupied by smokers or is a kitchen

with a grease film, you'll need to wash the walls with a TSP cleaner and then wipe them down with a damp cloth to get the paint to bond well. Spot-prime any newly patched surfaces and then mask the woodwork (**Photo 1**). If your room has wallpaper that's tough to remove, see p. 19.

As with any other new process, you should practice on a scrap before starting. Buy a damaged sheet of drywall at a home center, cut it 2 to 3 ft. wide and prime it. Then read this article and experiment with the process. It'll get you familiar with drying times and how best to use the application tool. This way when you get to your wall, you'll have a good feel for the technique and your results will be more consistent.

Step 1: Paint the room

The idea behind this step is to create a base color that completely covers the walls. It will show through only as background for the other two steps. First, cut in the corners and then roll it onto the wall, as you would with regular paint. The consistency is just like that of paint. You'll get excellent coverage with one coat even if you use a dark color over a light one, as we did. When you're finished, let this coat dry. Our room was ready for the next step in about an hour.

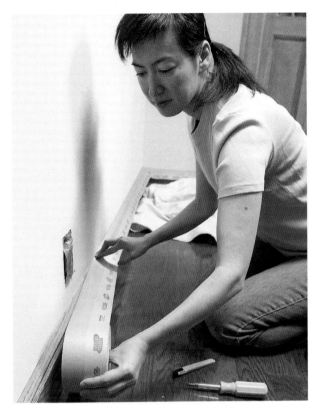

1 MASK the woodwork and the ceiling and remove the electrical cover plates. Repair walls and spot-prime as needed.

SAMPLE BOARD

STEP 1 PRODUCT

2 COMPLETE a 2 x 4-ft. sample to practice your skills. Apply the base coat (Step 1) to the corners and along the ceiling, baseboard, and window and door trim using a 2-1/2-in. brush.

3 IMMEDIATELY follow the brushwork with a 3/8-in. nap roller for smooth walls or a 1/2-in. roller for textured walls. Let the walls dry.

RUBBER-BOTTOM
FLOAT

APPLICATION
TRAY

4 POUR about 12 ozs. of Step 2 texture mixture into the application tray. Dip the edge of the float into the tray, then pull the float across the wall to deposit a thin layer over the base coat. Dip the float often with small amounts of product. Don't completely obscure the wall color behind; just create a thin buildup of material over the entire wall surface.

5 MIMIC the overall texture even in tight areas and along trim. Move the trowel edge at a different angle to produce a more random texture.

Step 2: Trowel the mud

This part is fun. Sure, it's a bit scary because there's no going back at this point. The product for this texture step is the consistency of runny drywall mud, or if you prefer, very thick gravy. There are as many ways to apply the texture as there are people who try it, so don't get uptight about doing it "right." The idea is to cover a bit less than half of the visible surface with random strokes of mud.

Pour a little mud into your pan. Get your float ready with your other hand and start applying. I like to work from the ceiling down, completing one wall at a time, but really, there are no rules. If you're uncomfortable on a stepladder, consider setting up a wide plank on top of sturdy crates to reach the top of an 8-ft. wall. Dip about half the float (lengthwise) into the pan, wipe off a bit of the excess and then lightly push the float onto the wall with the float pointing upward, as shown in Photo 4. Keep the float nearly flat against the wall and drag it across, pulling the mud mixture as you go. Repeat this about every 4 to 5 in. along the wall. If you repeat this process over the entire wall, holding the float in this upward fashion, you'll produce an even, consistent pattern. You can also achieve a more random, hand-troweled look like the walls in our room have if you turn your float 45 or more degrees every other dip. Try both methods on your sample board, then step back and see which you like best.

 Tip You're bound to drip some mud onto the floor or the wall beneath, so have rags ready to swab the wall or clean up the drop cloth. You don't want to step into the mud and track it onto carpeting.

Tip If a run from the mud dries on the wall and hardens before you notice it, shave it off with a putty knife and apply mud over it.

Don't get bogged down in one area; keep the motion going and refill your pan as necessary. After you've completed an area about the size of a coffee table, step back and examine the wall. You may need to go back and add strokes to certain spots to get a more "even" look. Remember, don't apply too much texture at this time; there's another layer of texture to come. You can always go back and apply more. As it dries, you can start to see how the room will look.

Step 3: More mud

By the time you've finished the last wall with the first texture application, the starting point will be dry and you can open the last can and get started. You'll notice that this mix is about the same consistency as the previous one. Dip your float into the pan and repeat the previous method. Try to cover some of the background color from Step 1 that you didn't cover earlier, but also overlap onto

6 APPLY the final product from the Step 3 can in the same manner as Step 2, letting the two previous applications show beneath. The slightly different shade from the previous product will give the wall a deeper, three-dimensional appearance.

7 GENTLY slice through the texture surface to release the masking paper and tape from the textured surface after it dries.

MASKING PAPER

the Step 2 texture as well. Vary the starting points of the strokes at the corners and along the wall and base trim to avoid making a similar pattern along the length of the trim. Try to imagine that the trim, windows and doors aren't there, and have the texture flow across the wall.

Step back occasionally to see "the big picture" and try to maintain a random uniformity.

Finishing touches

Once you've completed the project, take a break for an hour and then go back and examine it. You can still apply more mud to areas you missed or those that look too plain.

If your newly completed room is in a heavy traffic area such as a bathroom or hallway, you can protect the texture

with a clear water-based satin finish once the wall is dry. Just cut in the corners and along the trim with a brush and use a 1/2-in.-nap roller to cover large areas. You can also use a product called Tile Lab Grout Sealer, which is available at home centers. Keep in mind that clear finishes can darken the color slightly.

Buyer's Guide
To find Manda Mudd, go to www.MANDAMUDD.com. You can look at color samples and order online. If you don't purchase over the Internet, call Manda Mudd at (877) 626-3268 for more retail information.

Editor's Note: Problem walls
If you've tried to remove stubborn wallpaper and the result was a lot of torn edges, this color/texture finish is a great way to cover them. Because wallpaper paste can lift when water-based latex paint is applied, you'll need to seal the entire wall with an oil-based primer/sealer like Cover Stain by Zinsser. But first remove any rough wallpaper edges with a scraper and then sand lightly to feather the edges. If there are air bubbles in the wallpaper, cut them with a utility knife and scrape the surface with a putty knife. Wipe the wall clean with a lightly dampened cloth, let the wall dry and then prime the entire surface with the primer. Use an organic respirator, which is available at hardware and paint stores. Once the primer is dry, you can start with the Step 1 product.

If your walls have an old texture that's been compromised by smoother-looking spot repairs, you can go right over the old and create a new texture using Manda Mudd. —David

ORGANIC RESPIRATOR

PRIMER

TORN EDGES

150-GRIT SANDING BLOCKS

HandyHints®

FLASH FIND

If you lose a contact lens, turn off the lights and shine a flashlight beam across the floor. The lens will glimmer and make it an easy find.

NO-SLIP SEAT CUSHIONS

The rubber mesh designed to keep rugs from sliding around can also make seat cushions stay put. Get the mesh at a home center or discount store and cut it to fit. This trick works on wooden chairs and upholstered furniture too.

PRESERVE PICTURE HOLES

A fresh coat of paint can fill in and hide small nail holes. So if you plan to hang pictures in their same locations when the job is done, stick toothpicks into the nail holes. Leave the toothpicks protruding about 1/8 in. so you can roll right over them. After painting, you can pull out the toothpicks and then put nails and pictures exactly where they were.

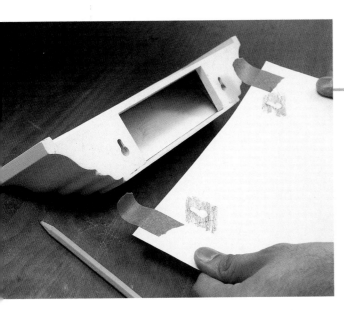

LAG SCREW
HANDLE

LAG
SCREW
HANDLE

PIVOT
POINT

DOOR PAINTING REVOLUTIONIZED

If you have a door that needs painting, you'll flip for this tip. You'll be able to paint both sides without waiting for the first to dry. Rest the door on sawhorses and drive a 1/4-in. x 2-1/2-in. lag screw into each corner of one end and another in the middle of the other end for a pivot.

Slide the sawhorses to each end of the door so the screws rest on the edges of the sawhorses. Paint one side of the door and then, using the two screws as handles, lift and rotate the door on the pivot screw to expose the unpainted side. Paint that side and go out for coffee while it dries.

GET AN EXTRA HAND FROM JACK

Hanging cabinets solo is slow, frustrating work. A car jack, boosted by scrap wood, can hold a cabinet steady for as long as needed and without a complaint.

PERFECT KEYHOLE TEMPLATE

When you're installing a wall hanging that has keyhole slots on the back, create a template to help you position the wall screws. Lay a piece of paper over the slots and do a pencil rubbing a la Sherlock Holmes. Level and tape the guide to the wall. Mark the top of the keyholes with a nail and your screws will be in perfect position.

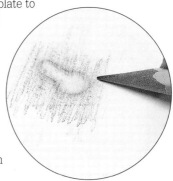

HandyHints®

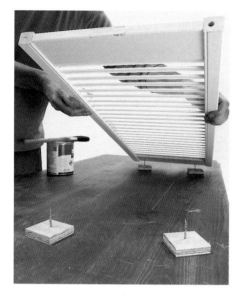

PAINTING SUPPORTS

Here's how to paint both sides of a project without waiting for the first side to dry. Drive screws through small plywood blocks. Paint the back side first, then set the project on the screws and paint the other side. The tiny marks left in the paint by the screw tips will be barely visible.

NO-SLIDE KNEE PADS

Knee pads that slip down your shins every time you stand up are a huge nuisance. Avoid the slide by strapping on a pair of hockey or baseball catcher's shin guards instead. You get comfortable knee pads that stay put, and shin protection, too. You can try a second-hand sports store or get a pair for about $30 online (www.amazon.com).

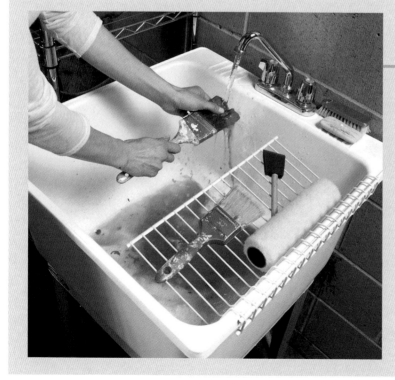

UTILITY DRYING RACK

Finally, a great place to dry brushes, rollers or rags in your utility tub. Form a hook in a wire shelf section by hammering one side around a scrap of 2x4. Hang it over the tub's edge for a clever shelf.

SCRATCH-FREE TECHNOLOGY

Digital screens on devices like cell phones, digital cameras and camcorders get knocked around and their fragile displays can get scratched. Cut PDA screen film protectors (10 for $15 at electronics stores) to fit all your electronic toys. When they're scuffed, simply pull them off and replace.

PET REPELLENT FOR FURNITURE

To train your pets to stay off furniture, place plastic carpet protectors—prickly side up—on their favorite perch. Available in office supply stores and the carpet/flooring department of home centers for about $2 per ft., the protectors can be cut to the size you need with a scissors or a utility knife. The plastic teeth will train your pet to associate the couch with "uncomfortable." Soon they will seek cozier spots to relax on and leave the easy chair to you. Just remember to remove the protector before you sit down.

TABLECLOTH DROP CLOTH

Vinyl tablecloths—the kind usually used on picnic tables—make great drop cloths. They're tougher than plastic sheeting, and if you put the smooth side face down, they don't slip around on hard flooring the way canvas drop cloths do. On carpet, put the smooth side face up. These tablecloths are cheaper than drop cloths, too: $2 to $4 at discount stores.

HandyHints ®

SQUEAKY-CLEAN VASES

It's difficult to clean out the cloudy residue left in slim flower vases. You can make any vase sparkle by adding warm water and denture cleaning tablets. Let it fizz for a few minutes and rinse well.

KEEP RIM RUST OUT OF PAINT

You can get a clean pour out of an old paint can that has dirt and rust in its rim. Just wrap the rim with tape to seal in the debris while you pour.

WET THE BRUSH BEFORE YOU PAINT

To minimize crusty paint buildup on bristles and make brush cleaning easier, dip your brush in water and shake out the excess before you paint with latex paint. If you're using an oil-based finish, dip the brush in mineral spirits. In hot, dry weather, dip the brush occasionally during painting.

COLORED COMPOUND FOR TOUCH-UPS

After applying a final coat of joint compound on drywall, you'll probably find a few minor scratches and craters. Before you fill these blemishes, mix a few drops of food coloring into joint compound. That way, the patches will stand out from the surrounding joint compound and you won't miss them during the final touch-up sanding. To prevent the color from bleeding through, spot-prime the patches with a stain-blocking primer.

PREP FOR
PAINTING

Fixes for the 8 most common drywall flaws

by Travis Larson

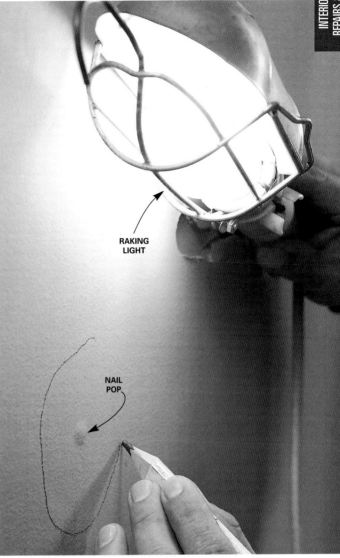

RAKING LIGHT

NAIL POP

et's face it—no wall is perfect. And if you want to rejuvenate a room with fresh paint, it'll look a whole lot better if you repair and smooth out those beat-up walls first. Some flaws, such as shoddy taping work, have been around since day one. Others, like cracks and nail pops, start showing up months or years later as the house ages. And still others are just insults from day-to-day living: holes from doorknobs, dents from furniture, holes from shelving and picture hangers. The good news is that you can fix all these problems. You only need a few inexpensive tools and a bit of finesse. With our tips, some patience and a keen eye, even beginners can get good results.

In this story, we'll show you how to repair and cover the most common drywall flaws so that they'll be all but invisible after that new coat of paint. The fixes are ordered from the most common and easiest to ones that are less common and more challenging.

To find the problems, inspect the entire wall surface by holding a light close to the wall and "raking" across the surface. The light will highlight wall flaws that aren't obvious to the unaided eye (**at right**). Circle each problem area with a pencil (not a pen or marker, which may bleed through paint later) to mark it for repair.

Editor's Note: Mud basics

Most of the fixes in this story require at least two coats of drywall taping compound. Compound is too thick to use right out of the bucket, so mix in small amounts of water until you get a smooth, mashed potato–like consistency. Use a slightly runnier mix for embedding paper tape. Let each coat dry completely (usually overnight) before applying another coat. If you have leftover ridges from tools, let them dry and scrape them off with a putty knife before adding the next coat. With the first coat, don't worry about craters, scratches or other small flaws. Just try to avoid large humps and make sure any patches are covered. The second coat is to fill in and smooth out any voids or low spots.

Generally, larger patches call for wider coats of drywall taping compound to mask them. That way, higher areas from patches or existing humps can be feathered out over wide areas so the wall will appear flatter. The most common mistake is to use narrow rather than wide swaths of compound over patches and humps. Strive for a thickness of 1/8 in. or so over the fix and feather the edges flush with the drywall. Sand all the fixes with 120-grit drywall sandpaper. Use a handheld sander for small jobs and a pole sander for big jobs. Check your work with the light again after sanding to look for areas that need more work. You can always add a third or even fourth coat of drywall taping compound to fix any remaining problems.

— Travis

1. FILL **NAIL POPS** AND **SMALL HOLES**

Small holes from brads or picture hangers are simple to fix. Gently tap on the wall with the handle of your putty knife to drive any standing drywall facing paper below the surface and create a tiny crater, and then hide it with filler.

Nail pops are usually caused by fasteners that are driven through the drywall paper during installation, or by a gap

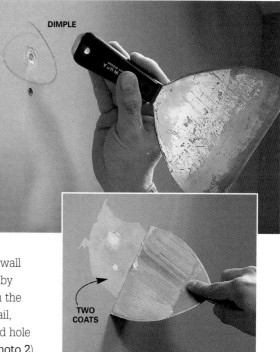

DIMPLE

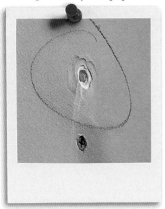

between the drywall and the stud. Then vibration and seasonal wood swelling and shrinkage cause the overlying filler to pop out from the wall. Drive in another 1-1/4-in. drywall screw near the nail pop so the head penetrates just below but not through the drywall paper. Then remove the old screw by pushing the screw gun tip through the middle of the nail pop and backing out the screw. If it's a drywall nail, drive it into the stud with a nail set and leave it. Then dimple the old hole (**Photo 1**) and fill it and the new screw head with two coats of filler (**Photo 2**).

TWO COATS

2. CAULK **CRACKS** AT INSIDE CORNERS

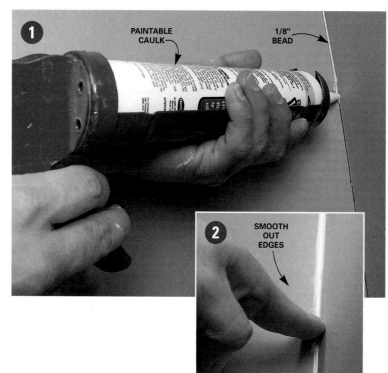

① PAINTABLE CAULK — 1/8" BEAD

② SMOOTH OUT EDGES

Hairline cracks at inside corners usually signal slight movement between adjoining walls. Choose any type of latex caulk and cut the tip just short enough to leave a 1/8-in. hole in the end. Squeeze a narrow line of caulk directly over the crack (**Photo 1**). Then mold the wet caulk into the corner with a moistened finger (**Photo 2**). The caulk will remain flexible and keep the crack from reappearing. Avoid thick layers of caulk, which may look too rounded in a square corner.

3. PATCH MEDIUM-SIZE **HOLES**

Large holes still require old-fashioned fixes that include cutting out a square chunk of drywall around the hole, installing backing, adding a drywall patch and then taping the wound. But holes under 6 in. in diameter can be more easily repaired with a self-adhesive drywall patch. Find 4 x 4-in. or 8 x 8-in. squares at home centers and specialty paint stores.

Select a size that'll overlap the sides of the hole by at least 1 in. Pick away any loose chunks of paper or gypsum that protrude above the surface. Then peel off the backing and stick the patch in place.

Spread a wide, thin layer of mud over the patch and the surrounding wall. The thin metal patch is perforated so the mud can penetrate and lock it in place. After the first coat dries, spread a second layer of mud to fill in imperfections and low spots, then sand.

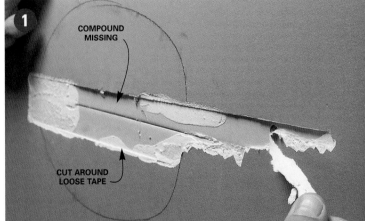

DOORKNOB HOLE

SELF-STICK PATCH

12" TAPING KNIFE

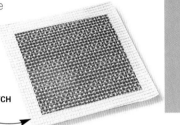

DRYWALL PATCH ($4 TO $6)

4. CUT OUT AND REPLACE **LOOSE TAPE**

If the tape is blistering or lifting away from the wall, it's because there wasn't enough joint compound under the tape to anchor it to the drywall. The solution is to cut through the paint and joint compound and peel every bit of loose tape away from the wall to expose the surface behind (**Photo 1**). Be aggressive with this step, even cutting and peeling tape beyond the evident crack. There's bound to be more poorly anchored tape that just hasn't come loose yet. You can tell just by looking at the lack of compound on the drywall surface behind. After cutting loose material away, fill the hole with setting compound (**Photo 2**). When that hardens, embed a strip of paper tape in taping compound a few inches beyond and directly over the patch. Then overlay two wide swaths of taping compound to blend the patch into the wall.

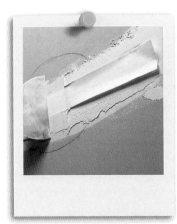

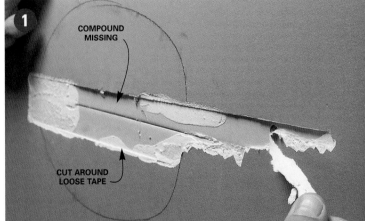

COMPOUND MISSING

CUT AROUND LOOSE TAPE

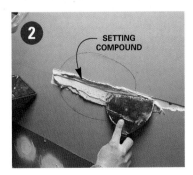

SETTING COMPOUND

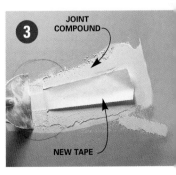

JOINT COMPOUND

NEW TAPE

5. NAIL, RETAPE AND MUD **CRACKED CORNERS**

If a metal corner bead is badly dented or damaged, your only option is to pry it off and replace it. That's a big job because you'll have to remove and reinstall the base trim as part of the project. But if only the edges are popping through the surface or there's a hairline crack along the flange, you can fix it. (Chances are the flange of the corner bead wasn't nailed securely or the taper neglected to tape the edges.)

NAIL LOOSE FLANGE

Drive 1-1/4-in. drywall nails through any corner bead edges that are loose, using as many nails as needed to hold the flange flat to the wall (**Photo 1**). Center fiberglass mesh tape over the flange over the entire length of the corner bead (**Photo 2**). Spread two coats of joint compound over the mesh tape, using the corner of the bead as a guide for the taping knife. If you have a corner that's in a vulnerable spot and constantly gets bumped, use "setting" compound for the first coat and regular joint compound for the second one. Setting compound is much tougher and won't crack nearly as easily. But be careful to apply even coats that don't project beyond the corner or leave humps or tool marks. Setting compound is very hard to sand.

FIBERGLASS TAPE

6. TAPER **HUMPED JOINTS**

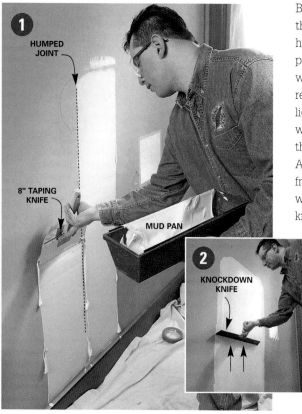

HUMPED JOINT

8" TAPING KNIFE

MUD PAN

KNOCKDOWN KNIFE

Butt joints (where drywall joins at the ends) often have unsightly humps left from built-up and/or poorly feathered edges when the walls were originally taped. (These really show up with the raking light.) Fix them by overlaying a wider layer of compound to blend the hump in with the surrounding wall.

Apply the first layer of compound with a taping knife, working from the bottom to the top of the hump (most of the time these will be vertical joints; **Photo 1**). Use a little more pressure on the knife edges on both sides of the hump to help feather (taper) the edges. Strive for an overall width of at least 2 ft. for the patch. Immediately after applying the first coat, drag a knockdown knife over the wet compound, smoothing the edges flat against the drywall (**Photo 2**). (A knockdown knife, $15, has a 22-in.-long rubber blade.) Wait too long with this step, even a few minutes, and the rubber blade will drag in the mud and you'll have poor results. Let the first coat dry and apply a second, slightly wider and thinner coat with the same techniques. Check out your patch with a raking light while sanding, and add more coats if needed to fill in low spots, craters or grooves.

7. CARVE OUT AND FILL **JOINT CRACKS**

Midwall cracks are tricky to fix and may crack again, so there are no promises here. That's because the cracks usually occur at the corners of windows, doors and other openings, which are the weakest points in the framing. Seasonal movement or foundation shifting shows up there, especially if the drywall hanger put a joint at that spot. If so, the only sure fix is to tear off the drywall and seam new pieces near the center of the opening.

However, try this fix first. Carve a 1/2-in.-wide by 1/2-in.-deep "V" with a utility knife in the center of the crack (**Photo 1**). Fill the crack with setting compound and let it harden (**Photo 2**). Then embed paper tape in taping compound directly over the patch (**Photo 3**) and overlay it with two or more wide layers of taping compound.

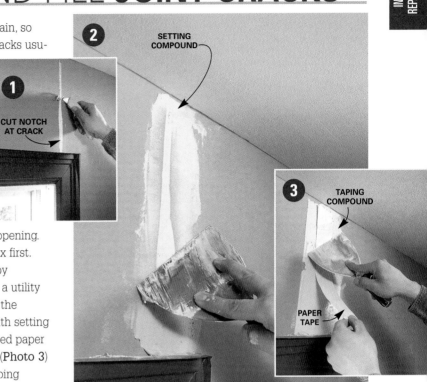

8. "SKIM COAT" LARGE **DAMAGED AREAS**

If there's significant damage over a large area of drywall, the only answer is to "skim coat" the entire area. That means covering the surface with a thin layer of joint compound to bury the damage. Tackle one area at a time, preferably areas no larger than 4 x 4 ft., at least until you get the hang of applying and smoothing larger areas of compound.

Prepare the wall by picking away any loose edges of drywall facing paper. Prime the leftover raw paper with any type of priming paint to seal the raw paper. (Kilz is a great product to use for this step because it seals well and dries fast.) Dab at the wet paint with a foam brush or rag to saturate the paper and wipe away any runs. Let the paint dry and lightly sand away any standing paper nubs. If you sand through the paint and expose fresh paper, paint it again or the paper will absorb moisture from the taping compound and paint and show through later.

Trowel on the compound with overlapping vertical strokes as we show in Fix No. 6. Then make a series of overlapping vertical strokes with a knockdown knife to smooth out tool marks and fill in low spots (**Photo 1**). Next make a series of overlapping horizontal strokes, again with the knockdown knife (**Photo 2**). Work quickly so the thin coat of mud doesn't begin to dry. If you did a good job of applying and smoothing the joint compound, you'll only need one coat. But if after sanding the wall, you find some uneven areas, trowel on more taping compound wherever it's needed to fill in problem spots and sand again. 🏠

PREFINISHED
WOOD FLOOR

Lay this hardwood floor, start to finish, in one weekend

by **David Radtke**

Installing a new hardwood floor used to be a lot of commotion. You had to schedule an installation and have the installer haul in a pallet of raw hardwood flooring and bang it in with a huge mallet and floor nailer. The next day the work area had to be sealed from the rest of the house as the big sanding machines rolled in and created bags of sawdust. For the next three days, the staining and finishing process made the whole house smell bad, and it took at least a week for the finish to harden before you could bring in the furniture.

However, prefinished flooring has changed all that. Now you can install a new wood floor that's completely finished from A to Z in a single weekend. You'll be amazed at the beauty, practicality and speed of installation of a staple-down prefinished wood floor. You can literally start installing one day and be using the room the next day. And don't confuse this flooring with wood look-alike plastic laminate flooring. The type we show here (Robbins, Huntington Plank style, red oak with walnut stain, www.armstrong.com, 800-233-3823) has a wear layer that

can be resanded a couple of times years down the road when the tough factory finish is finally compromised. Most experts agree that this is a 50-year or more floor.

In this article, we'll show you how to install your own prefinished wood floor. We'll give you tips on buying, cutting and layout and explain how much prep is needed before you start. We'll also give you tips on how to deal with transitions from one room to another.

We chose a special type of prefinished flooring, called "engineered" flooring. It's about 3/8 to 1/2 in. thick and usually made of three layers of wood laminated together. The wood grain in the middle runs opposite the grain in the bottom and top layers. This method of construction creates a floor that's more stable than one made of solid wood, with less seasonal movement and fewer cracks between planks during the dry season. In fact, engineered flooring is so stable that manufacturers allow its use in areas like basements as long as there isn't a moisture problem. Most engineered flooring can be glued down instead when stapling isn't possible, for example, where in-floor heating lies directly below. The thin profile of engineered wood flooring makes it a great candidate for remodeling because you can install it over an existing floor without significantly changing floor heights and transitions from one room to another. It costs about $5 to $9 per square foot.

For tools, you'll need a flooring stapler (rent one for $30 a day; **Photo 4**) and an air compressor. An air-powered finish nailer is handy but not necessary. A jigsaw will cut lengths and intricate cuts around vents and doorways, and a table saw is best for rip cuts near a wall. The other tools are inexpensive. You can get a tap block (**Photo 5**) and a pull bar at a home center for about $7 each. Follow the step-by-step photos for the basics and then read the text for tips and special instructions.

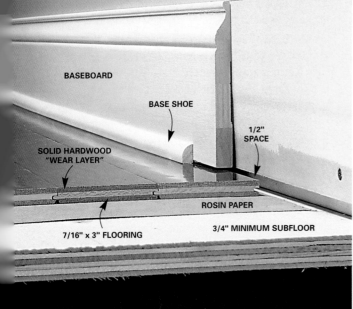

BASEBOARD

BASE SHOE

1/2" SPACE

SOLID HARDWOOD "WEAR LAYER"

ROSIN PAPER

7/16" x 3" FLOORING

3/4" MINIMUM SUBFLOOR

Figure A
Engineered Wood Floor Details

Engineered wood flooring is a prefinished tongue-and-groove flooring that has alternating wood grain laminations much like plywood, but with a 1/8-in. or thicker solid hardwood layer on top. The factory finish is very durable, but it can be sanded if it ever needs refinishing.

FLOORING STAPLER

Use a special narrow crown stapler to fasten engineered wood flooring to wood subfloors. The stapler has a special nose that guides the staple through the tongue at the perfect angle. You can rent staplers and compressors at a local rental outlet.

FLOORING STAPLES

1 **REMOVE the baseboard. Undercut the bottoms of the doorjambs and casing so the flooring can slide under them. Place a piece of flooring under a flexible trim saw and carefully cut the trim.**

FLEXIBLE JAPANESE SAW

HAMMER TACKER

ROSIN PAPER

2 **TAPE AND STAPLE rosin paper to the subfloor. If your manufacturer prefers 15-lb. felt, use that instead. Snap a line 1/2 in. plus the width of the flooring from the straightest wall in the room.**

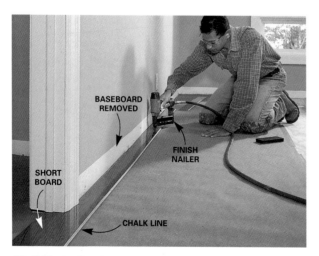

BASEBOARD REMOVED

FINISH NAILER

SHORT BOARD

CHALK LINE

3 **NAIL the flooring (tongue out) along the line every 16 in. Use long pieces of flooring to establish an absolutely straight start. Slip a short piece into the doorway behind this first strip if a doorway is along the starting wall. It would be difficult to place later.**

Picking out the flooring that's best for you

For a wide selection, shop for engineered wood flooring at any retail store that specializes in flooring. Bring a few samples home and live with them for a few days. Then choose the type of wood, the texture (some look hand-planed for a rustic look), the stain color and a satin or gloss finish.

Calculate the area you want to cover and buy an extra 10 percent for waste. Just remember to buy your flooring several days before you start and leave it in the house to acclimate to the ambient temperature and humidity. Also ask the flooring retailer to recommend the appropriate floor stapler and the right length nails. If the store doesn't rent floor staplers, check with your local tool rental outlet. We rented a stapler (**Photos 4 and 5**) and purchased staples at a home center.

Get your room ready

Engineered wood flooring can be stapled down over a sound plywood or OSB underlayment grade subfloor. You can also staple it over an existing hardwood floor or a vinyl floor (one layer only). Just be sure the existing subfloor or floor is solid underfoot. You may need to add screws to get rid of squeaks or remove carpet or even a layer of floor covering.

If you're laying your new floor over subfloor like we did, make sure the edges of the plywood meet smoothly without ridges between them. If there's a slight raised edge, try adding a few screws, or as a last resort, use underlayment filler and trowel it to feather out imperfections. Scrape away any paint globs or drywall chunks and thoroughly vacuum the whole area before starting the project. Also slide a 6-in. scraper along the surface to find any raised nails or screws and drive them down.

I like to remove the baseboard in the room so I can install the flooring closer to the wall. Most manufacturers want you to leave at least a 3/8-in. and sometimes a 1/2-in. expansion gap between the wall and the flooring.

If you have doors between rooms instead of archways, cut the bottoms of the casing and the jambs with a block of flooring and a crosscut saw. A Japanese saw (available at home centers) works great here because it has a thin, flexible blade. Concentrate on keeping the blade parallel to the floor for a clean, even cut. Vacuum the sawdust.

Cover the subfloor with rosin paper as shown in **Photo 2** to create a slip area between the floor surfaces and help quiet any potential squeaks. Some manufacturers prefer 15-lb. felt instead of rosin paper, so be sure to follow your manufacturer's suggestions.

Start along the straightest wall

Decide which direction you'd like the flooring to follow. Hallways look best with the planks running in the long direction; other rooms are a matter of taste. Some manu-

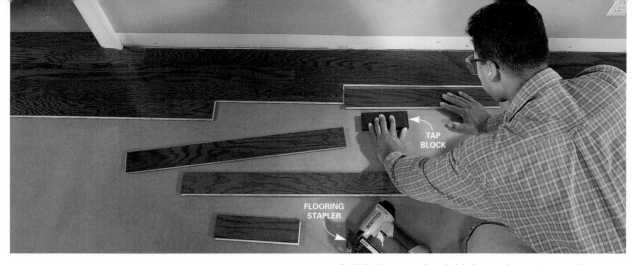

facturers recommend laying the floor perpendicular to the direction of the joists, but if you have a solid 3/4-in.-thick subfloor, either direction is fine.

Measure the width of a plank including the tongue and then add the appropriate wall clearance measurement to that. We needed 1/2-in. clearance. Mark that distance out from the wall at two spots about 1 ft. away from the corner. Measuring from the corner isn't always accurate because of a buildup of drywall compound. Tap in a nail at one mark and then pull your chalk line tight through the marks and snap a starting line onto your paper (**Photo 2**).

If this starting wall has a doorway, be sure to fit a strip of flooring under the casing and jamb because it'll be difficult to slip in later. However, don't nail this piece in until you nail the first row into place. Bring in three boxes of flooring and then select boards from them randomly. Some boxes might contain more light or dark boards, so drawing from several boxes will keep the floor from looking patchy.

Select long strips for the first couple of rows because it's easier to align them with your chalk line (**Photo 3**). Start 1/2 in. away from the end wall. Face-nail the flooring with pairs of nails every 16 in. Make sure your nail gun sets the nail head just below the surface. Fill these holes later with a matching color putty. The face nailing is necessary because the stapler won't fit that close to the wall at this stage. If you have a piece in the doorway, tap it in and nail it now. Continue with a second row, making sure to alternate end joints by at least 4 in. from the previous row.

By the third row, you'll have enough space to use the floor stapler. Before you use it, check the pressure at your compressor. Dial it to about 75 psi and test-staple a piece through the tongue somewhere along the floor. If you drive it flush with the wood surface at the tongue, it's perfect. If the staple is too deep or is still protruding above the tongue, adjust the pressure. Drive staples every 8 in. along the rows and get at least two staples in short planks. Tap the ends together and knock the plank sides together with the edge of your tap block (**Photo 5**).

The flooring is precisely milled, so you should never have to drive the tap block hard with your hammer. If the

4 TAP the second and third rows into place, making sure the ends and the sides fit snugly. Power-staple through the tongues every 6 in. Avoid placing joints of adjoining rows closer than 4 in., and place the joints as randomly as possible by choosing varying lengths of flooring.

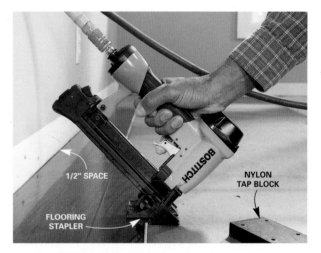

5 STAPLE through the tongues of the flooring, making sure the boot of the stapler is in full contact with the floor surface. Practice a few shots before you begin, and adjust the pressure from your compressor to 70 to 80 psi, so the driven staple is flush with the wood of the tongue.

6 CUT the flooring from the back side with a fine-tooth blade to avoid splintering. A jigsaw works well, especially for intricate cuts in doorways or around floor vents. Use a small table saw to rip pieces that lie against the end wall. Cut in another room to avoid dust.

grooves aren't fitting into the tongues, check for splinters or crushed tongues and remove them or cut them back with your utility knife.

Continue installing the flooring, leaving a 1/2-in. expansion space on each end. Drive hard-to-get-at end pieces into place with a pull bar as shown in **Photo 7**. If you don't have a pull bar, you can position a pry bar between the wall and the end of the flooring. To avoid crushing the drywall, pry against a drywall knife.

Fitting special spots

You may encounter heating vents in the floor and along walls or even radiators in older homes. Floor registers (**Photo 11**) are easy to cut around. Just be sure to measure the bottom of the register so you get the opening the right size. Wall-mounted registers that meet the floor can often be removed and then repositioned on top of the flooring. Cast-iron radiators are the toughest and will have to be removed before you start and then reinstalled later. You may need a professional to help drain the system, remove the radiator, and then reinstall and refill the system later. Hot water baseboard heat has metal covers along the wall. Lift the covers off (look for clips), then unscrew the metal

7 TAP a special pull bar to tighten the end joints near the ends of rows when there's no room for a tap block.

back plates. You can reinstall them later over the flooring.

After working your way across the room, you'll find that the nailer won't fit for the last two rows. Face-nail instead (**Photo 8**) and rip the last piece to fit. Use a pull bar to tighten the gaps and then nail the last rows about 1/2 in. back from the tongue edge. There's no need to pair up the nails here because you won't be tapping other pieces into them as you did on the first rows. Rip the last strips using

Transitions to other flooring

Blending one kind of flooring into the next may call for a bit of improvisation and creativity. You can buy several options of prefinished transition pieces from your supplier to solve almost any floor height difference from one room to the next. You may have to modify them slightly with your table saw to make the transition as smooth as possible. For carpeting, it's best to position the last strip of flooring in the center of the doorway or directly under the door. If necessary, pull the carpeting up in the doorway and then restaple it as shown in the photo below.

When you're installing flooring up to an existing vinyl or wood floor, leave an expansion space between the floors and then nail a transition piece over the gap. Be sure to cover the edge of the vinyl to keep it from lifting.

If you can't get a prefinished transition piece to work, make a piece from the same type of wood and then stain it to match your new flooring. The idea is to make the transition as shallow as possible but still sturdy enough to take heavy foot traffic.

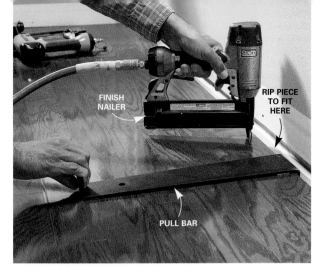

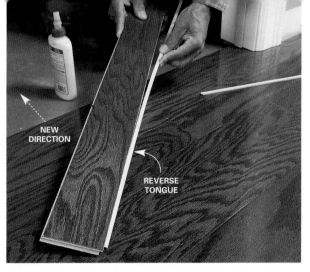

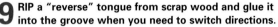

8 TIGHTEN the flooring seams near the end wall with a pull bar, then face-nail the pieces about 1/2 in. back from the tongue. The stapler won't fit into this tight space.

9 RIP a "reverse" tongue from scrap wood and glue it into the groove when you need to switch directions.

a table saw and make sure to allow for an expansion gap as you did at the start.

Reversing direction

You can easily continue the flooring through a doorway into another room, but if you want to continue in the opposite direction from your starting point, buy or make your own tongue to glue into a groove as shown in **Photo 9**. Rip a thin piece from 3/4-in.-thick stock on your table saw and then cut it to width with a straightedge and a utility knife. Check the fit and then glue the tongue into the groove of the plank and tap it into the groove of the existing spot as shown in **Photo 10**. This is a great way to avoid face-nailing through planks, especially in doorways, where they're most visible.

10 TAP the reverse tongue into the groove of the existing piece and then reverse direction, nailing into the factory tongues as before.

Finishing touches

Once your flooring is completed, nail your baseboard back into place and cut your base shoe to fit. Fill the nail holes with matching putty. Don't nail the baseboard or the base shoe through the flooring, only into the wall studs. If you need to move heavy appliances like stoves or refrigerators back into the room, roll or scoot them onto thin sheets of Masonite or 1/4-in. plywood and jockey them into position. Use felt pads under tables or heavy chairs to avoid scratches. 🏠

Editor's Note: Edge options

As you shop for flooring, you'll find three basic edge designs. We chose the square edge design that looks just like traditional wood flooring. This type may have a bit of "over" wood (a slight edge variation from board to board that you can feel with your bare feet). To avoid this, you can choose a micro-beveled edge that is hardly noticeable underfoot (or visible, for that matter). You can also choose a larger, bolder bevel to visually separate the individual planks.   — David

11 MIX OR BLEND stains to get a match for wood flooring vents or special transition pieces.

GreatGoofs®

Don't make 'em like they used to

After gutting a bathroom down to the wall studs in a 50-year-old house, I was feeling pretty good. I hauled out the last bag of debris and decided to take a coffee break to celebrate having the worst part behind me.

But as I grabbed my mug, loud cracking sounds filled my ears. Huge drywall slabs pummeled me and loose insulation swirled all around my dazed head and into my coffee cup. The ceiling had completely caved in.

Clobbered but not conquered, I examined the joist. Securing the entire 5 x 8-ft. ceiling were only eight nails of various shapes and sizes. Turns out there was a steel shortage during World War II, causing a nail shortage. Guess they had to skimp a little. Needless to say, I have a new appreciation for local history.

Ticked off

After months of enduring a soft, annoying ticking sound from my ceiling fan, I got up the nerve to finally take it apart.

I removed the fan, took it apart, cleaned and inspected all the parts, then reassembled and reinstalled it. When finished, I was left with four extra bolts—and the tick.

The next day I repeated the whole tedious process and managed to have no extra parts, but still the soft tick continued—from a battery-operated clock on the shelf.

Underwear whereabouts?

After 12 years, the old dryer finally died. I immediately loaded the appliance into my truck, dropped it at the recycling center, bought a new dryer and installed it. In less than two hours, our laundry room was back in business. I was sure my quick response would go into the record books and I waited for my well-deserved praise. Then my wife asked me where I had put the wet clothes from the old dryer.

Then it dawned on me—the clothes were still in the old dryer! I called the recycling center and learned that the old dryer had been hauled away only moments before. Sometimes, it pays to delay.

Great balls of fire

Last spring we found our house being invaded by mice. My husband went into the crawlspace below to see where the critters were getting in and found a hole under the pantry and near the water heater. Using an aerosol can of spray foam, he got to work filling the hole. The pilot light on the water heater suddenly ignited the foam and flames shot across the kitchen floor. I grabbed my son and flew out the door yelling to my husband. Luckily he was able to put out the small fire and no one was hurt. I later noticed the warning label on the can. Now we're a bit more careful about pilot lights and spraying foam just anywhere!

Insulation conflagration

While paneling his basement, my neighbor drove a nail into a copper water pipe. No big deal. He just turned off the water, cut the pipe and slipped on a repair coupling. But while soldering, he set the insulation's paper facing on fire. As the small fire grew, he ran for the garden hose and his wife called 911. Only after dragging the hose into the basement did he remember that the water supply was off. Luckily, there was a fire extinguisher handy and he finished off the flames just as a fire truck arrived.

HANG IT
STRAIGHT, LEVEL & SOLID

*With these four techniques, you can hang
just about anything on your walls, and keep it there*

by **Jeff Gorton**

HANG **HEAVY MIRRORS** WITH CONFIDENCE

Take extra precautions when hanging a heavy mirror. If the mirror has a hanging wire, remove it and screw D-rings to the frame (Photo 1). (Mirrors without frames should be hung with special mirror hangers.) Locate the D-rings an equal distance from the frame's top, about one-third of the total height down. Measure the exact distance between the centers of the D-rings (**Photo 1**). The trick is to hook your tape measure on one edge of a D-ring, and measure to the same edge of the second D-ring. Record this measurement. Then measure down to the top of the D-rings (**Photo 2**).

Photo 3 shows how to transfer the measurements to the wall. But first you'll have to hold the mirror up to the wall and choose the best position. Start with the center of the mirror at about 60 in. from the floor. When you like the position, mark the top center with a sticky note.

Some picture hangers are rated to support heavy mirrors, but it's stronger and safer to install hollow-wall anchors instead. We recommend the screw-in type anchor shown below. It's rated to support 40 lbs. Weigh your mirror and choose the appropriate type of anchor. Use toggle-type anchors (**Photo 3**, p. 44) for heavier mirrors. Measure from your reference point to position the anchors (**Photo 3**). Make starter holes with an awl or Phillips screwdriver. If you hit a stud with the awl, simply drive a screw. **Photo 4** shows how to hang the mirror. If the top isn't level when you're done, wrap a few turns of electrical tape around the D-ring on the low side.

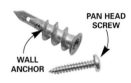

PAN HEAD SCREW

WALL ANCHOR

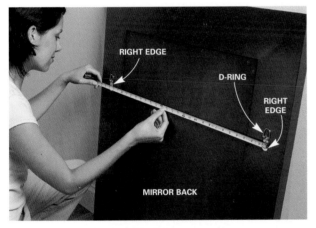

1 MEASURE from the right edge of one D-ring to the right edge of the second D-ring to find the exact distance between the centers of the hanging D-rings.

RIGHT EDGE

D-RING

RIGHT EDGE

MIRROR BACK

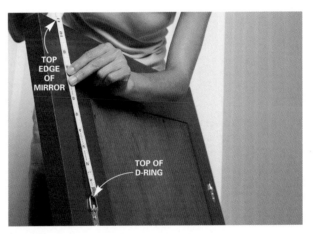

2 MEASURE from the top of the D-ring to the top of the frame to determine the distance down.

TOP EDGE OF MIRROR

TOP OF D-RING

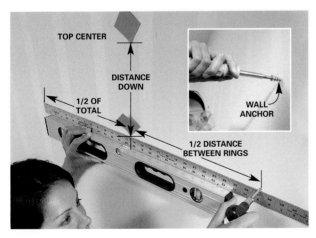

3 USE a level and ruler to plumb down the correct distance. Mark the spot with the corner of a sticky note. Use the level and ruler to find the exact hanger positions. Drive an anchor into the drywall at each hook location (inset).

TOP CENTER

DISTANCE DOWN

1/2 OF TOTAL

WALL ANCHOR

1/2 DISTANCE BETWEEN RINGS

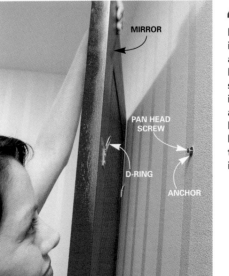

4 SCREW a pan head screw into the anchor. Leave the screw sticking out about 1/4 in. Hook the D-rings onto the protruding screws.

MIRROR

PAN HEAD SCREW

D-RING

ANCHOR

HANG **PICTURES**
STRAIGHT AND LEVEL

The first challenge in hanging a picture is deciding exactly where you want it. It's not so hard with just one picture. You can ask a helper to hold it up while you stand back and judge the position.

Most experts recommend hanging a picture with its center about 60 in. from the floor, or bottom edge 6 to 8 in. above a piece of furniture. Use these heights as a starting point. Then adjust the position of the picture to your liking, and mark the top center with the corner of a sticky note. Use the technique shown in Photos 2 – 6 to complete the job.

A group of pictures is trickier. First cut out paper patterns and arrange them on the wall with low-adhesive masking tape. The temporary red line from a laser level is helpful for aligning a series of photos level with one another (**Photo 1**). The laser level is ideal because you get a perfectly straight line without having to mark up the walls. A standard carpenter's level will also work.

When you arrive at a grouping that's pleasing, mark the top center of each pattern with the corner of a sticky note (**Photo 1**). You'll use the bottom corner of each sticky note as a reference point for locating the picture hangers.

Now you're ready to position the picture hangers (**Photos 2 – 4**). Use two hangers for each picture for extra support and to help keep the picture from tipping. Choose picture hangers that are rated to support the weight of your art. We recommend professional hangers like the one shown on p. 41. They work

1 PROJECT a level line and tape exact-size paper patterns on the wall. Mark the top center of each pattern with the corner of a sticky note.

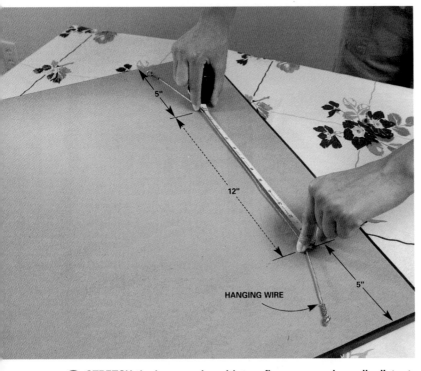

2 STRETCH the hanger wire with two fingers spaced equally distant from the edges of the picture frame. Keep the wire parallel to the top of the frame. Measure the distance between your fingertips.

> **Tip**
>
> Before you hang the picture, stick a pair of clear rubber bumpers on the back lower corners of the frame to protect the wall and help keep the picture level. You'll find these with the picture hanging supplies or in the cabinet hardware department (they're called "door bumpers").

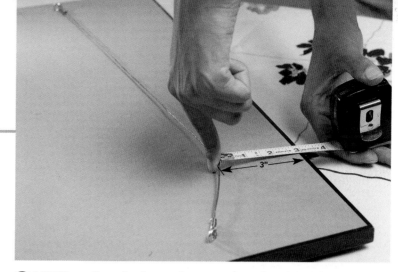

fine in drywall. These are available at home centers or from most picture-framing shops. OOK is one popular brand. Plaster may not support pictures as well as drywall does. To hang heavier art on plaster walls, use picture hangers with double or triple nails.

Photos 2 and 3 show how to measure the space between the hangers and the distance from the top of the picture frame. The distance between hangers isn't critical. Just space your fingers several inches from the outside edges of the picture frame. Transfer these measurements to the wall (**Photo 4**). An inexpensive level with inches marked along the edge is a great picture-hanging tool (**Photo 4**). Otherwise, just stick masking tape to the edge of a level and transfer measurements to the tape (Photo 2, p. 44). Then line up the bottom of the hooks with the marks and drive the picture-hanger nails through the angled guides on the hooks (Photo 5).

3 LEAVE one finger in place and measure from the wire to the top. Use this dimension and the dimension from Photo 2 to position the picture hangers.

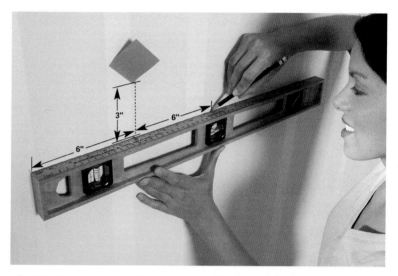

4 FIND the hanger positions by measuring down from the sticky note and to each side from center. Keep the hangers level.

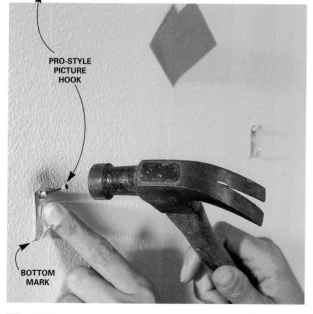

PRO-STYLE PICTURE HOOK

BOTTOM MARK

5 ALIGN the bottom edge of a picture hook with the mark and drive a nail through the hook's guide.

6 SLIP the wire over both hooks. Slide the picture sideways across the wires until it's level. Use the same process to hang the remaining pictures.

HANG A **QUILT** WITHOUT DAMAGING IT

One good way to display a quilt is to hang it on a wall. But don't just tack it up by the corners or it'll stretch out of shape. Instead, use this method for hanging quilts or other decorative textiles because it distributes the weight evenly for smooth hanging and minimal stress to the fabric. The hand stitching (**Photo 1**) used in this method doesn't damage the quilt because it only goes through the backing, and it's easy to remove when you no longer wish to display the quilt.

Measure the top edge of the quilt and purchase the same lengths of 1-1/2-in.-wide sew-on hook-and-loop fastener strip and 2-1/2-in.-wide cotton or synthetic webbing. We found the hook-and-loop strip at a fabric store and the webbing at an upholsterer's shop. You'll also need a length of 1-1/2-in.-wide pine or poplar, a staple gun and several 2-1/2-in. wood screws.

Photos 1 – 3 show how to prepare and hang the quilt. If the quilt pattern allows, it's best to rotate the quilt 180 degrees every month or so. This relieves stress on the fabric and helps prevent uneven fading. To be able to rotate the quilt, you'll have to sew another strip of hook-and-loop along the opposite edge.

HERRINGBONE STITCH

"LOOP" SIDE OF THE HOOK-AND-LOOP

WEBBING

BACK OF QUILT

1 SEW the loop side of the hook-and-loop to the webbing. Then stitch the webbing to the back of the quilt using a herringbone stitch as shown.

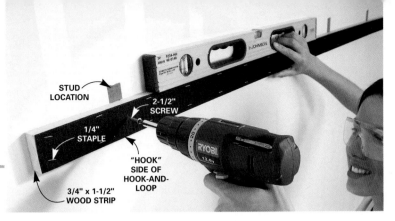

STUD
LOCATION

2-1/2"
SCREW

1/4"
STAPLE

"HOOK"
SIDE OF
HOOK-AND-
LOOP

3/4" x 1-1/2"
WOOD STRIP

2 STAPLE the hook side of the hook-and-loop to the wood strip. Determine the best position, and level the wood strip and screw it to the studs.

3 HANG the quilt by smoothing the hook-and-loop tape that's sewn on the back of the quilt along the tape stapled to the wood strip.

Editor's Note: Additional hanging tips

It's usually not hard to hang things on drywall. You can drive nails easily, and studs are simple to locate. Other types of walls present unique challenges. Plaster is harder than drywall and can crumble. But the pros we talked to say as long as you use professional picture hangers like the ones we show here (these have sharper nails and built-in angle guides), and use hangers a little larger than required, you'll usually be OK. In brick or stone, you can often drive a thin nail into the space between the mortar and the brick or stone. In brick, stone and concrete, you want to avoid making large holes because they're virtually impossible to hide if you move the picture. A good method for brick, stone or concrete walls is to drill a hole that's slightly smaller than the threaded part of a drywall screw. Use a masonry bit in a hammer drill and drill the hole at a slight downward angle. Then thread the screw into the hole, leaving about 1/4 in. sticking out for use as a hanger.

—Jeff

NewProducts

Ball-and-cup laser level

The LaserBall 360 by Zircon stands out from the pack of portable laser level tools for its ease of use and ability to mount anywhere quickly, leaving your hands free.

The four-way bubble level, lighted by an internal LED, allows you to find level or plumb for a perfectly level line. Or, use it to generate a line at any angle you want. The ball has magnets inside, which hold it to the cup mounting system. Once you set the ball in the cup (it takes delicate nudging to get it level and plumb), it maintains its position. You can even attach it to the wall with the adhesive pad included.

The LaserBall costs just $20, but it doesn't project as long a line as higher-priced tools. It's available at most home centers and hardware stores.

Zircon, (800) 245-9265. www.zircon.com

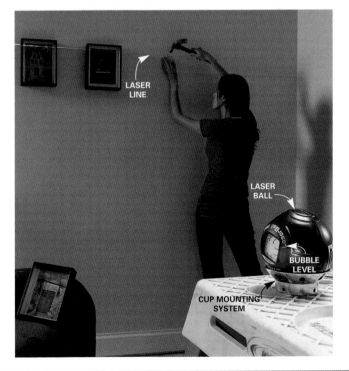

LASER
LINE

LASER
BALL

BUBBLE
LEVEL

CUP MOUNTING
SYSTEM

ALIGN KEYHOLE-SLOT **SHELVES**

Many light-duty shelves have keyholes in the back. The keyholes slide over protruding screws for support. The trick is to precisely place the screws so they align with the keyholes.

Photos 1 – 5 show a foolproof method that doesn't require any measuring or math.

Photo 2 shows a trick for transferring the keyhole locations to the wall. If the mounting screw locations don't land over studs, use wall anchors to support the shelf. We're using a slick toggle-type anchor that holds 60 to 100 lbs. and is easy to install. This brand, Snaptoggle, is available at most home centers (find them online at www.toggler.com). Make sure the screw heads supplied with the anchor fit the keyhole slot before you install the anchor. Otherwise go to a smaller size anchor.

Drill holes for the anchors at each mark and mount the anchors in the wall. Let the screws protrude enough for the keyholes to slide over them. Test-fit the shelf by aligning the keyholes with the screws and sliding it down. If the shelf won't slide on or is too loose, remove the shelf and adjust the screws until you get a snug fit. 🏠

TOGGLE ANCHOR

COLLAR

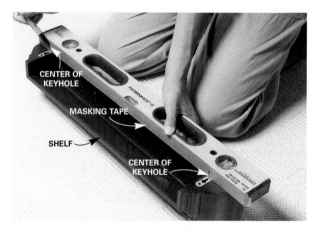

CENTER OF KEYHOLE

MASKING TAPE

SHELF

CENTER OF KEYHOLE

1 STICK masking tape to the edge of your level and mark the keyhole centers on the tape.

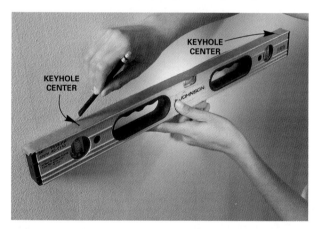

KEYHOLE CENTER

KEYHOLE CENTER

2 PLACE the level against the wall at the desired shelf height. Adjust it to level it and mark the wall at the two keyhole locations.

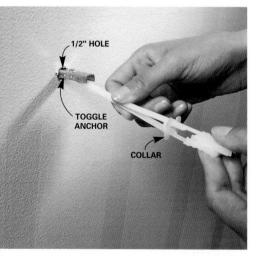

1/2" HOLE

TOGGLE ANCHOR

COLLAR

3 DRILL a hole into the drywall at each mark and slip the toggle through the hole. Push in the plastic collar tight to the drywall.

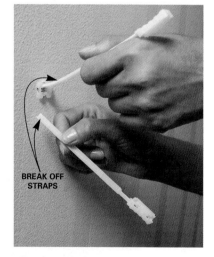

BREAK OFF STRAPS

4 Then BREAK OFF the straps flush with the collar.

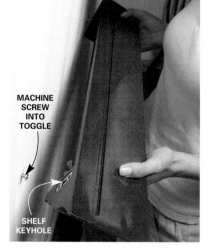

MACHINE SCREW INTO TOGGLE

SHELF KEYHOLE

5 DRIVE the included machine screw into the toggle, letting it protrude about 3/16 in. Test-fit the shelf.

HOW TO AVOID

7 UGLY DRYWALL MISTAKES

Our enthusiastic but clueless handyman here doesn't know it, but there are 7 mistakes in this photo—can you find them?*   by **Jeff Gorton**

*Here are 7 mistakes to avoid

1. Leaving out backers at inside corners

2. Forgetting to mark framing before installing the drywall

3. Forcing drywall over outlet boxes (four occurrences in photo)

4. Cutting for a "too-tight" fit

5. Creating extra joints by using small pieces

6. Joining pieces at the corner of a door

7. Installing tapered edges along corners

Providing poor support at edges

TOO LITTLE BACKING

Add 2x4 backing

ADDED 2x4 BACKING

Framing at inside corners is often inadequate or lacking altogether, making it impossible to fasten the edge of the drywall.

The solution is to inspect the framing before you start hanging drywall. Make sure there's at least 1 in. of exposed framing at corners. If not, add another 2x4 alongside the existing framing (**photo right**). Especially check along the top of walls that run parallel to the ceiling framing. Normally blocking is nailed to the top plate of the wall during the framing phase, but it's often missing. If you have to add blocking and don't have room to swing a hammer, drive screws into the blocking at an angle from below.

If you forget to mark the location of framing members before you cover them with drywall, you'll have a hard time placing the screws accurately (**top right**). For foolproof screw placement, make these marks and use them as a guide to draw a light pencil line across the sheet (**bottom right**). Then you'll be able to place screws quickly and accurately. And you won't have to waste time removing screws that miss the framing.

Mark the location of ceiling joists on the top plate of the wall framing. Then mark the center of each stud on the floor. Make note of unusual framing so you'll know where to place screws after it's covered with drywall. After the ceiling drywall is hung, mark the stud locations on the ceiling with a pencil before you start to hang drywall on the walls.

Guessing at framing locations

NO FRAMING MARKS

SCREWS MISS

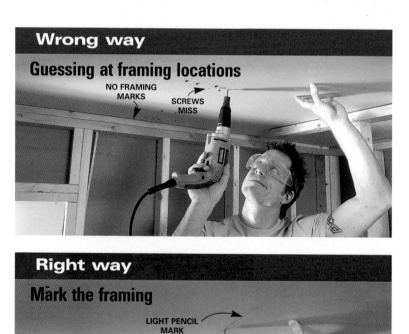

Mark the framing

LIGHT PENCIL MARK

JOIST CENTER MARK

Wrong way

Forcing the drywall over outlet boxes

BROKEN DRYWALL

TIGHT FIT

RID

Right way

Trim around boxes, then fasten

TOO TIGHT

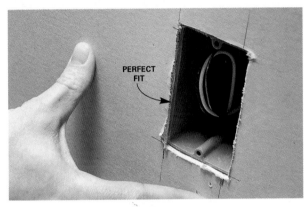

PERFECT FIT

Even with careful measuring, you'll often run into an outlet hole that doesn't quite fit. The common mistake is to screw the drywall to the framing before trimming the opening. Then the drywall will break around the electrical box (**photo above**), requiring extra time to patch. The key to solve this problem is to check the fit before you press the drywall tight to the wall.

After carefully measuring and cutting out the openings in your sheet of drywall, hold the drywall in place. If the fit is close, fasten the sheet with a few screws along the top edge or well away from the outlet openings. Trim excess drywall away along tight box edges with a utility knife (**top right**) until the drywall slides easily over the outlet boxes (**bottom right**). Then finish fastening the drywall.

There's no reason to measure and cut drywall for an exact fit. It'll usually just cause trouble. Jamming in a piece that's too tight will crumble the edge or break out a corner (**first photo at right**). And removing a piece to shave a too-tight edge is messy and time consuming. A loose fit avoids this problem. Cut it to leave about a 1/8-in. gap at edges. In fact, when you're hanging the ceiling, keep in mind that 1/2 in. along the perimeter will be covered by drywall on the walls. And the same is true

Wrong way

Cutting for a tight fit

TOO TIGHT

Right way

Leave 1/8-in. gaps at edges

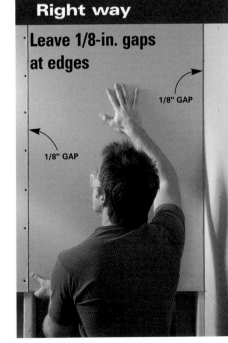

1/8" GAP

1/8" GAP

of inside wall corners. So you can safely cut these pieces 1/4 in. less than the actual measurement and leave a gap in the corner if necessary. Even a piece whose edges aren't

covered should be cut a little short. It's easier to fill a 1/8-in. gap with setting-type compound than to cut and repair a broken edge or corner.

Wrong way

Creating unnecessary joints

8' SHEET OF DRYWALL

BUTT JOINT

8' SHEET OF DRYWALL

BUTT JOINT

Taping drywall is time consuming and tedious enough without adding extra joints, especially those hard-to-tape butt joints (**photo left**). So plan your job to use the longest and largest sheets possible. And don't scrimp on materials. Drywall is cheap.

If the walls you're planning to drywall are between 8 ft. 1 in. and 9 ft. 1 in. tall, consider ordering special 54-in.-wide sheets of drywall to avoid an extra horizontal joint. You'll find 54-in.-wide drywall at drywall suppliers, or you can special-order it from most home centers and lumberyards. You'll also speed up your job by using 12-ft.-long sheets of drywall rather than standard 8-footers (**photo below**). However, hauling 12-ft. sheets is difficult and getting them into the house can be challenging. For large jobs, have the drywall delivered. Many drywall suppliers will even stack the drywall in the house for an extra fee.

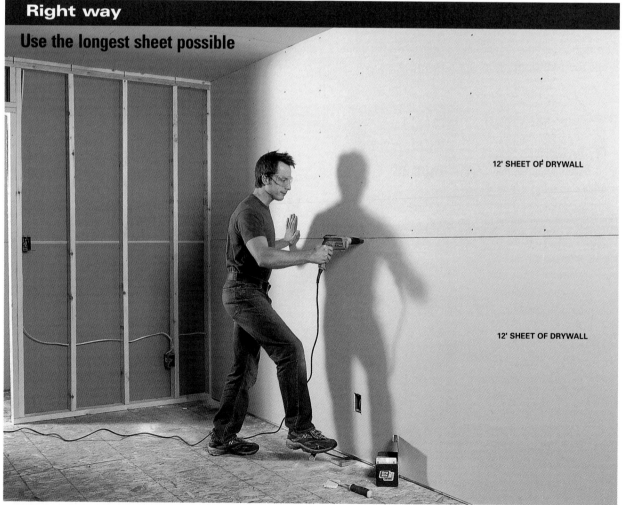

Right way

Use the longest sheet possible

12' SHEET OF DRYWALL

12' SHEET OF DRYWALL

A void lining up a sheet of drywall with the edge of a door or window opening (**first photo at right**). Your home tends to shift and settle slightly, and that movement shows up at the corners of windows and doors. A joint at this location, even if it's well taped, is weaker than solid drywall. Chances are it'll crack in the future.

It's better to notch drywall around openings rather than to make a joint. For interior walls, simply continue over the opening with a full sheet and cut out the opening after you fasten the sheet (**photo far right**). Windows on exterior walls are a little trickier. Measure and notch the sheet before hanging it. Get help when hanging notched sheets because the skinny section above the opening is often fragile. It's OK to join sheets over an opening (and often easier if you're working alone) as long as the joint isn't in line with either side.

Wrong way
Creating a joint at corners

BAD JOINT LOCATION

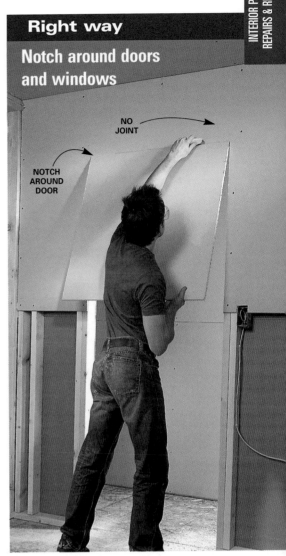

Right way
Notch around doors and windows

NO JOINT

NOTCH AROUND DOOR

Wrong way
Installing tapered edges along corners

TAPERED EDGE

I f you hang a sheet of drywall with the tapered edge along an outside corner, it will be hard to install the corner bead accurately. The corner of the bead will lie too low, making it difficult to cover with joint compound. The solution is to place cut edges along an outside corner (**photo right**).

Right way
Use non-tapered edges only

NO TAPER AT CORNER

CUT EDGES; NO TAPER

SUPER-SIMPLE
STORAGE

PROTECT TABLE LEAVES

When you're storing table leaves, protect the edges with pipe insulation (about $4 per four-pack of 3-ft. foam). It will keep your dinner table picture perfect and free of scuffs.

SHOE POCKET

Hanging shoe bags are great for closets, but they can also cut the clutter in your garage, workshop or laundry room. A shoe bag like this one costs about $12 at discount stores.

IRONING BOARD

Ordinary coat hooks on the back of a closet door keep your ironing board out of the way but close at hand when you need it.

TWO OPEN-STUD-WALL STORAGE TIPS

'Tween studs shelving

Store smaller containers—spray paint, putty cans, glue bottles—right in the wall! Screw shelf brackets (6-ft. lengths cost $1.50 each at home centers) to the studs, then install shelves, cut from standard 1x4 boards, on adjustable clips ($2 for a bag of 12). The boards fit perfectly; there's no need to saw them to width.

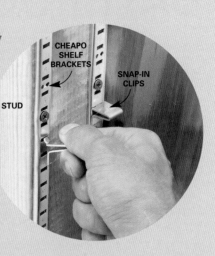

CHEAPO SHELF BRACKETS

SNAP-IN CLIPS

STUD

Studly clamp storage

Clamps scattered and hard to find when you need them most? Here's a way to keep them in one spot. Hang bar clamps on horizontal scraps of 2x4 screwed between open-wall studs. Add another board or two for glue bottles, dowels and biscuits. To hold C-clamps and spring clamps, drill holes in the studs and install lengths of 3/16-in. threaded rod, tensioned with 1/4-in. fender washers and nuts.

3/16" NUT

3/16"-DIA. THREADED ROD

1/4" FENDER WASHER

UNDER-BED STORAGE RACK

If you're getting rid of your old dishwasher, hang on to the lower dish rack. Slip it under a bed for convenient roll-out storage. 🏠

TOP 10
BATHROOM UPGRADES

Our favorite ways to increase comfort and convenience without busting your budget

by **Gary Wentz**

1 Whirlpool tub

Bathtubs that provide a massage aren't just for million-dollar homes anymore. Smaller tubs that fit into a standard 5-ft.-long tub space, with smaller price tags (starting at about $500), have made whirlpool tubs affordable. When you look at prices, remember to add at least $200 for the faucet, plumbing and electrical supplies. You may want to replace your water heater too. Your water heater capacity should be about 75 percent of the tub's capacity.

There are two types of whirlpool tubs. Traditional "water-jet" tubs provide a more powerful water stream. The other type of whirlpool, an "air-jet" tub, massages by blasting air through tiny holes. Some people prefer the tingle of air massage; others find it too gentle. Air-jet tubs are often louder and incoming air cools the water faster. Expect to spend at least $1,200 for an air-jet tub.

soothing soak

2 A soap dispenser

cut the clutter

Many hotels no longer provide tiny bars of soap and miniature shampoo bottles. They've discovered that push-button dispensers mean less clutter, more convenience and quicker cleaning. The version shown here dispenses three liquids (such as soap, shampoo and conditioner). Either screw it to the wall or fasten it with adhesive and two-sided tape. You might find a dispenser at a home center or discount store, but you can check out a variety of models online; just type "soap dispenser" into any search engine. The Aviva III model shown is available from comforthouse.com for about $40.

3 A towel warmer

Any bathroom feels luxurious when there's a warm towel waiting as you step out of the shower. But towel warmers have practical benefits too. Towels dry faster, so they're less likely to develop a musty odor. A towel warmer can also take the chill out of a cool bathroom. Small versions produce only as much heat as a 100-watt light bulb, but larger models can noticeably raise the temperature in an average-size bathroom. All versions have switches, so they don't waste power when you don't want the extra heat. Some even have timers. Prices range from $40 to $250.

warm luxury

Adding a heated towel rack isn't any more difficult than installing a new towel bar—just fasten it to the wall and plug it in. There are even a few freestanding versions that don't require any installation at all. If you're doing an extensive bathroom remodel, consider a hard-wired model, which provides a neater look by eliminating the power cord. If your home is heated with water, consider a "hydronic" towel warmer, which works like a radiator. Hydronic versions generally produce more heat more economically. You might find a few towel warmers at a kitchen and bath showroom or other retailer, but to browse a wide variety of models, visit www.comfortchannel.com or just type "towel warmer" into any search engine.

4 A dimmer switch

If your bathroom is a quiet refuge where you escape from the world, let the lighting match your mood. A simple dimmer switch ($8 to $20) lets you choose bright light for shaving or applying makeup and gentle light to accompany that soothing shower or bath. You can install one in just a few minutes, but to do it safely you have to check the grounding and the size of the junction box.

cut the glare

5 A recessed medicine cabinet (or two)

Every bathroom can use more storage space. And most bathrooms have a spot—usually next to the door—that's perfect for an extra medicine cabinet. If you install a "recessed" cabinet that fits inside the wall between the studs, you won't lose an inch of space in the bathroom. If wall space allows, you can even install two cabinets this way, side-by-side or over-under. Another good spot for a medicine cabinet is above the toilet. But in that case, you'll most likely need a surface-mount cabinet, since there's usually a large vertical vent pipe in the wall behind the toilet. Medicine cabinets are available at home centers and kitchen and bath showrooms starting at about $30. Here are some Web sites to check out: www.broan.com, www. nutone.com, www.robern.com and www.kitchensource.com.

extra storage

6 A big mirror

If you're looking for dramatic results on a limited budget, you can't do better than to install a big mirror. It will provide a larger view, of course, but the real wow effect of a big mirror is that it makes a dim, cramped bathroom feel bright and spacious. Home centers and kitchen and bath showrooms carry or can special-order large framed or unframed mirrors. For a wide online selection, go to www.simplymirrors.com. If you want a large, unframed mirror cut to the size and shape you like, call a business that specializes in mirrors (in the yellow pages under "Mirrors").

bright, spacious feeling That way you can even get a huge mirror (typically up to 6 ft. x 10 ft.) with polished or beveled edges. You can also have holes cut so the mirror fits neatly over switches, outlets or light fixtures ($20 to $30 per hole). Either build your own mirror frame or leave the edges exposed and hang the mirror with clips or adhesive. A 4-ft. x 5-ft. mirror with polished edges costs about $160.

7 New faucet & hardware

If the main elements of your bathroom—like the flooring, tub and vanity—are in good shape, a new set of matching hardware might be all you need for an updated look. Seemingly small items like a stylish faucet, light fixtures, towel bars or cabinet door hardware can have a big impact. While you're at it, replace grimy old light switch and outlet covers. You'll find everything you need at a home center or a kitchen and bath showroom.

fast facelift

8 Frameless shower & tub doors

Frameless shower doors will save you countless hours of tedious cleaning over the years. They aren't entirely frameless; you fasten metal channels to tub or shower walls. But the glass doors themselves have no frames and no crevices to collect soap scum. Some models, such as Sterling's Finesse series or Kohler's Purist line, also feature clever designs to make installation easier (www. kohler.com). The model shown here (Sterling Finesse 6305-34, about $400) has no crossbar above the door opening, so there's no head hazard for tall folks and one less part to clean for the rest of us (www.sterlingplumbing.com).

easy cleaning

9 A quiet bath fan

You might be tempted to leave your noisy bath fan off. But don't. Humidity from hot showers feeds mildew, causes condensation and can support rot inside your walls. Instead, upgrade to a quiet fan.

Fan noise is measured in "sones." The lower the number, the quieter the fan. "Quiet" fans usually hum at 1.5 sones or less; some are as low as .3 sones (find them at www.broan.com). If a fan doesn't carry a sone rating, it's probably loud (3 to 5 sones). Quiet fans start at about $100.

cut the noise

Replacing a fan and ductwork takes one day. But often you can connect a quiet fan to existing ductwork and save hours of work. Most quiet fans require duct that's at least 4 in. in diameter. To determine the size of your existing duct, pull off the fan's grille and find the manufacturer and model number. Then go online and type them into a search engine such as Google. At Web sites of manufacturers and parts retailers, you'll find the specifications for your fan. If your fan uses 4-in. duct, you'll have a wide range of quiet fans to choose from at home centers. If your fan is connected to 3-in. duct, check out the WhisperFit line of fans at www.panasonic.com.

To remove moisture from your home, it's best to let a fan run for 15 to 30 minutes after you shower or bathe. So consider replacing the fan's switch with a timer. Rotary timers, which work well but make a buzzing sound, cost about $20 at home centers. For silent operation, get an electronic timer (www.levitonproducts.com, item No. 6230M, $40). Another option is to install a fan that switches on when humidity levels rise (www.broan.com, item No. DH100W).

10 Heated floor

Bare feet and bathrooms go together, so your feet will appreciate a warm floor all winter long. There are two basic types of floor heating systems: electric resistance wires, which operate like an electric blanket; and hydronic systems, which pump hot water through flexible plastic tubing. Hydronic systems churn out more heat more economically. Some upscale homes are heated entirely by hydronic "radiant" floor heat. If you just want warm toes when you step out of the tub, you may find electrical heat more practical. The system costs less and is usually easier to install.

With either type of system, there are only two ways to add heat to your floor: You can install new flooring (ceramic tile is the most popular flooring for heated floors). Or—if the floor is accessible from below—you can fasten wires or tubing to the underside of the subfloor. For any type of floor heating system, expect to spend $10 or more per square foot.

The electric mat shown here is embedded in mortar beneath ceramic tile. For more information, go to www.suntouch.net.

For a mat that's installed on the underside of the floor between floor joists, check out www.calorique.com.

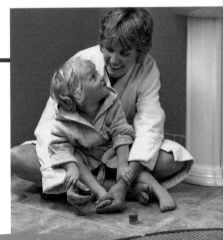

warm feet

These suppliers specialize in helping do-it-yourselfers install hydronic systems: www.radiantcompany.com and www.radiantec.com.

Ask TFH™
The Family Handyman

TOO MUCH STATIC

In the winter, I have a big problem with static electricity. I have hot water radiator heat and rugs throughout my house. Is there a better solution than putting a humidifier in every room?

Yes, you have several other options. Static electricity is caused by your body picking up free electrons as you walk on the rugs. When you have extra electrons on your body and you touch a metal conductor, such as a door handle, the electrons flow into the object and you get a tiny shock.

During the summer, the humidity in the air helps electrons flow off your body, so you don't build up a charge. The air is drier in the winter, no matter what type of heating system you have, allowing a larger charge to build. Humidity will certainly help reduce static electricity, so installing a whole-house humidifier is one option.

Another option is to treat your rugs with an anti-static chemical as shown. Spray-on treatments are available at many carpet retailers and online at sites such as www.ultrastatinc.com and www.clausencarpet.com/anti.html. Carpet companies also have anti-static carpets available. Most residential carpets sold today have some sort of treatment applied at the factory.

A third option is to wear special shoes that dissipate static charge. The shoes have conductive strands in the soles that discharge static electricity as you walk. They start at about $70. You can find the shoes at select shoe stores and online at sites such as www.shoemall.com (800-704-5478).

Spray an anti-static treatment on rugs and carpeting to reduce static shocks.

CARPETING BELOW GRADE

We're planning to finish our basement. The floor is a concrete slab. Can I install carpet in some of the rooms even though they're below grade? We've never had any water problems.

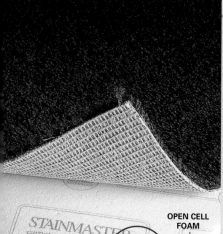

OPEN CELL FOAM

Any carpet that can be used in other areas of the house can be used in the basement. But as a precaution against moisture, use an open cell pad to allow the concrete to "breathe." Nearly all pads are open cell pads, which provide better insulation and are less expensive than closed cell pads. In addition, some pads have a film barrier or odor guard (**see photo**) that helps eliminate odors that sometimes come from basement floors. Look for a stamp or words on the pad that say it provides odor protection. These pads cost $1 to $2 more per square yard than traditional pads and are available at carpet stores.

Rubber pads (which are closed cell) are also available for carpet installed below grade, but most professionals don't recommend them because they can trap moisture between the pad and the concrete. This may cause moisture to move up the walls and get into the drywall.

The key is to think through and resolve any potential moisture problems in your basement before installing carpet. Once installed, carpets with open cell pads can withstand moderate wetting if you clean them with a wet/dry vacuum. But keep in mind that a flood of water will ruin both the carpet and pad, and you'll have to replace them.

REMOVE TILE FROM CONCRETE

The tile in my bathroom looks outdated and needs to be replaced. What's the best way to remove ceramic tile from a concrete slab? I want to do this with the least amount of work.

There's no easy way to do this. Unlike tile on cement board or wood, there's no underlayment or subfloor that can be pried up and thrown away. Removing tile from concrete requires knocking out the tiles and adhesive. It takes time and hard work. Even a small bathroom will take half a day, at a minimum.

Use a 3/4- or 1-in. masonry chisel and a 2-lb. hand maul. Start at a broken tile or between tiles where the grout has loosened. Work the chisel under the tiles, forcing them loose (**photo above**). Strike the face of stubborn tiles to break them up for easier removal. Wear safety glasses, gloves, pants and a long-sleeve shirt, since hammering the tile sends sharp shards flying. Also wear a dust mask.

Typically, older floors with mastic adhesive will come up easier than floors laid with thin-set mortar. Rent a small jackhammer with a chisel point if the tile refuses to come loose. For larger rooms, consider renting an electric tile stripper ($50 to $100 per day).

After you remove the tiles, chisel and scrape the adhesive off the concrete as well. If you can't get it all, don't worry. You can leave bits of adhesive up to 1/8 in. thick. Then use the flat side of a 12-in. trowel to apply a 1/8-in. layer of latex thin-set mortar over the floor (**photo at right**). This is to fill in voids and level around remaining

bits of adhesive. If you're installing new tile, use the same latex thin-set to set the tile. Thin-set holds ceramic tiles better than mastic and is easier to work with.

Keep in mind that the easiest solution of all is to leave the old tile in place and install new tile directly over the old. The new floor will be slightly higher, so you'll have to trim the door and extend the toilet ring. For more details, talk with an expert at a local tile store.

12" TROWEL

THIN-SET MORTAR

Ask TFH™
The Family Handyman

WILL YOUR REMODELING PAY OFF?

Our kitchen needs remodeling, but we're not sure how much to spend. We don't want to lose money when we sell. How can we learn how far to go?

If you're concerned about the future value of your remodeling investment, consult a local real estate agent or home appraiser. Home values are highly variable depending on your neighborhood, the regional market and the condition of your home. These real estate professionals will use local variables to estimate the market value of your home and tell you what upgrades will deliver the best return.

Another useful source of information is the annual Cost vs. Value Report on the Remodeling Magazine Web site (www.remodelingmagazine.com), which presents both the national picture and the regional breakdown for 22 major remodeling categories (kitchens, bathrooms, additions, windows, etc.). Generally it shows that bathroom and kitchen projects have strong paybacks (more than 90 percent), if kept in a mid-price range. The payback drops if the project includes major tearouts or upscale cabinets, appliances and fixtures. Mid-range remodeling of "space expansion" areas like attics, basements and decks also scores above 90 percent

payback. Additions, however, don't fare so well. Family rooms, master suites and sunrooms score only about 80 percent return. In general, "lifestyle" improvements such as swimming pools, spas and exercise rooms don't pay back very well either. But siding replacement scored high (fiber cement was 104 percent and vinyl 96 percent).

Check the regional breakdowns for these categories, however, because you'll find wide variations. For example, a major kitchen remodel in Phoenix returns about 99 percent, but the return in Burlington, Vermont, is only about 46 percent. The value of other homes on your block matters too. An expensive remodel won't deliver a high payback if it makes your home the most expensive one on the block. But a modest remodel that replaces an outdated kitchen, updates a grungy bathroom and upgrades a shabby exterior can pay off well.

BUBBLING WALLPAPER

I have several noticeable bubbles in my wallpaper. How can I get rid of them?

Fix the bubbles by cutting them with a razor knife. A small slit is all that's needed. Then insert the end of a glue applicator and squeeze in a little adhesive (**see photo**).

Wipe away excessive adhesive with a damp sponge and press the wallpaper against the wall to force out the air, using a plastic straightedge.

The glue applicators and proper adhesive are available at paint stores and home centers for less than $10.

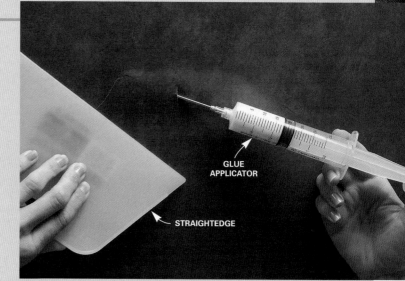

GLUE APPLICATOR

STRAIGHTEDGE

READER MYSTERY PHOTO

STAIN ON A VINYL FLOOR

There's a mysterious stain on my vinyl floor and it has gotten larger over the past several years. The vinyl is over concrete in my downstairs bathroom. What could cause the stain and is there a way to get rid of it?

You have a classic case of "bottom-up" staining—the stain is penetrating the vinyl from underneath. It may be the adhesive that was used to adhere the vinyl to the concrete, or it could be the result of moisture rising up through the concrete.

Since your stain is yellow, it's probably an adhesive stain. If it were black, gray, blue or pink, it would indicate mold growth. Then you'd have to solve a moisture problem before laying your new floor.

You have two options. Either rip up the flooring and scrape off the adhesive, or install a new floor (vinyl, laminate, carpet, wood or floating floor) right over the top of the vinyl, provided the old vinyl is well adhered. If it's coming loose, tear it out and start over. Otherwise, the second option is quicker and easier. Besides, the old vinyl will make a great underlayment. The stain won't come up through the old vinyl and discolor the new floor.

Bottom-up staining has become less common over the last 10 years because adhesive formulas have improved.

REMOVING BASE-BOARD NAILS

I'm trying to reuse the old baseboards in my living room, but when I tap the nails back out, they bend and the boards crack. What's the best way to remove the nails?

Instead of pounding the nails back out, pull them all the way through with nippers. Place the board face down, grab the nail with the nippers, then roll the nippers forward or backward (Photo 1).

The finish nail will come out the back side without marking or scuffing the face of the board (Photo 2). In fact, the nail hole filler on the front side won't even fall out!

1 PULL nails through the back side of baseboard with nippers.

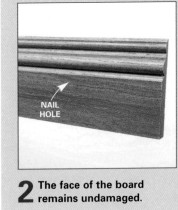

NAIL HOLE

2 The face of the board remains undamaged.

WAIT FOR THE ALARM

We have a carbon monoxide alarm with a digital readout. It sometimes shows carbon monoxide is present, but the alarm never goes off. How do I know if we have a dangerous level in our house?

CO ALARM

Pay attention to the alarm. If the alarm goes off, you have a potentially dangerous level of carbon monoxide in your home. Immediately follow these guidelines: Press the reset button, call the fire department or 911, get fresh air by going outside or standing next to an open window, and make sure every member of the household joins you.

The digital readout alone doesn't always tell whether you have a dangerous level of CO. A continuous low reading over a long period can be more hazardous than a momentary high reading. The alarm, on the other hand, senses both the concentration of CO and its duration, and is designed to sound when the combination of the two is hazardous.

The digital feature is useful, however, because it'll tell you when any CO is present, even a very low level. You can search out sources and correct a potential problem. Look for a correlation between using a gas appliance and a CO reading. If you can't find the source, call in a heating or appliance professional to track it down.

CO ALARM

OLD-STYLE CO "DETECTOR"

ORGANIZE YOUR
CLOSET!

This simple shelf-and-rod system will bring order to your cluttered closet and double the storage space

by **Lucie Amundsen**

Annoyed by an overstuffed closet packed so tightly that you can't find your favorite shirt or shoes? Where the closet rod bends under the weight of all of "his" and "her" clothing?

If so, the simple closet organizing system we show here is a great solution. It utilizes the closet space much more efficiently by dividing your closet into zones that give your slacks, dresses, shirts, shoes and other items their own home. As a result, your clothing is better organized and you can find your party shirt or power skirt quickly and easily. It also prevents "closet creep," where "her" clothing

tends to infringe on "his" zone. (Or vice versa!) Overall, you'll get double the useful space of a traditional single pole and shelf closet.

In this article, we'll show you how to build this simple organizer, step-by-step, and tell you how to customize it to fit closets of different sizes. We designed it for simplicity; you can build it in one weekend, even if you're a novice. However, to do a nice job, you should have experience using two basic power tools: a circular saw and a drill. A power miter box and an air-powered brad nailer ($90) make the job go a bit faster, but they aren't necessary.

Figure A: Closet Organizer

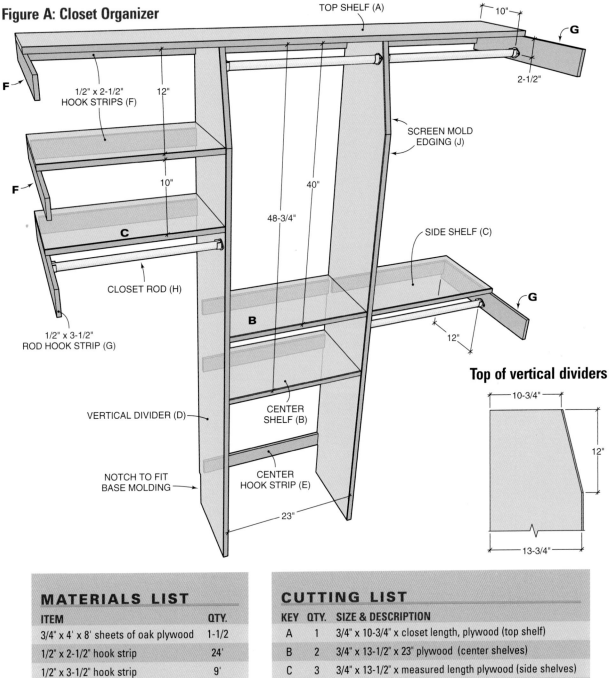

TOP SHELF (A)

10"

G

F

1/2" x 2-1/2"
HOOK STRIPS (F)

12"

SCREEN MOLD
EDGING (J)

2-1/2"

F

10"

40"

48-3/4"

C

SIDE SHELF (C)

CLOSET ROD (H)

G

12"

1/2" x 3-1/2"
ROD HOOK STRIP (G)

B

VERTICAL DIVIDER (D)

CENTER
SHELF (B)

Top of vertical dividers

10-3/4"

12"

NOTCH TO FIT
BASE MOLDING

CENTER
HOOK STRIP (E)

23"

13-3/4"

MATERIALS LIST

ITEM	QTY.
3/4" x 4' x 8' sheets of oak plywood	1-1/2
1/2" x 2-1/2" hook strip	24'
1/2" x 3-1/2" hook strip	9'
1/4" x 3/4" x 8' screen molding	4
1-1/16" closet rod	8'
Pairs of rod holders	4
6d finishing nails	1 lb.

CUTTING LIST

KEY	QTY.	SIZE & DESCRIPTION
A	1	3/4" x 10-3/4" x closet length, plywood (top shelf)
B	2	3/4" x 13-1/2" x 23" plywood (center shelves)
C	3	3/4" x 13-1/2" x measured length plywood (side shelves)
D	2	3/4" x 13-3/4" x 82" plywood (vertical dividers)
E	4	1/2" x 2-1/2" x 23" (center hook strips)
F	7	1/2" x 2-1/2" x measured lengths (hook strips)
G	3	1/2" x 3-1/2" x closet depth (hook strips for rods)
H	4	1-1/16" x measured lengths (closet rods)
J		1/4" x 3/4" x measured lengths (screen molding)

Don't buy it—build it!

While you may be tempted to buy a prefabricated organizer, it'll be surprisingly expensive when you tally up the
cost of all the pieces. The materials for our organizer cost
only $150. We used 1-1/2 sheets of oak veneer plywood,
plus several types of standard oak trim that you'll find at
most home centers and lumberyards. (See the Materials
List above left.) Keep in mind that if you use other wood
species, you may have trouble finding matching trim, and
you'll have to custom-cut it from solid boards on a table

saw. If you choose to paint your organizer, you can use less expensive plywood and trim, and cut your expenses by about one-third.

Begin by measuring the width of your closet. The system we show works best in a 6-ft. closet. If your closet only measures 5 ft., consider using a single vertical divider, rather than the two we show in **Figure A**.

Assemble the center unit

After referring to the Cutting List and your closet dimensions, rip the plywood into two 13-3/4-in. pieces for the vertical dividers. If you plan to rip plywood with a circular saw, be sure to use a straightedge to get perfectly straight cuts. We'll be using hook strips to attach the center unit and shelves to the closet walls, as well as for spacing the uprights (**Figure A**). If you want to save a bit of cash, you can rip these strips from the leftover plywood (and enjoy the gratification that comes from using the entire sheet). Cut the plywood to length using a factory plywood edge as a guide (**Photo 1**). Always check for accuracy by just nicking the plywood with the blade to make sure you're hitting your mark. Fully support your project with 2x4s so the cutoff doesn't fall and splinter. Also, for smoother cuts, use a sharp blade with at least 40 teeth.

You don't have to cut out the baseboard in the closet or even trim the back side of the dividers to fit its exact profile. The back of the organizer will be mostly out of sight, so square notches will do (**Photo 2**).

You'll have to trim the tops of the dividers back to 10-3/4 in. to make it easier to slide stuff onto the top shelf (unless you have an extra-deep closet). We angled this cut to the first shelf point (**Figure A**).

Apply the screen molding to hide the raw plywood edges on the dividers and shelves. You'll have to cut a 7-degree angle on the molding with a circular saw, jigsaw or miter saw to get a perfect fit on the dividers. Cut this angle first and when you get a nice fit, cut the other ends to length. You could also apply edge veneer (iron-on) or any other 3/4-in. wood strips to cover the edges.

Now sand all the parts to prepare them for finishing. A random orbital sander (starting at about $50) with 120-grit sandpaper will make quick work of this, but a few squares of sandpaper and a wood block will also do the trick. After sanding, wipe the surface of the wood with a clean cloth to remove dust.

It's easiest to apply your finish before assembly. We chose a warm fruitwood-tone Danish Finishing Oil. This

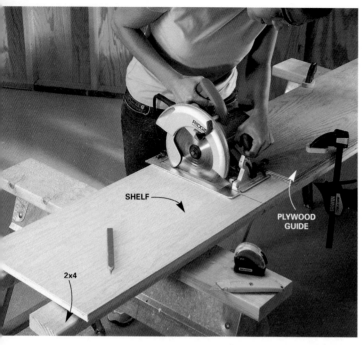

1 MEASURE your closet dimensions and cut the plywood vertical dividers and shelves to size (Figure A). Use a guide to make crosscuts perfectly square.

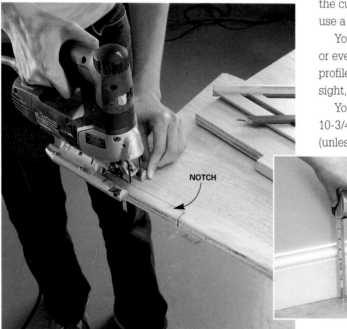

2 MEASURE the baseboard height and thickness and cut notches with a jigsaw on the vertical dividers to fit over it.

> **Tip**
> When you're gluing and nailing your screen molding (Photo 3), have a damp cloth handy to promptly wipe away any glue ooze.

type of finish brings out the natural grain of the wood, looks velvety smooth, and is easy to renew when you scratch or scuff it. Use a small cloth to rub a generous amount of oil into the surface until the plywood and hook strips have an even sheen, and allow it to dry overnight.

After the finish oil dries, assemble the center unit. Lightly mark the vertical dividers where the interior shelves and hook strips will be positioned and drill 1/8-in. pilot holes to simplify the nailing. Then spread a thin bead of glue onto the shelf ends and clamp the unit together. Use four 6d finish nails to pin the shelves securely (**Photo 4**), then countersink the nail heads with a nail set. Nails and glue are strong enough for holding garments and other light items, but if you plan to store your boat anchor collection on a closet shelf, put a cleat under the shelf to bear the weight.

Position one of the center unit's interior hook strips at the very top of the dividers and one above the bottom notches, and one under each shelf. The strips will shore up the unit and keep the plywood from bowing when you install it.

In the closet

If you have a thin carpet and pad, you can place the center unit directly on top of it. However, if you have a plush rug with a soft padding, stability is a concern. After determining the exact placement of your unit (by centering the unit on the midpoint of the closet; **Photo 5**), mark and cut out two 3/4-in.-wide slots in the carpet and pad so the dividers rest on the solid floor below.

Find the studs using a stud finder and mark them with masking tape. Also measure and mark the center of the

Editor's Note: Protect prime space

Your bedroom closet is valuable real estate, and the only way to protect it is to store off-season or rare-occasion clothing elsewhere.

Many of us use garment bags, plastic bins (stored off the floor in a humidity-controlled basement) or a freestanding wardrobe. However, many mid-century homes have closets on the main level that are 4-1/2 ft. deep or better, and they're perfect candidates for off-season use.

Deep closets can fit double rods mounted parallel to each other in the front and the back. It's an ideal setup for tightly stashing off-season outfits. Add a rolling bin on the closet floor to store accessories, beachwear or ski gloves in Ziploc Big Bags (about $1 each). This will keep your bedroom closet clear and your active gear at hand.

Every clothing item should be handled annually and those not worn in a given season cast off. Passing along unused attire creates the luxury of space and ease in any closet.

—Lucie

> **Tip**
> To make perfect crosscuts on plywood, score your pencil line with a utility knife. This will give you a finer cut with less splintering of the veneer.

SCREEN MOLDING

SHELF BRACKET CLAMPING SYSTEM

3 SMOOTH the cut plywood edges with 80-grit sandpaper and a block, then glue and tack 3/4-in. screen molding onto the edges that will show. Apply a stain or finish and let it dry.

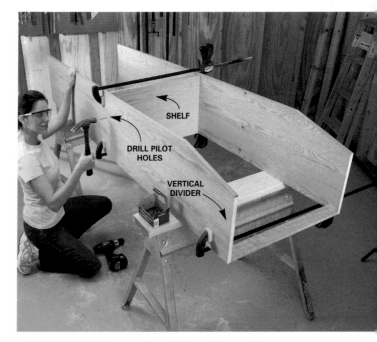

SHELF

DRILL PILOT HOLES

VERTICAL DIVIDER

4 LAY OUT the intermediate shelf positions with a square, spread glue on the shelf edges and nail the shelf to the dividers with 6d finish nails. Nail the 1/2-in. hook strips to the dividers as well.

5 SET the center unit in the closet, level it with shims, predrill and tack the hook strips to the wall studs with 6d finish nails.

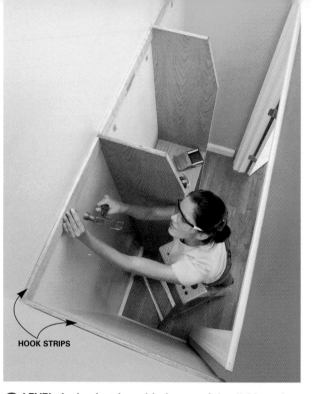

6 LEVEL the hook strips with the top of the dividers, then predrill and nail them to the studs. Continue the strip around the closet sides.

wall on tape. This way you'll avoid marking up your walls. Set the unit in its position against the wall. Level and shim as necessary (**Photo 5**).

Predrill the hook strips with a 1/8-in. bit, then nail the unit to the studs. Level and nail on the remaining hook strips (**Photo 6**), starting with wider hook strips along the side walls to accommodate the hanging rod hardware (**Figure A** and **Photo 8**).

The inside walls of the closet will never be perfectly square because of the mudding and taping of the drywall

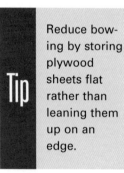

Tip Reduce bowing by storing plywood sheets flat rather than leaning them up on an edge.

corners. Measure your closet width and cut your shelf to the widest dimension, then tilt the shelf into position. At the corners, mark a trim line along each end to achieve a snug fit (**Photo 7**).

Getting the top shelf over the central unit and onto the hook strips may take some finagling. Once you have the shelf resting squarely, drill pilot holes and nail it into the tops of the dividers and the hook strips (**Photo 7**).

Clothes rods and hardware

To avoid having to Harry Houdini yourself around shelves, install all your closet rod hardware before you put in the side shelves.

The hardware for the closet rods should be positioned about 1-1/2 to 2 in. down from the shelf above and about

10 to 12 in. from the back wall. In our closet, we hung our top rods 10 in. from the back, which is good for pants, and our bottom rods, for shirts and blouses, at 12 in. If you want your top rod 12 in. out, make the top shelf 12 in. wide and trim less off the top of the vertical dividers.

Installing side shelves

To best secure the side shelves, sand the cut edge that will be in contact with the center unit with 100-grit paper. This will break up any finishing oil and provide a cleaner surface for the glue.

Lay out the remaining shelves on their side wall hook strips and use a level to determine their exact position on the center unit.

Mark and drill the pilot holes through the center unit, then lift out the shelf and apply a thin bead of glue. To prevent smearing, put the center unit side in first while tipping up the wall side of the shelf. Keep a cloth handy to wipe up the inevitable glue smudges.

Nail the shelves in place and you're done. Fill 'er up! ⌂

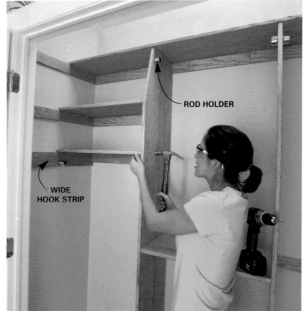

7 TRIM the top shelf ends to fit the side walls, drop the shelf into place, and nail it to the tops of the vertical dividers and to the hook strip with 6d nails.

8 SAND the cut edge of the side shelves to prepare them for glue. Determine the exact shelf placement and drill pilot holes. Spread glue on the shelf end and secure it with 6d nails.

New Products

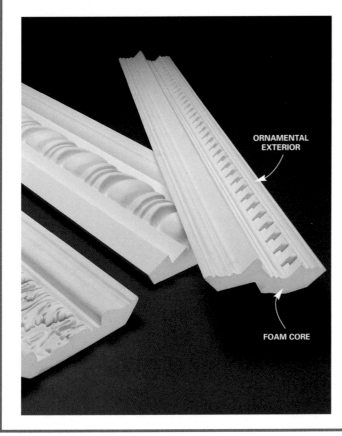

Wood trim without the work

Fypon's low-maintenance composite trim isn't wood, even though it looks just like it. Instead, it's an extruded sandwich with a lightweight urethane core that's covered with a paintable PVC coating. Lightweight yet durable, the trim is easier to install than wood (it can be glued rather than nailed). You cut it using the same tools as for wood. Other advantages it has over wood is that it won't rot—ever—and it holds paint much better. Great for inside or outside work.

Smaller trim pieces cost about the same as similar clear wood millwork profiles. But start comparing bigger, fancier profiles and you'll find it's much less expensive than wood. In fact, most of these profiles aren't even produced in wood—you'd have to pay a fortune to have them custom milled.

Starting at $4 per foot, the products are available at some lumberyards and home centers. However, most profiles are custom order. Go to the Web site for more details and to see hundreds of photos.

Fypon, (800) 446-3040. www.fypon.com

RemodelRight

BATHROOM REBORN IN STONE

Enter this bathroom and you'll find stone ranging in size from 5/8-in. flecks to 500-lb. slabs. It's installed on the ceiling, walls and floors; used as baseboard molding, shower seat and backsplash; laid in herringbone, mosaic and diagonal patterns; tumbled, polished and honed. It's a testament to the versatility, workability and beauty of stone as a building product.

The designers—by carefully selecting not only the tile, but lights, plumbing fixtures and cabinetry as well—created a room with an underlying "Old World" feel.

Other features include:

■ **A perfect makeup area.** Candlestick sconces on each side of the large framed mirror provide excellent lighting, and the mirror—while having a built-in look—cleverly disguises a close-at-hand storage space behind a swinging door.

■ **A focal point mural in the shower.** A variety of companies offer an array of murals and medallions that add a special touch. The design can range from geometric to pictorial, the subject matter from aquatic to classic art reproductions, the material from stone to glass and ceramic.

■ **Custom cabinetry.** The vanity cabinets were given an aged look through an eight-step process that involved distressing the wood with ice picks and chains, hand sanding, sealing the wood, more hand sanding and finally several coats of paint and clear lacquer.

From April 2006, page 28. See bottom of page 237 for information on ordering photocopies of complete article.

ULTIMATELY ORGANIZED

These homeowners wanted a larger kitchen, a larger dining room, a butler's pantry and a dedicated "communication hub"— all without adding on. Something had to give. For this family, the thing that "gave" was the formal living room; in fact it was eliminated.

Behind the simple white cabinet doors in the kitchen lie hard-working accessories for maximum storage, efficiency and utility. Base cabinets with rollout trash and recycling receptacles are positioned next to the sink. The cabinet with the butcher-block top at the end of the island has drawers with sliding plastic tops to store snacks and to keep bakery goods fresh. Full-extension glides were used for all drawers and rollouts to provide complete access to storage spaces.

Other features include:

■ **Hidden outlets.** Continuous electrical strips with outlets positioned every 12 in. are positioned along the back, lower edge of the wall cabinets. A valance built into the cabinet helps hide the outlets.

■ **Disappearing pocket doors.** To help separate the kitchen from adjacent spaces, pocket doors were used. Swinging doors take up valuable floor space; pocket doors take up none.

■ **Loads of light.** Spectacular windows bring in loads of daylight, while unobtrusive recessed fixtures work the late shift. Pendant lights over the island hang low enough to illuminate the countertop and cooktop, but high enough to avoid shining directly into the eyes of those standing or sitting.

BEFORE

From May 2006, page 34. See bottom of page 237 for information on ordering photocopies of complete article.

RemodelRight
ROOM TO BREATHE

These homeowners felt their kitchen was too dark, too outdated, too cramped and too separated from the rest of the house. And storage space was at a premium. The two things they had going for them were an underused entryway and a large, poorly designed half bathroom, adjacent to the kitchen. Their architect took advantage of the underused space and, employing some ingenious space-saving ideas, created the open, welcoming kitchen shown here.

Step one involved downsizing the mudroom and bathroom to create more space for the kitchen. It meant sacrificing an exterior door and shower stall, but the end result

BEFORE

was an extra 60 sq. ft. of kitchen space. Crown molding and hardwood flooring were extended into the new kitchen from the existing living room to help pull the old and the new spaces together.

Other features include:

■ **A reach-in pantry** that occupies a corner that might otherwise be wasted space. A pocket door provides excellent access and the frosted-glass panel fools the eye into thinking the space is larger than it really is.

■ **A recycling center** is concealed in the centrally located island cabinet, making it easily accessible to all parts of the kitchen.

■ **Drawers with full-extension guides** provide complete access to the contents—even things in the very back.

From November 2006, page 32. See bottom of page 237 for information on ordering photocopies of complete article.

2

Electrical & Hi-Tech

IN THIS CHAPTER

REMOTE
MOTION
DETECTOR
LIGHTING

A remote sensor automatically lights up dark sidewalks, yards. And it'll operate any light fixture.

by **Gary Wentz**

A gangly-looking motion detector floodlight is fine for scaring off a backyard intruder, but it doesn't look good on your house. A remote-style motion detector is a better choice. You can connect it to any type of decorative fixture—even existing ones—and mount it discreetly off to the side.

This article will show you how to install and connect a remote sensor to new or existing lights. The wiring is a little more complicated than it is for most electrical projects, but even a novice can handle it by following the wiring diagrams we provide. We won't detail the most basic aspects of electrical work, so you may need to do some further reading or online research before you begin. Apply for an electrical permit at the local inspections department so an inspector can check your work.

The toughest part of this project may be running the wires that connect the sensor to the light fixtures. In some situations, you can "fish" wires through finished walls. But in many cases, this project is only practical where you have open studs, as in an unfinished garage (as we show), or during a major remodeling project. If new wiring isn't an option for you, consider sensors that give you similar results but with little or no rewiring (see "Sensors That Don't Require New Wiring," p. 73).

Choosing a sensor

Home centers and hardware stores carry motion sensors ($20) that look like the ones you see mounted on flood-lights. They're usually labeled as "replacement" sensors for floodlight fixtures, but you can attach one to a mounting plate ($5) and use it as a remote sensor. For a less obtrusive look, we chose a Tuff Dome sensor ($51) manufactured by RAB Lighting. To order one, go to www.prolighting.com (item code: stuff500) or call (877) 852-9373.

Before you buy a sensor, add up the wattage ratings on the fixtures it will control. The wattage

Figure A: New Junction Boxes and Cable

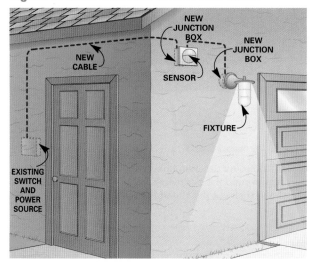

NEW JUNCTION BOX

NEW JUNCTION BOX

NEW CABLE

SENSOR

FIXTURE

EXISTING SWITCH AND POWER SOURCE

Figure B: Sensor Between Switch and Lights

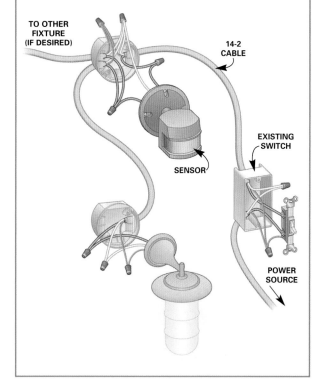

TO OTHER FIXTURE (IF DESIRED)

14-2 CABLE

EXISTING SWITCH

SENSOR

POWER SOURCE

rating of the sensor must be at least as high as the total watts of the fixtures. For example, if you have two fixtures, each rated to hold a 100-watt bulb, the sensor must be rated to handle at least 200 watts. Most sensors sold at home centers are rated for 300 watts (the rating is listed on the packaging and/or on the sensor itself). The Tuff Dome sensor is rated for 500 watts. For $65, you can buy a sensor that will handle up to 1,000 watts. To find high-wattage sensors, call an electrical supplier (in the yellow pages under "Electrical Equipment and Supplies") or go to www.electricsuppliesonline.com.

Install junction boxes

The sensor and each light fixture require electrical boxes ($3) set into the wall (**Figure A**). You can rewire boxes at existing fixtures as well. Choosing a location for your motion sensor isn't complicated: Check the manufacturer's directions for viewing range and

Figure C: Sensor Between Lights

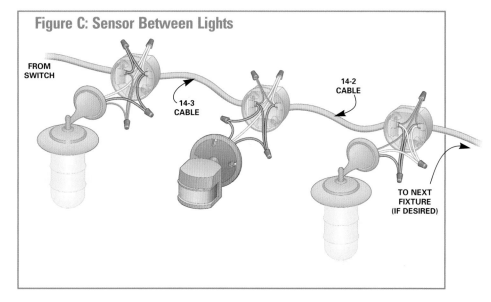

FROM SWITCH

14-3 CABLE

14-2 CABLE

TO NEXT FIXTURE (IF DESIRED)

place it where it can "see" visitors or intruders as they approach your house. Typically, the sensor will detect motion best if you place it 6 to 10 ft. above ground level.

The sensor we used can be mounted on a round or rectangular box. If the interior walls are unfinished, buy boxes mounted on an adjustable bar (**Photo 2**). This design lets you position the box anywhere between studs. If the wall is enclosed, use "remodeling" boxes, which clamp to the siding and wall sheathing and fish in the cable.

Hold the box against the wall and trace around it with a pencil. Avoid placing the box directly on a stud or other

framing. With brick or stucco, use a 1/4-in. masonry bit to drill a series of holes all around the circle. Then break out the middle with a chisel (**Photo 1**). On stucco, you'll have to cut the exposed metal mesh with snips. Cut out the sheathing behind stucco with a jigsaw.

If you have wide lap siding made from wood, cement board or hardboard, cut your hole near the center of a board so you can mount the fixture on the flat surface. If you have vinyl siding or siding courses that are too narrow to provide a flat mounting surface, you'll need a mounting block that fits over lapped edges. Plastic blocks cost about

$5 at home centers. To cut a hole in any type of siding, drill a 3/8-in. starter hole through the wall and then cut out the circle with a jigsaw.

Wiring options

Before you run electrical cable to the junction boxes, you have to determine how you'll wire your system. We show the simplest method here: drawing power from a switch box and running cables to the sensor and then light fixtures (**Figure B**). You can also run the cable to a fixture and then to the sensor (**Figure C**). But cable and connection details will vary a bit.

Simply choose the method that will make running cable easier. If your sensor will be placed close to the switch, the method shown in **Figure B** is probably best for you. If a light fixture is closer to the switch, the method shown in **Figure C** is probably best. Both illustrations include additional light fixtures. If you have a single light, just eliminate the wiring that feeds the second fixture. Your system must have a switch that can turn off the power to the sensor and light fixtures. We used an existing switch in an existing junction box; you may need to add a box and switch.

With either method, you can add as many fixtures as you like as long as you don't exceed the wattage rating of the sensor. Boxes have to be a certain minimum size to contain the wires. A 16-cu.-in. box is adequate for all the wiring configurations we show here. See "Sizing the Box," p. 90, for details.

Run cable to the boxes

Once you've determined how you'll wire the system, run the electrical cable between the junction boxes (**Photos 3 and 4**). First, look at the existing cable you'll use to power the sensor and lights. On the cable's plastic sheathing you'll find one of these numbers: 14-2, 14-3, 12-2 or 12-3. The first number (12 or 14) indicates the gauge of the wire. The second lists the number of wires in the cable (plus the bare ground wire).

CAUTION: Turn off power at the main breaker panel before removing the cover of the electrical box you intend to use as a power source. Then check the wires inside with a voltage detector to verify that the power is off.

Be sure to buy cable that's the same gauge as the existing cable. If you plan to follow **Figure C**, you'll need some cable that contains two wires and some that contains three wires.

Stand back and take a few minutes to plan the paths of the cables. The shortest route isn't always the best. Avoid a path that will force you to drill holes in tight spots

1 CUT holes for junction boxes. On stucco, drill a series of holes around the perimeter, break out the stucco with a chisel and then cut the sheathing with a jigsaw.

or through heavy framing members. In an unfinished garage, run wire high in the walls or along rafters where it's less likely to be damaged. If you only have a few holes to drill, an inexpensive 5/8-in. spade bit ($4) works fine. But if you have lots of drilling to do, buy an auger bit ($10). The screw at the tip of the bit makes for faster drilling with much less strain. When you've created a path for the cable, run the cable from box to box and then fasten the cable to framing with plastic staples. Place the staples within 8 in. of each box and no more than 4 ft. 6 in. apart.

Connect the sensor and the lights

When all the cable is in place, you can connect the sensor and the fixtures (**Photo 5**). It's tempting to rush through this part of the project so you can see the results of your work. But take your time. With one wrong connection, your system won't work. And finding where you went wrong is a hassle. If you're connecting to existing wires, cut off the old bare ends and strip off insulation to expose fresh wire for your new connections. With all the connections complete, turn on the power and set the sensor to "test" mode so you can make sure the system works correctly. Then aim and adjust the sensor (**Photo 6**). ⌂

Energy-saving bulbs and sensors

Power-saving compact fluorescent (CF) light bulbs designed for outdoor use are becoming more popular and economical. Unfortunately, most motion sensors aren't designed to handle CFs. Some sensors tell you right on the packaging whether they work with CFs. With other sensors, you have to check the wattage rating in the specifications. If the wattage rating specifies "incandescent" lighting but doesn't mention "fluorescent," assume it won't handle CFs. The Tuff Dome sensor shown here is CF-compatible.

2 INSTALL junction boxes so they're flush with the exterior surface of the wall. Have a helper outside position the box while you fasten it.

3 DRILL 5/8-in. holes in the center of the wall framing to create a path for cable. Then run the cable between the junction boxes. Fasten the cable to framing with plastic cable staples.

4 STRIP OFF 12 in. of the cable's sheath and feed wires into the box. If two or three cables enter a box, label wires with masking tape and a marker to avoid confusion.

5 CONNECT the sensor and the fixtures as shown in the wiring diagrams. Hang fixtures on a leftover piece of wire while you make connections.

6 ADJUST the sensitivity and "on-time" of the sensor according to the manufacturer's instructions.

Sensors that don't require new wiring

Built-in sensors

Some outdoor fixtures have a built-in sensor. These decorative lamps operate like floodlight motion detectors but are more stylish. Like any other light fixture, they take just a few minutes to install. They're not designed to control other light fixtures and are available in a limited range of styles. Most home centers carry three or four models. Prices start at about $35.

Wireless sensors

A wireless sensor works like the remote control for a garage door opener. It sends a radio signal to a receiver that switches on a light. No wiring is necessary to control existing lights. Just screw the receiver into a light socket and mount the sensor anywhere you like. There are some limitations to this system, though. The sensor requires batteries, which you'll have to change every few months. In rare situations, the radio signal can't reach the receiver because of interference or blockage. Finally, the shade or globe on your light fixture has to be large enough to hold the receiver along with a light bulb. A kit containing a sensor and two receivers costs about $50 at home centers. You can find similar products online at www.smarthome.com or www.homesecuritystore.com.

GFCI PROTECTION IN GARAGES

I'm planning to add more electrical receptacles in my garage. Will installing a GFCI receptacle in every outlet increase the safety factor? I do a lot of woodworking and often use power tools.

The National Electrical Code requires that all the receptacles in a garage have GFCI (ground fault circuit interrupter) protection, with a couple of exceptions. Garages have a high potential for dangerous shocks because of damp concrete floors or even standing water. GFCIs guard against fatal electric shocks by instantly shutting off the power as soon as they detect a small current "leak."

Keep in mind that you don't have to buy a GFCI for each receptacle. GFCIs have an extra set of terminals (the "load" terminals) that allow you to wire standard receptacles to the existing GFCI and gain the required GFCI protection.

The code lists two exceptions: You don't need GFCI protection for receptacles (outlets) typically out of reach, for example, the receptacle on the ceiling for the garage door opener. And you don't need GFCI protection for a receptacle dedicated to an appliance, like a freezer, that stays in one location.

Woodworking tools that are fixed in place, like a dust collector that's hooked into ductwork, satisfy the second exception. But mobile tools, such as table saws and portable dust collectors, must have GFCI protection. Ask your local electrical inspector about tools that you think might be exceptions.

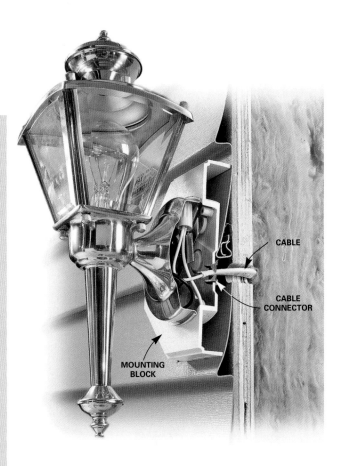

CABLE

CABLE CONNECTOR

MOUNTING BLOCK

SAGGING EXTERIOR LIGHTS

My outside lights are screwed to the vinyl siding and are drooping. How can I make the light fixtures solid?

For adequate support, mount the fixtures to a solid block or base, which you usually install before or during the siding process. However, you can also buy special blocks that fit right over the siding (about $15 at home centers). We show a block made by Arlington Industries, (800) 233-4717, www.aifittings.com. The mounting blocks are paintable and available in different sizes and profiles to fit most types of flat and lap vinyl siding styles. You don't have to cut into the siding to mount the block. However, light fixtures must be secured to an electrical box. The block we show here has a built-in electrical box, so you don't need the one in the wall. If you use a block without an electrical box, shift the existing electrical box out so you can mount the fixture to it.

MOUNTING BLOCK

To install the kit, insert the cable connector in an opening in the center of the mounting block, then feed in the cable(s) from the back. Set the block into place as shown and screw it to 1/2-in. (minimum) wood sheathing. Or mount it to a stud. Connect the wires, mount the fixture and caulk around the block so it's watertight.

GFCI

"LINE" NEUTRAL (TO POWER SOURCE)

"LOAD" NEUTRAL (TO OTHER RECEPTACLE)

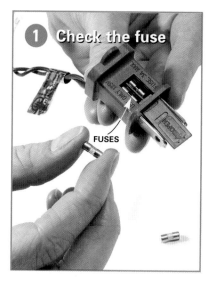

① Check the fuse

FUSES

② Check the bulbs: Tester #1

ELECTRICAL & HI-TECH

BULB
TESTER

BURNED-OUT HOLIDAY LIGHTS

I'm putting up my outdoor Christmas lights that I used last year. Half of the lights won't work. I know it's cheaper to just replace them, but I hate to throw them away. Yet I also hate to pull out every bulb to find the bad one. Any solutions?

③ Check the bulbs: Tester #2

BULB
TESTER

Judging by our mail, it seems that most of us have experienced the frustration of uncooperative holiday lights. There's a simple way to solve the problem. First, slide back the plastic covering on the plug to check the fuse (**Photo 1**). Some strings have more than one fuse, in which case they'll be next to each other. Replace any blown fuses. New ones are available where holiday lights are sold and at some electronics stores.

Second, test the bulbs with an inexpensive tester (less than $10), available where holiday lights are sold and online. Usually, changing a problem bulb (or tightening it) will fix the entire strand. The tester will indicate which bulbs are bad and need to be replaced. (For the tester to work, the lights must be plugged into the electrical outlet correctly—the narrow "hot" blade into the narrow slot and the wide neutral blade into the wide slot.)

Some testers work by having you slide each bulb through a hole (**Photo 2**). With other testers, you simply touch each bulb (**Photo 3**). You can test an entire strand in a few minutes. Sometimes you have two or

more defective bulbs, so only identifying one bad bulb may not fix the problem.

Keep in mind that inexpensive strings of lights aren't durable. At the end of the holiday season, take down the lights with care. Don't pull too hard on the wires. A loose bulb, broken socket or frayed wire is sometimes all it takes for the strand to malfunction.

After taking down the lights, plug them in before storing them, to make sure they still work. Then carefully wrap the lights in their original or similar containers, making sure the bulbs don't bang together. Proper storage is key to their continued success. Wadding them up in a coil and stuffing them into a box will almost guarantee they won't work next year.

Also be aware that most holiday light bulbs have short life expectancies, about 1,000 to 1,500 hours. This means the lights are designed to last one to three seasons, depending on your usage. Newer style LED (light-emitting diode) lights are the exception. They can last 10 times longer than traditional lights.

Ask TFH™
The Family Handyman

FISHING CABLES

I want to install a chandelier in my dining room ceiling. Since I have a bedroom above, I don't have easy access. How do I run a cable from the switch location on the wall (I can get to that spot) to the light with the least damage to the walls and ceilings?

You'll have to cut some holes in the walls, but you can minimize ceiling damage by using a "fish tape." A fish tape is a long strip of spring steel used for pulling wires through walls and ceilings. They're available at hardware stores and home centers, starting at $25.

To map out the best path for the cable run from the switch to the light, first determine the ceiling joist direction. Generally, it's best to run the cable in the space between the joists so you won't have to cut a lot of holes in the ceiling. Then figure how to get the cable through the wall to that joist space.

Since you can't run the cable through the attic, the next best choice is to go down into a basement or crawl space, then go back up through the stud cavity directly below the joist space. If you can't go down, follow the procedure we show here, which is to go horizontally across the studs until you're below the joist space. As you can see in **Photo 2**, you'll have to notch each stud and the top plate.

Once you know the path of the cable, cut a hole in the ceiling for the chandelier outlet. At each location where the cable will cross a framing member, cut away the drywall. Where the cable will turn from the wall to enter the ceiling, cut out a 3-in.-wide section of drywall in the wall and ceiling (**Photo 1**). Extend the openings at least 2 in. from the edge of the top plate.

With a sharp 5/8-in. or 3/4-in. chisel, trim the stud or plate back about 1/8 in. so that the guard plate will sit flush with the face of the framing (**Photo 4**). Then chisel the notches for the cable (**Photo 2**).

Feed the fish tape from the opening at the top plate to the lighting outlet, connect the cable and pull it through (**Photo 3**). Then feed the fish tape from your wall switch to the top plate opening, connect the cable and pull it through the wall.

Be sure to install nail guards that completely cover the cable where it crosses the framing (**Photo 4**). Wire the switch and the lighting outlet, then patch the holes in the wall and repaint.

1 CUT a 3-in.-high by 5-in.-wide opening in the drywall, using a keyhole saw, at each framing member and the top plate.

2 CHISEL a 1/2-in.-wide x 1/2-in.-deep notch in the studs or joists to hold the cable. You can also use a reciprocating saw to cut the notches.

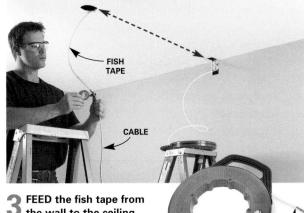

3 FEED the fish tape from the wall to the ceiling box. Connect the cable to the fish tape and pull it back through the ceiling.

4 PRESS the cable into the notches and cover it with a nail guard for protection.

Handy Hints ®

DISAPPEARING REMOTES

If your remote controls are cluttering up your coffee table and getting lost behind sofa cushions, here's how to neaten up. Apply adhesive-backed hook-and-loop strips to the underside of the coffee table and to the backs of the remotes. To avoid snags on upholstery and clothing, put the soft (loop) material on the remotes. Now all the controls are hidden from view, but you'll always know where to find them. Hook-and-loop strips are available for about $7 a package at home centers and discount and hardware stores.

COLOR-CODED CHARGERS

Strips of colored masking or electrical tape take the confusion out of mating cordless tools with their chargers. No more matching by trial and error!

CIRCUIT BREAKER ID

When you need to turn off the power to a circuit, there's no need to flip circuit breakers on and off until you find the right one. To end the guesswork, just write the corresponding circuit breaker number on the backs of the outlet covers and switch plates.

Hi-TechSolutions

YOU CAN HAVE **TUNES** IN ALL YOUR ROOMS

New high-tech components make it easier than ever to install your own whole-house audio system. We'll show you how.

by **Jeff Gorton**

Bringing music into every room isn't the complex, high-cost project it was several years ago. Now, thanks to simplified systems, you can easily install speakers and remote control access throughout your house for a modest cost. We'll tell you what to buy and show you how to run the wires and mount the speakers and controls. The rest is simple plug-in hookups.

The whole-house audio system we're showing in this article uses a technology called A-BUS. A-BUS technology uses a standard Cat-5e cable (four-pair communication wire) to carry all the signals from a central source. The wires carry audio signals to each room, where they're amplified to speaker-level audio by the keypads. In addition to amplifying the sound signals, the keypads transmit infrared remote control signals back to the audio equipment source. Anything you can do with your source equipment's remote control, you can also do from any room that has a keypad.

With this system, the audio source chosen from any one room plays in all of the rooms. Systems that allow you to play different audio sources simultaneously are significantly more expensive and complicated to set up, and we won't deal with those in this article.

A-BUS components are available from many manufacturers (see the Buyer's Guide on p. 84). The Channel Vision kit we purchased includes speakers and controls for four rooms and cost about $1,000. You'll also need Cat-5e cable, speaker cable and a few other parts that we've listed on p. 84. Keep in mind that you won't get

Amplifying keypad and speaker

Keypads amplify the sound signal and send it to the speakers. You can control the speaker volume by pressing the keypad or by using a remote control. The keypad also relays infrared remote control signals back to the system components, allowing you to change songs, switch from a radio station to a CD player, or activate any other command available on your receiver's remote control.

Optional connection for iPod or MP3 player

Installing a universal input module before the keypad in any room allows you to use the keypad and speakers as a single-room stereo system. Just plug your iPod, MP3 player, portable radio or computer into the RCA jacks on the module and it'll play through the speakers. Install the universal input module in a convenient location, near the computer for example. Run the Cat-5e cable from the panel distribution module to the universal input module first. Then run a Cat-5e cable from the universal input module to the keypad.

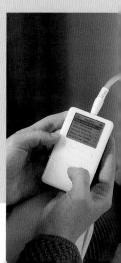

Figure A: Audio System Components and Locations

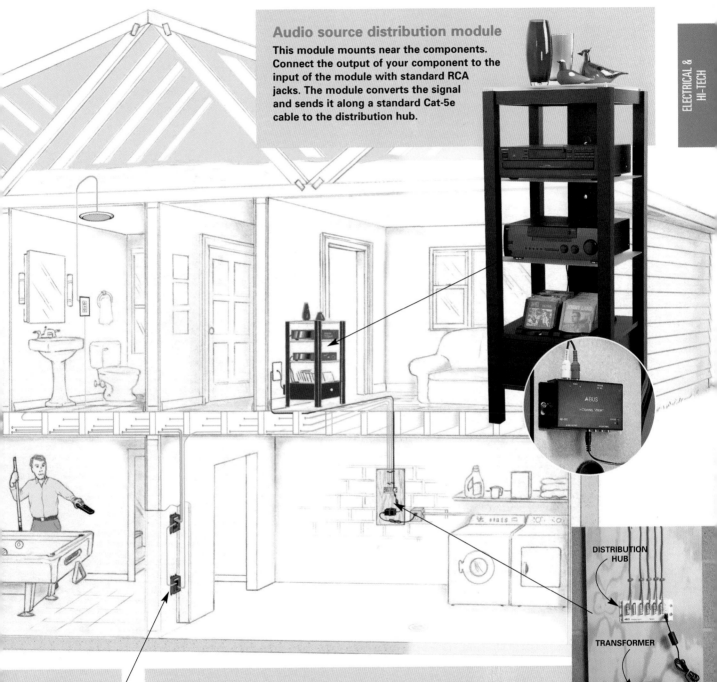

Audio source distribution module

This module mounts near the components. Connect the output of your component to the input of the module with standard RCA jacks. The module converts the signal and sends it along a standard Cat-5e cable to the distribution hub.

DISTRIBUTION HUB

TRANSFORMER

UNIVERSAL INPUT MODULE

Audio source distribution hub

The distribution hub divides the signal from the audio source module into outputs, in this case for four rooms. Run a Cat-5e cable from an output to the amplified keypad in each room. A transformer plugs into the distribution hub and provides low-voltage power through the Cat-5e cable to the keypad amplifiers.

"rock the room" amplification like you would with powerful amps, but it's plenty loud enough for average listening.

The hardest part of this project is running the wires without tearing up walls and ceilings. If you live in a single-story house with open floor joists over the basement or crawlspace or if you have easy access to the attic, then fishing the wires will be straightforward using the techniques we show in **Photos 3 and 4**. In this

1 CHOOSE a location for the keypad and trace around the box, making sure to mark the notches for the clips. Probe for obstructions with a stiff wire, then cut along the lines with a drywall keyhole saw.

LOW-VOLTAGE REMODELING BOX

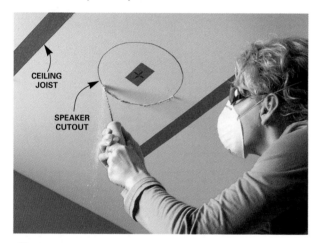

CEILING JOIST

SPEAKER CUTOUT

2 MARK both speaker locations with masking tape and probe for obstructions. Trace around the template and cut out the opening with a drywall saw.

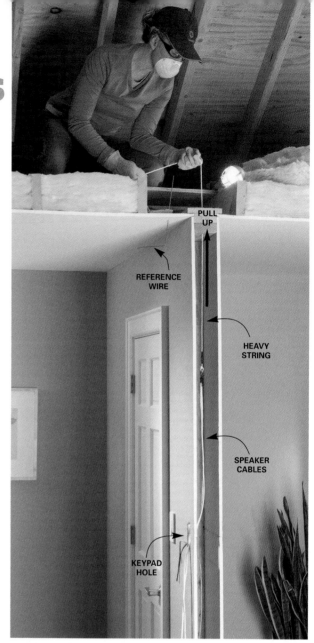

PULL UP

REFERENCE WIRE

HEAVY STRING

SPEAKER CABLES

KEYPAD HOLE

3 POKE a reference wire through the ceiling, then in the attic find the wire and measure over to find the center of the wall. Drill a 3/4-in. hole down through the top plate. Drop a weighted string through the hole. Attach the cables and pull them up into the attic.

situation, you'll come close to finishing a four-room installation in a weekend. But two-story homes and homes without basements or attic access present unique wire-fishing challenges. You may have to spend a little more time fishing wires and patching walls and ceilings. You'll need a drill and 3/4-in. spade or auger bit to bore through framing members. An electrician's fish tape ($25) is handy for pulling wires through the walls (**Photo 4**).

Connecting the equipment is straightforward and only requires a few tools. You'll need a scissors or side-cutting pliers to remove the cable sheathing and trim the wires. Buy a punch-down tool ($4 to $6) to press the wires onto the punch-down blocks (**Photo 7**). You'll also need a wire stripper ($12) to remove insulation from the speaker wires.

Choose the best locations for the components

Locate the panel distribution hub on a wall in a room that's easy to reach with wires from every room (**Figure A**). Put it right next to the audio equipment if you want. We chose a spot on the basement wall. Keep in mind that you'll need an electrical outlet nearby to power the transformer.

Keypads are most convenient if they're mounted near the light switch at the entry to the room where you're locating the speakers. But you'll also want to make sure to place them in locations that allow easy wire fishing from the panel distribution module and to the speakers. Make sure they're in the line-of-sight from where you plan to use the remote control.

4 PUSH a reference wire through a small drilled hole along the baseboard. Measure over from it and drill a hole up through the bottom plate. Push a fish tape (or stick) up from below. Attach the cable with tape. Pull the cable down through the hole.

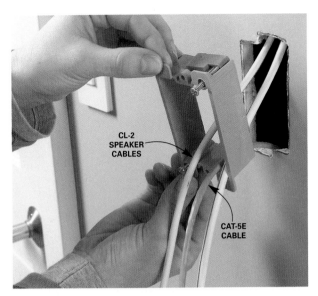

5 SLIDE the low-voltage remodeling box into the wall and tighten the screws until the clips are snug to the drywall.

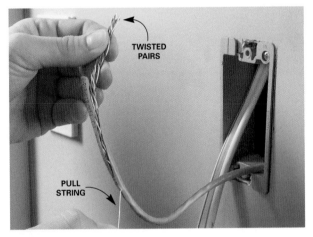

6 STRIP off a few inches of sheathing and pull the exposed string (unzip) to expose another 2 in. of wires. Snip the sheathing. Clip the wires to 2 in. and untwist the pairs.

You can mount speakers in the ceiling or walls. For the best sound, place wall speakers about a foot from the ceiling and centered on your listening position. Locate ceiling speakers above and to the side of your listening position. For example, in the dining room, the ideal location for ceiling speakers would be centered above the table and about 8 ft. apart.

Next cut the holes for speakers and keypads

Don't cut any holes for keypads or speakers until you've located framing members with a stud finder and probed the wall for obstacles. Mark framing members with blue tape. Then push a stiff wire (a cutoff clothes hanger works great) through the drywall to feel for obstacles like electri-

cal cables, heat ducts or wood blocking. Avoid exterior walls because they'll be packed with insulation. For round ceiling speakers, bend the wire at about 4 in. Push it into the center of your desired speaker location and spin it to see if anything's in the way. When you're confident that the space is clear, use the template included with the speakers to mark the hole, and cut it out with a keyhole saw.

Photos 1 and 5 show the installation of a low-voltage remodeling box (available at most home centers and hardware stores). After tracing the box outline, cut the hole carefully so the box fits tightly in the drywall. There isn't much room for error. Pull the wires first, then mount the boxes. It'll be easier to reach into the wall and grab the fish tape or string.

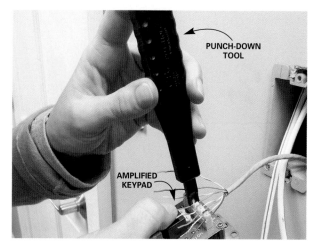

7 LAY each wire into its corresponding groove on the back of the amplified keypad and punch them down with the punch-down tool. Trim the ends of the wires with a scissors or end cutter.

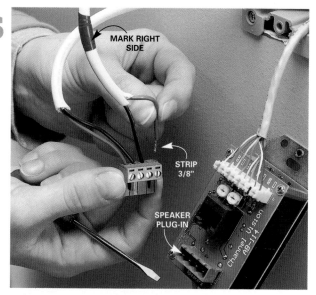

8 STRIP 3/8 in. of insulation from each speaker wire, twist the strands together and push each wire into the speaker hook-ups (red to positive and black to negative). Tighten the screws. Plug the block into the keypad and mount the keypad in the wall box.

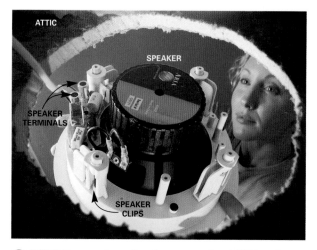

9 STRIP the speaker wires to expose about 3/4 in. of stranded wire and connect them to the speaker. Press the speaker against the ceiling and tighten the screws until the clips are snug to the drywall.

10 RUN the Cat-5e cables through the attic, crawlspace or basement to the distribution hub. Prepare the Cat-5e cables using the technique shown in Photo 6. Punch them down, using a separate block (labeled 1 through 4) for each set of speakers.

Fish Cat-5e to the keypads and speaker wires to the speakers

For this system, you'll need to run one Cat-5e cable from the distribution hub (**Photo 10**) to each keypad location. You'll also need to run one Cat-5e cable from the distribution hub to a Cat-5e modular jack located near your audio equipment. And finally you'll run speaker cables from the keypad location to the speakers in the same room. Use CL-2 speaker cable. It's rated to run inside walls.

Photos 3 and 4 show how to reach interior walls from the basement or attic. Use a coat hanger or other stiff wire as a reference point to locate your drilling spot. Snip off a

10-in. length of coat hanger wire and tighten it in your drill chuck. Then, from inside the room you're fishing to, drive it through the wall or ceiling next to where you want to drill. Locate the coat hanger from the basement or attic and figure out how far to shift the hole in order to come up inside the wall. Drill the hole and you're ready to fish the cable. After pulling the wires, seal the holes with foam or insulation.

To maximize the efficiency of the Cat-5e cable, it's important to take a few precautions when you're installing it. For the best performance, follow these guidelines:

■ Make bends gradual with no less than a 12-in. radius.

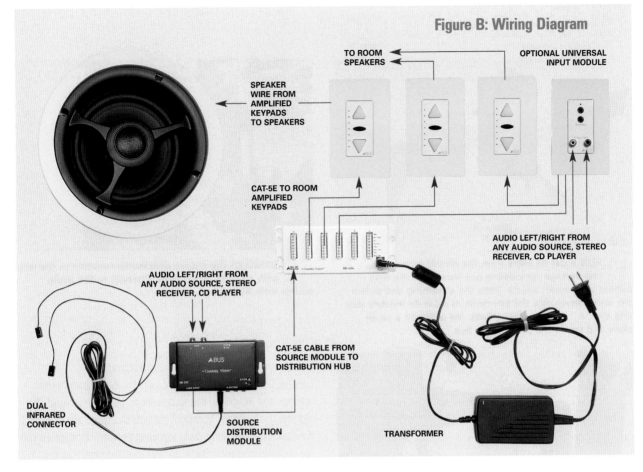

Figure B: Wiring Diagram

TO ROOM SPEAKERS

OPTIONAL UNIVERSAL INPUT MODULE

SPEAKER WIRE FROM AMPLIFIED KEYPADS TO SPEAKERS

CAT-5E TO ROOM AMPLIFIED KEYPADS

AUDIO LEFT/RIGHT FROM ANY AUDIO SOURCE, STEREO RECEIVER, CD PLAYER

AUDIO LEFT/RIGHT FROM ANY AUDIO SOURCE, STEREO RECEIVER, CD PLAYER

CAT-5E CABLE FROM SOURCE MODULE TO DISTRIBUTION HUB

DUAL INFRARED CONNECTOR

SOURCE DISTRIBUTION MODULE

TRANSFORMER

- Pull gently; don't tug the cable.
- Support it with special cable staples made for communication cables.
- Cross existing electrical cables at a right angle. Never use the same holes or run the new cable side by side with electrical cables unless there's a 12-in. separation.

The next step is to connect the wires

Connecting Cat-5e wires is easy. You simply remove a section of the plastic sheathing, untwist the pairs of wires, and use a punch-down tool to push them onto special "punch-down" blocks. You have to be careful not to nick the tiny wires when you're removing the sheathing, though. That's why we recommend the unzipping method shown in **Photo 6**. **Photo 7** shows how to punch the wires down onto the keypad connectors. The wiring order is indicated by small icons with color codes written on them. The slanted lines indicate striped wires. Line up each wire with its matching icon before punching it down. Use the same punch-down technique to make connections at the distribution hub (**Photo 10**) and at the Cat-5e modular jack (**Photo 11**).

Strip the sheathing from the speaker wires using the technique shown in **Photo 6**. Then strip and connect the wires (**Photos 8 and 9**). Make sure the bare stripped sec-

tion fits completely into the holes with no bare copper showing. Connection details may vary slightly from one manufacturer to another.

To prevent heat loss through the ceiling, build a sealed enclosure over the speaker from drywall scraps or foam insulation, taped together with foil duct tape. Then cover the enclosure with insulation.

Wall-mounted speakers will sound better if you plug the stud space above and below the speaker with fiberglass batts.

Connect the equipment with standard cables

Photo 12 shows how to connect the source module. You can connect any audio source to the module. If you're connecting a receiver, plug the RCA cable into the "tape out" outputs on the back. With this setup, you'll be able to listen to any component (CD player, radio or turntable, for example) that's plugged into the receiver.

If a component has remote control capability, you can control it from the keypads. But first you have to stick a flasher in front of the components' infrared (IR) receiver. This isn't as complicated as it sounds. **Photo 13** shows how. You may have to experiment a bit with the placement of the flashers, since it's not always easy to spot the exact

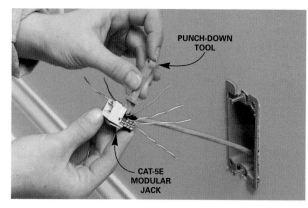

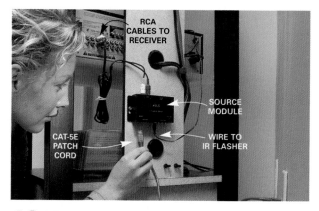

11 RUN a Cat-5e cable from the distribution hub to a low-voltage remodeling box located in the wall behind your audio source. Strip the sheathing and punch the wires down into the terminals of a Cat-5e module jack. Use the "A" wiring pattern. Snap the jack into a cover plate and screw the plate to the box.

12 CONNECT the source distribution module to the jack with a Cat-5e patch cord. Connect to the audio source with RCA cables.

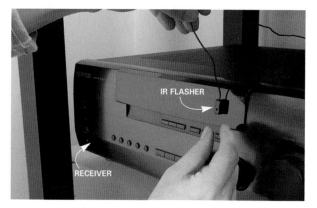

13 POSITION an infrared (IR) emitter over the IR receiver of each audio source component you wish to control from the amplified keypads. Plug the IR emitters into the source distribution module (Photo 12).

location of the IR receiver on the equipment.

The Channel Vision remote control is programmed to operate the keypads, but you have to teach it to send IR signals to the other components. Instructions are included. You can also use your own learning remote or programmable remote, but you'll have to use the Channel Vision remote to teach it to control the keypads.

With a little luck, you'll turn on the music and everything will work perfectly. If it doesn't, you most likely have a loose connection or mixed-up wires. Double-check all your connections. Be sure the wires are punched down completely and connected in the right order. If you're still having trouble, contact your salesperson for help. ⌂

MATERIALS LIST

Channel Vision Kit No. AB-901 includes these items:

1 single-source module

1 distribution hub

1 24-volt transformer

4 amplified keypads

4 pairs of ceiling speakers

2 dual IR flashers

1 punch-down tool

1 universal remote

You'll also need:

Cat-5e cable

Cable staples

CL-2 speaker cable

Low-voltage remodeling boxes

Cat-5e modular jack and cover plate

Cat-5e patch cable

RCA connecting cables

Optional: Universal input module (see p. 79)

NEW ELECTRONIC SWITCHES

Make life (a little) more convenient

by **Travis Larson**

Say "so long" to at least some of your old light switches and mechanical timers. Ever-shrinking and smarter microelectronics containing "embedded intelligence" can help you save a bit on energy costs, but more important, they'll add convenience. The ones featured here don't require you to add wires within the walls; you just have to replace the old switches with new electronic ones. All of these switches can be controlled manually at the switch as well.

A clumsy, finicky, hard-to-program mechanical timer can be replaced with an electronic one that even has an internal atomic clock that resets itself after power outages. Lights on old three-way switches were impossible to dim from more than one location—no longer true. Replace a mechanical-dial shutoff timer switch with a new unit that has preset intervals so that with the touch of a button, you can decide how long a bath fan or other fixture will run. And when you enter a room with your hands full, let a new electronic occupancy sensor (above right) turn on the lights—and turn them off again when you leave.

Home centers carry a version of most of the switches shown here. But for the widest selection, go to the manufacturers' Web sites listed below.

Buyer's Guide

Intermatic: (815) 675-7000. www.intermatic.com
Leviton: (718) 229-4040. www.leviton.com
Lutron: (888) 588-7661. www.Lutron.com

Occupancy detector

In rooms that you often enter with your arms full, like the kitchen or laundry room, it's handy to have the light come on automatically when you enter. No one around? It turns off the light and saves on those energy bills.

Featured switch: Leviton PR180 ($20)

ELECTRICAL & HI-TECH

Three-way dimmers

This new electronic three-way dimmer system calls for a main dimmer that works in conjunction with a "slave" dimmer at the second switch location. The slave and main dimmer switches use radio signals to let each one know what the other is up to.

Switch models, both by Leviton: Main Switch, TPI06 ($38); Slave Switch, MS00R-10W ($30)

Programmable timer switches

Would you like some lights to turn on and off at certain times? Say you'd like to schedule your outdoor lights to come on at 6 in the evening and shut off at 10 that night. It's simple with a programmable switch. This switch can be separately programmed for every day of the week.

Featured switch: Intermatic EJ500C ($33)

Timer switches

This class of switches is perfect for lights or fans that you'd like to leave on for a set amount of time. Bathroom heat lamps and exhaust fans are perfect candidates. Push the 10-minute button and the bathroom fan will turn itself off in 10 minutes—long enough to clear out the moisture after a shower, for example.

Featured switch: Leviton 6260M ($42)

Remote-controlled dimmer

Keep the remote by your bedside, favorite movie-lounging spot or near the dining room table. No more climbing out of bed to turn off the lights when you're ready for a little shuteye; just reach for the remote!

Featured switch: Lutron MIR-600-THW ($53)

Hi-TechSolutions

SAVE YOUR
HOME MOVIE TAPES

Put your video collection on DVDs and eliminate the clutter!

by **Travis Larson**

f you're over 30, you probably have drawers full of bulky VHS tapes that chronicle family highlights. With the compact, high capacity of DVDs, you can now reduce that jumble of tapes to a neat (short) stack of discs. They take less storage space, you can burn endless copies and mail them to anyone, and they're simpler to play.

You can easily make this conversion with an "analog to digital converter" even if your computer skills are a bit "lite." You'll need your VCR, a computer that sports a DVD burner (sorry, you Apple fans—no Mac version available for the Dazzle converter shown), blank recordable DVDs and the converter. The heart of the system is a piece of hardware that converts the analog signal from your VCR into a digital signal so your computer can then burn it onto a disc.

Load the software into your computer, and then hook up the VCR to the DVC and the DVC to the computer. While the tape plays, digitized video is fed into the computer, where it's stored on the hard drive ready for disc burning. However, this isn't a

Turn These

Into These

high-speed operation. You'll have to run the VCR tape at real time (standard play speed) to complete the digitizing process. The system shown also has built-in editing features, which allow you to delete or shorten boring (or embarrassing!) scenes, type in on-screen notes and even add a sound track. And more, the software even has options to enhance washed-out colors and stabilize shaky movies. You can order this system directly from the company or contact the company to find a retail store that carries it.

Tip

Convenience isn't the only reason to digitize those treasured recordings. VHS tapes aren't much more than magnetized plastic ribbons that will eventually degrade. The plastic wheels and bearings they run on won't last forever either. And every time you play a tape, there's always the risk that it will be eaten by a hungry machine!

What you need

DVD BURNER

From Here

VCR PLAYER

SOFTWARE

ANALOG TO DIGITAL CONVERTER

To Here

Buyer's Guide

The converter shown, called Dazzle, comes in several versions, which range from $50 to $130 (shown). Dazzle is available from Pinnacle Systems (800-293-2948, www.dazzle.com).

For more choices, type "VHS DVD conversion" into any search engine.

Converter connections

Hook up the VCR to the converter with S-connectors for the best signal. If those jacks aren't available on your VCR, use the red, yellow and white RCA connectors.

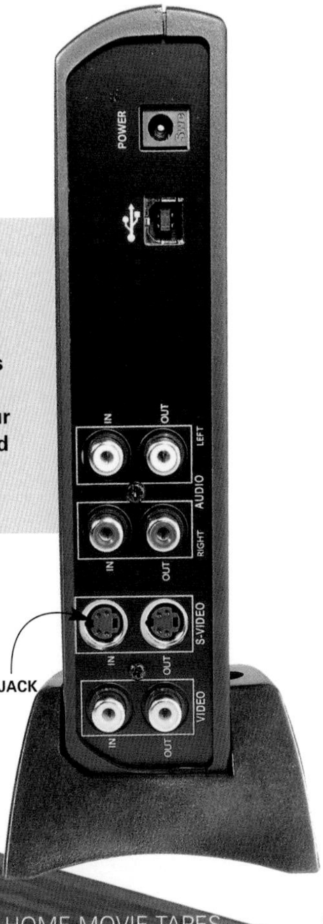

S-JACK

MAKE LIFE EASIER WITH
3-WAY SWITCHES

The simple technique for adding a second switch to that kitchen or stairway light

by **Brett Martin**

Tired of having to walk up a flight of stairs or across the room to turn on a light? The solution is to add a second switch in a convenient location. No more extra trips across the room or fumbling up a dark stairway.

Controlling a light from two switches is a bit more complicated than first meets the eye, especially if you're dealing with finished walls. The key ingredient is a special type of switch called a "three-way" switch. You'll need two of them, one to replace the existing switch and another for the new switch location. With these, you'll have the convenience of turning a light on and off from two spots.

In this article, we'll show you how to run a new electrical cable and connect the two switches. We'll also tell you how to resolve the most common complication—replacing an undersized electrical box so your work is safe and conforms to the electrical code.

While this project isn't difficult, it does require basic electrical skills: running cable correctly and making solid wiring connections. If you don't have wiring experience or if you get in over your head, don't hesitate to call in a licensed electrician. Apply for an electrical permit at your local inspections department before starting so an electrical inspector can check your work.

If your wall framing is open (an unfinished basement or garage, for example), you can easily run the new cable and complete this job in only two hours. However, if the cable has to run through closed walls, allow several more hours. In addition to standard tools, you may need a "fish tape" ($25) to pull wire in closed walls. Also, if you don't have a voltage detector, buy one ($10) so you can check for live wires and avoid hazardous shocks. You can find them at a home center or hardware store.

Plan the wire path

To start, decide where you want the second switch. You'll run cable from the existing switch to this new switch location, so look for the most accessible path between the two (**Figure A**).

If possible, start at one switch location, run the cable straight up through the stud cavity in the wall to the attic, then come back down through the wall to the second switch. Or feed the cable down into the basement or crawl space, then come back up. If neither option works for your situation, you may have to run cable horizontally through the walls or through the ceiling. This takes extra effort because you have to cut into, and later repair, finished surfaces. Avoid exterior walls, where you'll run into

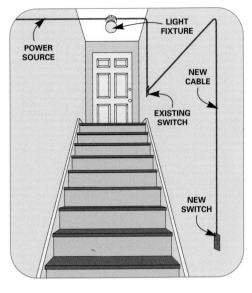

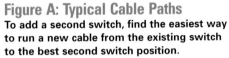

Figure A: Typical Cable Paths
To add a second switch, find the easiest way to run a new cable from the existing switch to the best second switch position.

obstacles such as windows, doors and insulation.

If you can't find an unobstructed path for the cable, move the new switch location.

Once you decide on a path, measure the amount of cable you need, then add 10 ft. so you'll have plenty to work with. It's better to waste a couple of feet than to come up short!

You'll also need a wire stripper ($5), 14-3 or 12-3 cable (match existing wire gauge; $12 for 25 ft.), two three-way switches ($5 each) and two remodeling boxes ($3 each).

Prep the switch locations

Shut off power to the existing switch, unscrew it from the electrical box and pull the switch out of the box. Avoid touching the screw terminals until you confirm that the power is off with your voltage detector. If the detector lights up, then the power is still on. Find the circuit breaker (or fuse) that shuts it off.

Unhook the wires to the switch (**Photo 1**). In most cases, the existing electrical box will be too small to contain the additional wires and connectors needed for the three-

CAUTION: Turn off power at the main circuit breaker panel before unhooking the existing switch, then check the wires with a voltage detector to verify that the power is off.

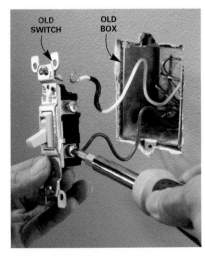

1 REMOVE the cover plate to the existing switch (the power is off). Then unscrew and remove the switch. Cut the electrical box loose and remove it.

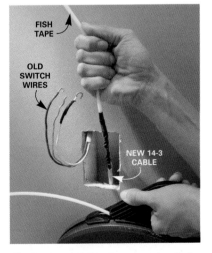

2 CUT a hole for the second switch box. Drill holes as needed in the framing and fish a new cable through the wall back to the old switch position.

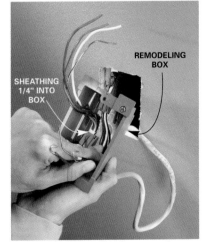

3 INSERT the cables into a remodeling box from the back side at each box location. Pull the cables from the front as you push the boxes back into the wall.

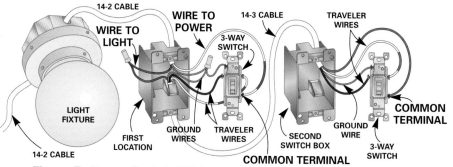

Figure B: 3-way Switch Wiring

The key to wiring two three-way switches is to run the two wires that were originally connected to the old switch (Photo 1) to the "common" terminals. The "travelers" can go to either terminal.

way switch (see "Sizing the Box," at right, to find out). You'll have to replace the old box with a remodeling box anyway so you can pull in the new cable (**Photo 3**). A remodeling box has clamps that secure the cable to the box. You can mount it solidly in drywall without cutting open the wall.

Label and unhook any wire connections that are inside the existing box (wires that weren't connected to the switch). Then unscrew the grounding screw and cable clamps (if any) in the box. Slip a hacksaw blade between the old box and the wall stud and cut the nails. (You may have to pry the box away from the stud slightly to create space for the blade.) Saw with short strokes to avoid damaging the drywall on the other side of the wall.

You'll probably have to enlarge the wall opening slightly for the new box. Simply use the new box as a pattern, trace around it on the wall, and enlarge it with a drywall saw. Don't cut the hole too large; you want a tight fit.

Next, fine-tune the position for the second switch. Use a stud finder to find potential obstacles, such as framing. If possible, keep the second switch the same height off the floor as the first switch. Trace an outline of the box on the wall, then cut the opening with a drywall saw. Don't mount the new boxes until you run the new cable.

Run 14-3 cable between the switches

We won't go into the details of running the cable, because each

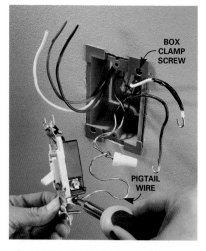

4 CLAMP the first electrical box to the wall. Connect a three-way switch, the ground wires and all other wires following Figure B.

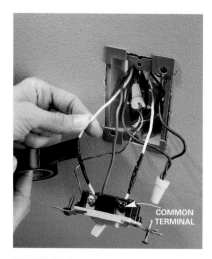

5 WRAP the second white wire with black tape to show that it acts as a hot wire. Fold the wires back into the box and screw the switch into place.

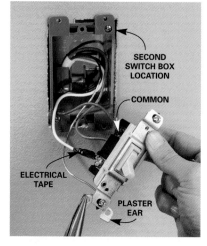

6 CLAMP the second electrical box to the wall and wire a three-way switch, following Figure B. Snap off the plaster ears and install the switch.

situation is different. But if the walls are open, your job is easy. Drill a 3/4-in. hole into the center of each stud between the box locations and run 14-3 cable from one box opening to the other. If you're going up through an attic or down through an open basement, drill through the center of the wall plates (top and bottom framing members).

If you can't go up or down, you may have to run the cable horizontally through finished walls. If so, cut a 3-1/4-in. by 5-in. slot into the drywall at each stud, notch the studs, fish the cable though the wall, leaving at least 18 in. of cable projecting from each opening, then tuck it into the stud notches. Cover the notch and cable with special nail guards and patch the drywall holes.

Strip 12 in. of sheathing off the ends of the new cable. Insert the cable into the electrical boxes from the back side (**Photo 3**). It's easier to push cable through the back than to pull it from the front. The first switch location has an existing 14-2 cable running to the light. Wrap the cable with electrical tape where the sheathing ends to help it slide into the box.

Pull the cables from the front as you slide the box into the wall opening. Pull the cable at an angle that minimizes pressure on the plastic cable clamp in the box. Otherwise, the sheathing could snag or the clamp could break. The cable sheathing should extend 1/4 in. into the box (the clamps should push against the sheathing and not the wire; see **Photo 6**) and make sure the wires extend at least 3 in. past the outside edge of the box when the box flanges are snug against the wall.

Tighten the screws at the top and bottom of the box to clamp it into place.

Wire the switches

Strip 3/4 in. of insulation from the end of each wire, then connect the wires following **Figure B** and **Photo 5**. The black electrical tape on the white wire indicates that it's a hot rather than a neutral. For secure connections, hook the ends with a needle-nose pliers before placing them under the screw terminals (**Photo 4**). Make sure the wire ends face clockwise around the screw for better clamping strength.

Clip the plaster ears off the switches so they'll fit tight on the remodeling box (**Photo 6**). Gently fold any excess wire into the boxes, then screw the switches into place. Be careful not to apply so much pressure that you loosen the box.

Install the cover plates, then turn on the power. Ideally, both toggles should be in the up or down position when the light is off. If necessary, remove the second switch, rotate it 180 degrees in the box, then reattach it so the two toggle positions are coordinated.

Extra wires in the box

You might find two 14-2 cables in the existing electrical box instead of the one we show in **Photo 1**. There may also be other cables present. Don't worry. Regardless of what you find in the existing box, the wiring for the three-way switches will not change.

You only need to focus on the two wires connected to the existing switch. Keep the other connections the same, even if you have to disconnect them when you change to a larger box.

The two wires you unhook from the old switch and the three wires you'll add from the new 14-3 cable are the only wires you need to work with.

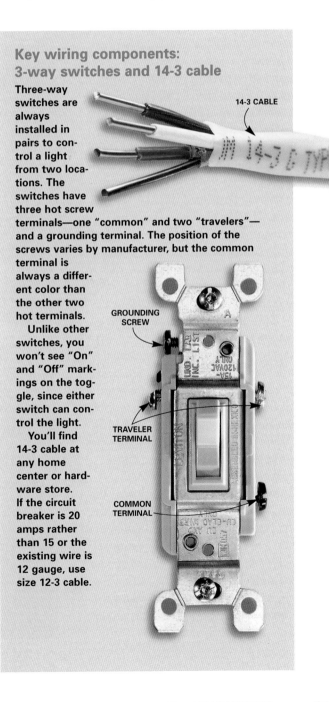

Key wiring components: 3-way switches and 14-3 cable

Three-way switches are always installed in pairs to control a light from two locations. The switches have three hot screw terminals—one "common" and two "travelers"—and a grounding terminal. The position of the screws varies by manufacturer, but the common terminal is always a different color than the other two hot terminals.

Unlike other switches, you won't see "On" and "Off" markings on the toggle, since either switch can control the light.

You'll find 14-3 cable at any home center or hardware store. If the circuit breaker is 20 amps rather than 15 or the existing wire is 12 gauge, use size 12-3 cable.

14-3 CABLE

GROUNDING SCREW

TRAVELER TERMINAL

COMMON TERMINAL

TAME A HYPERACTIVE MOTION DETECTOR

An outdoor motion detector light can save electricity and scare off intruders. But if passing cars or the neighbor's dog constantly triggers the light, you don't get either benefit. To stop unwanted "trips," you have to limit the "detection zone," the area where the sensor can see moving objects.

First, aim the detector. Turn the sensor head right or left and up or down so that its field of vision is roughly centered on the area you want to cover. To make the head stay put, you may have to tighten screws or ring nuts (**Photo 2**) on the arm that supports the head. Next, set the "on-time" switch to "test" (**Photo 1**). This will let you determine the detection zone by walking across the detector's field of vision. When it sees you, the light will go on for a couple of seconds. (Your detector may need a one- or two-minute warm-up period before it starts to work.)

If the detection zone in front of the detector is too long, aim the head down slightly. If the zone is too short, raise the head, but keep it at least 1 in. from lightbulbs and lamp covers. When the range is about right, make finer adjustments using the range dial (**Photo 1**). It may be labeled "range" or "sensitivity." Start with the dial set at the maximum range and turn it down to shorten the zone.

If the zone is still too wide, narrow the lens opening with electrical tape (**Photo 2**). This is a trial-and-error process that can take a few minutes. Normally, you need to apply narrow blinders only to the right or left ends of the lens, but you can cover as much of the lens as you like. When the length and width of the zone are just right, reset the on-time switch.

SENSOR HEAD

1 **SHORTEN** the sensor's detection zone by adjusting the "range" dial. Start with the dial set to "max" and turn down until the range is correct.

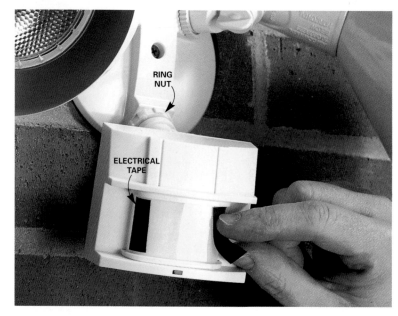

RING NUT

ELECTRICAL TAPE

2 **NARROW** the detection zone by sticking electrical tape blinders on one or both sides of the sensor's lens.

SILENCE A HUMMING DIMMER SWITCH

You might think that a dimmer turns down the lights by turning down the power flow. But it actually works like a super-fast strobe, switching the power on and off dozens of times per second. This electrical pulsation causes the filaments in light bulbs to vibrate and that creates the humming sound you hear. An easy solution—which usually works—is to try different brands of bulbs. Some bulbs have beefier filaments, which vibrate less. You can even try "rough-use" bulbs meant for garage-door openers or trouble lights. These bulbs have heavy filaments but are pricey ($3 each). If bulb switcheroo doesn't stop the hum, upgrade your dimmer switch. Dimmers that cost about $20 usually dampen the electrical pulse better than models in the $10 range. Swapping out a dimmer switch is usually a simple matter of disconnecting and reconnecting three wires. Just be sure to work safely. Turn off the power to the circuit—and make sure it's off using a noncontact voltage detector.

CHANGING BULBS USUALLY STOPS THE HUM.

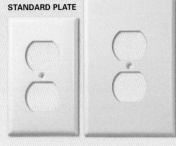

HIGH-QUALITY DIMMER

High-quality dimmer switches are less likely to cause humming.

OVERSIZE PLATES HIDE MISTAKES

When you're installing drywall or paneling, small mistakes can leave big gaps around electrical boxes. Luckily, there's a product made just for this situation. "Oversize" cover plates ($1) for switches and outlets are available in standard colors at home centers and hardware stores. They're 1/2 in. to 3/4 in. longer and wider than standard plates, so they can be a bit conspicuous. Electrical codes don't allow gaps wider than 1/8 in. around boxes, so fill gaps with joint compound or caulk before you screw on the cover plate.

OVERSIZED PLATE

STANDARD PLATE

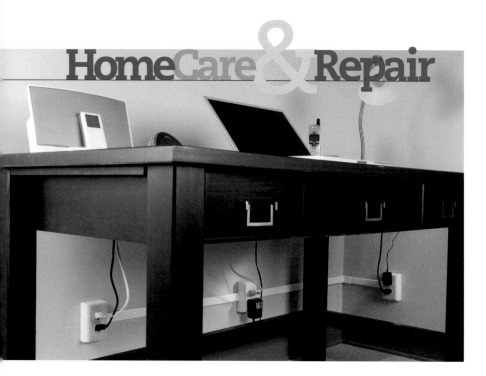

HomeCare & Repair

ADD OUTLETS WITH SIMPLE SURFACE WIRING

Surface wiring is a system of channels and boxes that let you put outlets, switches or light fixtures anywhere you want—without the hassle of cutting into walls, fishing wire and patching holes. And it can look neater than you might think, since you can paint the parts to match the walls. Mount outlets low on walls where they'll be hidden by furniture.

All the parts you need are available in metal or plastic at home centers. We chose plastic because the channel was easier to cut. You'll also need wire, connectors, outlets and cover plates. The total bill for the added outlets shown here was $60. (You can use a similar system to run low-voltage wiring for a telephone, TV or computer.)

You'll need some wiring know-how to complete this job safely. To find articles on wiring techniques, go to www.familyhandyman.com and type "wiring" into the search box. You can usually add outlets to an existing circuit unless you plan to plug in a device that draws a lot of power, such as an air conditioner or a space heater. Your electrical inspector will review this with you when you apply

for a permit. Be sure to have your work inspected when it's complete.

Start by mounting a box base at an existing outlet (**Photo 1**). You'll later draw power from that outlet to serve the new outlets. Cut out the back panel of the box with a utility knife before you screw it to the junction box. Then use a stud finder to locate studs and mark them with masking tape.

Run channel to the first outlet location (**Photo 2**). If the channel won't make any turns or run around

corners, just cut it to length with a hacksaw. But if the channel turns up or down or goes around a corner, miter the adjoining ends at a 45-degree angle. A power miter saw will do this fast, although you can also use a miter box to guide a hacksaw blade ($7 at home centers and hardware stores). To mount the channel base, drill 1/8-in. holes at each stud and 1/2 in. from the ends. Wherever an end doesn't land on a stud, use a drywall anchor.

With the first section of channel in place, fasten a box base to the wall. Don't cut out the back panel. If the base lands on a stud, simply screw it to the stud. If not, use two drywall anchors. Continue adding channel and boxes.

Next, run wire from the existing junction box to each box base. The size of the wire you add must match the size of the existing wire. Use the labeled notches on a wire stripper to check the gauge of the existing wire

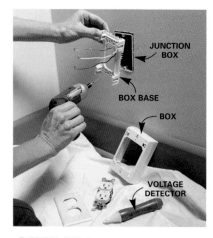

1 **TURN OFF the power and make sure it's off** using a voltage detector. Remove the old outlet and screw a box base to the junction box.

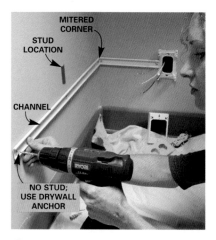

2 **CUT the channel to length, drill holes and screw it to studs.** If the ends don't land on studs, fasten them with drywall anchors.

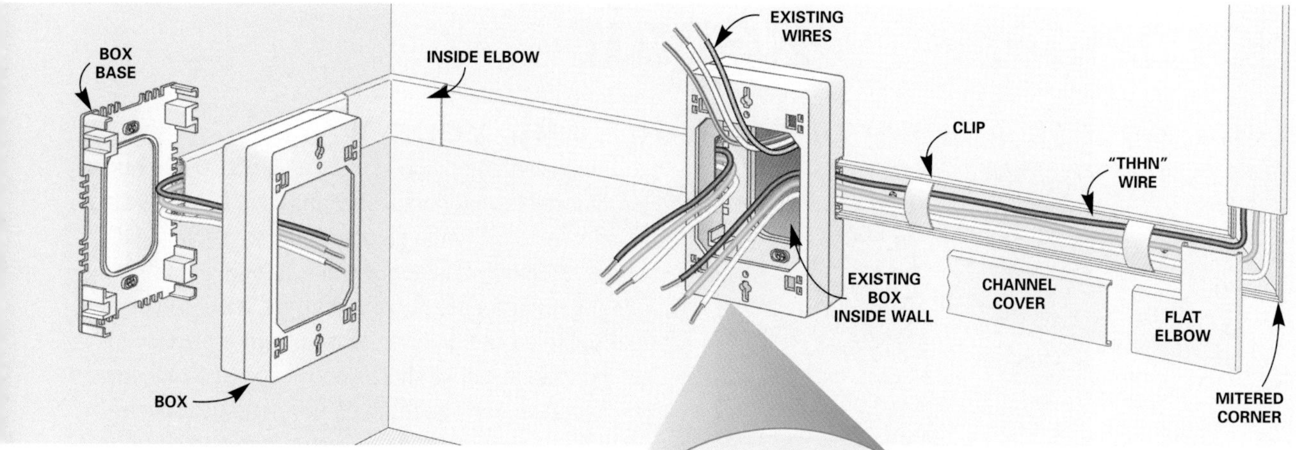

Figure A: Surface Wiring Parts

Surface wiring can extend from the existing junction box in one direction (as in our photos) or in two or three directions. It can run around corners or up and down walls.

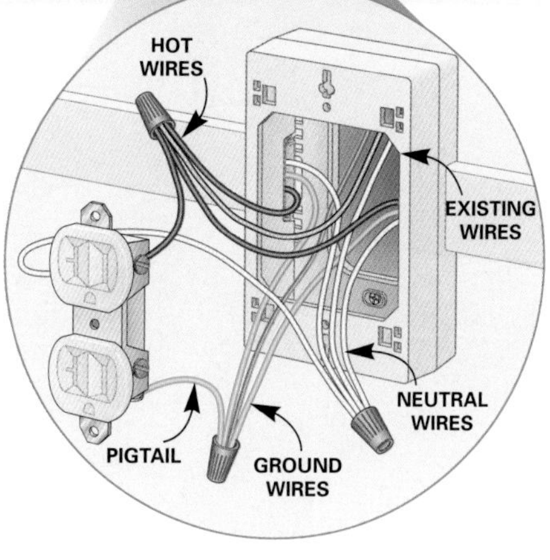

Labels in Figure A: BOX BASE · INSIDE ELBOW · EXISTING WIRES · CLIP · "THHN" WIRE · EXISTING BOX INSIDE WALL · CHANNEL COVER · FLAT ELBOW · MITERED CORNER · BOX

Figure B: Wiring at Existing Outlet

In general, join all hot wires, all neutral wires and all ground wires and add pigtails to the proper terminals on the outlet.

Labels in Figure B: HOT WIRES · EXISTING WIRES · NEUTRAL WIRES · PIGTAIL · GROUND WIRES

(14-gauge is most common, but you may have 12-gauge wire). Use only individual wires labeled "THHN," which is sold in spools or by the foot at home centers and hardware stores. You'll need three colors: green for the ground, white for the neutral, and red or black for the hot wire. Don't simply buy plastic-sheathed cable and run it inside the channel.

Cut channel covers to length (no need to miter them). At turns or corners, hold an elbow in place when you measure for the covers—the elbow will overlap about 1/4 in. of the cover. Snap the covers onto the channel base followed by the elbows and boxes (**Photo 3**). Wiring the outlets is similar, whether you added several outlets or only one. If you ran two channels from the existing junction box (as in Figure A), you'll have two new sets of wire to connect to the old wiring (**Figure B**). If you ran channel only one direction from the box (as in our photos), you'll have fewer wires, but the process is the same: Join all the hot wires together, all the neutrals together and all the grounds together. Wiring is similar at the new outlet boxes that fall between sections of channel (**Photo 3** shows "pigtails" ready for an outlet). At the last box in the run, you'll have only three wires (see **Figure A**); connect them directly to the new outlet.

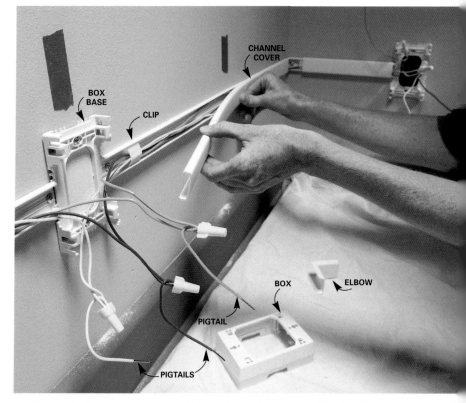

3 MOUNT a box base on the wall. Run wire and secure it with clips. Snap the cover and elbows over the channel. Then snap the boxes onto the bases. Add outlets.

Labels in Photo 3: CHANNEL COVER · BOX BASE · CLIP · BOX · ELBOW · PIGTAIL · PIGTAILS

HomeCare & Repair

UNSCREW the old outlet cover and pull off the foam gasket behind it. Press the new gasket over the outlet and screw on the in-use cover.

If you keep anything plugged into an outdoor outlet during wet weather—a pond pump, Christmas lights, a low-voltage lighting transformer—the plug is bound to get wet and create a potentially dangerous shock hazard.

The solution is an in-use outlet cover, which keeps the outlet sheltered and dry even while a cord is plugged in. That reduces the risk of shocks and keeps GFCI outlets from getting wet and shutting off power. In-use covers help to protect your walls too. When a standard outlet cover is held open by a cord, it can let water into your walls—not much water, but enough to encourage slow wood rot and peeling paint.

Home centers and hardware stores carry in-use covers to accommodate horizontal, vertical, rectangular and duplex outlets. A tough metal cover like the one shown here costs about $10. The gasket that comes with the cover forms a watertight seal over smooth surfaces, but seal around the cover with caulk if you have rough brick or stucco siding.

STUCK-BULB SOLUTIONS

When a light bulb is stuck in its socket, the culprit is usually corrosion between the socket and the bulb's metal base. This is most common outdoors and in damp places like basements and bathrooms. If you have a bulb that won't budge, put on heavy gloves and eye protection. Make sure the light switch is off. Then go ahead and twist as hard as you like. Don't worry about breaking the bulb. In fact, if the bulb just won't turn, your next step is to break it intentionally. Hold a screwdriver tip against the bulb and give the handle a firm whack with a hammer. This leaves the bulb's metal base in the socket.

Often, you can unscrew the base by inserting a pliers and holding the jaws open as you turn. A potato might work too: Round the end of the potato with a knife, jam it into the socket and turn. But if your bulb base is really stubborn, use hot glue and a 1/2 x 1/2-in. stick of wood (**Photo 1**). If you don't have a scrap of wood, buy a 5/8-in. dowel ($3) at a home center or hardware store. Save yourself all this hassle in the future by applying a special lubricant such as Bulb EZ to the new bulb ($4, www.bulbez.com, 530-478-0707).

1 APPLY a heavy blob of hot glue to a stick and press it into the broken bulb's base. If the glue doesn't fill the base, inject glue into any voids. Let the glue cool for five minutes and turn the stick to screw out the base.

2 COAT the threads of the new bulb with a special lubricant designed for light bulbs. The coating inhibits corrosion and makes future removal much easier.

3 Plumbing, Heating & Appliances

IN THIS CHAPTER

Handy Hints®

"Slight blockage in the waste tee. I'll have to operate immediately."

RIGHT-ANGLED CUTS ON PIPES

Scratching your head over how to mark a cutting line all the way around a cylindrical workpiece? No problem. Measure and mark the cutoff location on the front and back sides of the cylinder, then wrap a sheet of construction paper around the cylinder, aligning the paper edge with both marks. Next trace the cutting line, then saw along that line to create a square-cut end.

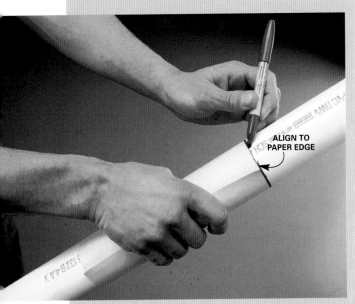

ALIGN TO PAPER EDGE

PIPE-FINDING PRESCRIPTION

A stethoscope ($20 at drugstores) lets you locate plumbing lines inside walls when you're planning a remodeling project. You need a steady flow of water, so turn on faucets full blast to find supply lines. To locate waste lines, have a helper flush toilets or fill sinks and let them drain. You'll hear the flow from several feet away, and the sound will get noticeably louder as you get closer. You'll be able to locate pipes within a foot or so. A stethoscope also lets you hear the hiss of larger leaks in supply lines.

DRAIN VACUUM

When a hard object like a toothbrush, comb or toy plugs a toilet or drain, a plunger may not be the solution—it might only push the obstruction in deeper. Instead, suck out the water and the obstruction with a wet/dry shop vacuum. You'll feel like Superman!

REFRIGERATOR RODEO

A 10-ft. piece of rope makes pulling your refrigerator easy. Loop the rope over and behind the unit. (Be sure your model doesn't have the coils on the back of the refrigerator, as you don't want to damage them.) Whenever you pull out a fridge, protect your floor with plywood, hardboard or cardboard. Yee-haw!

POWER SCOUR

Now that discount and dollar stores carry cheap ($1 to $5) electric toothbrushes, you can add a modern twist to routine cleaning. Rapid vibration will quickly scrub out stubborn dirt, while the long handle can get to hard-to-reach places without all the elbow grease.

STOP LEAKS IN PLUMBING JOINTS

Foolproof methods for connecting valves, faucets and sinks, and drain parts

by **Jeff Gorton**

ALIGN SLIP JOINTS PRECISELY FOR A TIGHT SEAL

The rubber slip-joint washers on the joints of chrome trap assemblies often leak. If you're reassembling a chrome trap, buy new slip joint washers and nuts. However, new washers sometimes stick to the pipe, causing them to twist or distort as you push them tight with the slip joint nut. To avoid this, lubricate the drain tubing and slip joint with a little pipe joint compound (**Photo 1**). The compound helps the washer slide smoothly and creates a tighter seal.

Start the slip joint nut by hand, and twist it on until the threads are engaged correctly. Hand-tighten all joints first (**Photo 2**). Then adjust the trap parts until they're aligned and pitched slightly for drainage. This is key; a misaligned joint will leak, even with new washers. Finally, use a large slip joint pliers to tighten the nuts an additional half turn.

Plastic trap parts use hard plastic slip joint washers for a seal. Make sure the flat part is against the nut with the tapered side facing the fitting.

SLIP JOINT NUT

TEFLON PIPE JOINT COMPOUND

SLIP JOINT WASHER

ASSEMBLED SLIP JOINT

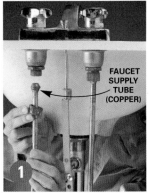

FAUCET SUPPLY TUBE (COPPER)

FAUCET SUPPLY TUBE (BRAIDED)

CHOOSE FLEXIBLE SUPPLY TUBES

The skinny copper or chrome supply tubes used to connect faucets and toilets (**Photo 1**) are tricky to cut, bend and align. But you don't have to put up with them. When you're replacing a faucet or toilet, use flexible supply hoses with a braided covering instead ($3 to $6 each; **Photo 2**). They have rubber gaskets at each end and don't require much force to seal. They're available in many lengths and are flexible enough to fit almost any configuration. The only trick is buying a connector with the correct size nuts on the ends. Take your old tubing and the nuts on each end along with you to the store to be sure of an exact match.

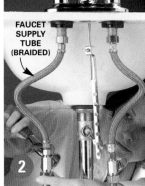

RUBBER SEAL

Start the nuts carefully and hand-tighten. Then tighten an additional half turn (**Photo 2**). Avoid overtightening. It's easy to tighten the nuts a little more if the joint leaks.

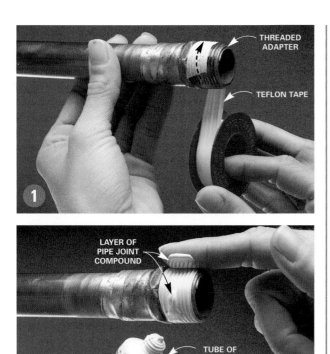

THREADED ADAPTER

TEFLON TAPE

LAYER OF PIPE JOINT COMPOUND

TUBE OF TEFLON PIPE JOINT COMPOUND

TEFLON TAPE PLUS PIPE JOINT COMPOUND

USE TWO TYPES OF TEFLON ON THREADED JOINTS

Connections that rely on threaded pipes and fittings are prone to leaks if they're not sealed with either Teflon tape or Teflon pipe joint compound. Careful plumbers use both on every joint for extra security. They don't want to come back.

Start by wrapping the male threads with Teflon tape (**Photo 1**). With the end of the threaded pipe facing you as shown, wrap the tape clockwise. Usually three layers is enough. Once in a while, you'll run into a loose fitting that requires four or five wraps. Stretch and tear the tape to complete the wrap.

Spread a thin layer of Teflon pipe joint compound over the tape (**Photo 2**). If you're working with plastic pipe, choose compatible Teflon pipe joint compound. Then start the threads by hand before tightening the connection with wrenches (**Photo 3**). Wipe away the excess.

LUBRICATE THE FERRULE ON COMPRESSION JOINTS

Compression joints are most common on shutoff valves, although you find them on other fittings as well. They have a brass or plastic ring (ferrule) that's compressed into a recess when you tighten the nut, forming a seal. Lubricating the pipe and the ferrule with a bit of Teflon pipe joint compound (**Photo 1**) helps the ferrule slide along the pipe and squeeze tightly into the recessed fitting with less wrench pressure (**Photo 2**). Tighten compression fittings firmly with two wrenches to crimp the ferrule onto the pipe (**Photo 3**). Also make sure the pipe or tube goes straight into the fitting. Misalignment will cause a leak. If the fitting leaks after you turn on the water, try tightening the nut an additional one-quarter turn. This usually stops the leak. 🏠

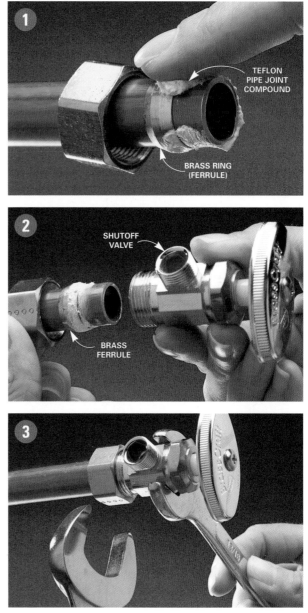

TEFLON PIPE JOINT COMPOUND

BRASS RING (FERRULE)

SHUTOFF VALVE

BRASS FERRULE

The Family Handyman

BUBBLING TOILET

I live in a ranch home with the washing machine and toilet in adjoining rooms. When the washing machine discharges water, air comes bubbling up through the toilet. Sometimes the water level in the toilet will drop, too. The washing machine connects to the house sewer line before the toilet does. What's going on, and what's the fix?

You're seeing signs of poor venting, that is, your drain line is gasping for air. When you pour liquid from a can, you'll notice that it doesn't flow evenly unless you have a second opening for air. The same holds true for plumbing. As water goes down a drain, air is needed to equalize the pressure in the drain line.

This is the purpose of a venting system. If the drain lines in your home have poor venting (as in **Figure A**, for example), water rushing down the drains will pull water from nearby P-traps. The drain in the toilet bowl is basically a P-trap. If the problem just started, it's probably a blocked drain or vent that needs to be "snaked" out. And since the water in the toilet is dropping and gurgling, it's likely that the problem is near that area.

Unfortunately, a clogged or missing vent is tough to fix, since it usually requires breaking into the walls to examine the drain system. Unless you have plumbing experience, this project is best left to a professional.

Figure A
Common Example of
Poorly Vented Drains
Venting in this system is missing, or the vents don't open to "free" air.

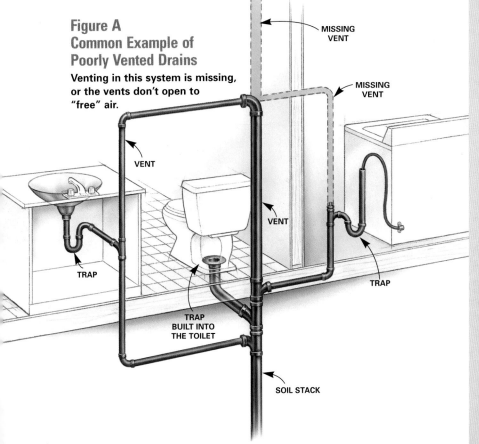

MISSING VENT

MISSING VENT

VENT

VENT

TRAP

TRAP

TRAP
BUILT INTO
THE TOILET

SOIL STACK

If I set my gas water heater temperature to 120 degrees F, it's often not hot enough. It was as low as 90 degrees. That's a 30-degree temperature swing. I don't want to raise the temperature setting because the water at times will be scalding hot. Is this normal?

No, the temperature range you're experiencing is not typical. A 17-degree swing is considered standard. The swing usually results in cooler, not hotter, water. The swing often occurs because the thermostat won't switch the heater on until the water cools a certain amount.

However, occasionally a water heater heats water beyond its temperature setting. This is usually caused by "stacking," which occurs when you use just enough water to switch on the burner but draw little off. Doing this repeatedly causes overheated water to rise to the top of the tank, where it could be drawn off extra hot.

Since you've tried adjusting your thermostat setting and you still get too large a temperature swing, you probably have a bad thermostat. Call a plumber. If you have a standard water heater that's more than five years old, buy a new unit. Gas water heaters cost about $400, and it would cost at least half that to have a plumber diagnose the problem and more for the fix.

WATER HEATER
TEMPERATURE
SETTING

Turn the thermostat down so the water is 120 degrees F. Setting the temperature too high can result in scalding water.

LEAKING WATER HEATER

I replaced our 50-gallon water heater two years ago and each year since I've had to replace a leaking T & P valve. We have hard water. Is that shortening the life of my valve?

The T & P valve, also known as the temperature and pressure relief valve, is a safety device that protects against excessive temperature and pressure levels in the water heater. The valve is located on or near the top of the tank. Part of the valve extends into the unit (**see photo**).

If water discharges (your "leak"), it usually means the valve is defective (it opened and didn't close) or the water heater is operating under too high a temperature or pressure.

First, check the water temperature and make sure the setting is about 120 degrees F (or "medium" if your thermostat doesn't have a degree reading). If the valve continues to leak, remove it and examine it for mineral buildup and signs of corrosion. The minerals in especially hard water can clog it or attack the metal parts, resulting in valve failure. This is especially common with water from a well. And if you have municipal water, check with your local water department to find out if the water supply has a high concentration of minerals. In either case, you'll have to soften your water.

If the valve looks clean, consider two other possible causes: high water pressure in the municipal system or some sort of backflow preventer around the water meter or main shutoff. You'll need a licensed plumber to diagnose and handle these problems.

TEMPERATURE AND PRESSURE RELIEF VALVE

WATER HEATER

RELUCTANT FLUSH

For years my downstairs toilet worked fine. Now it drains slowly. I've used a drain cleaner many times, but it hasn't helped. The toilet on the second floor and all of the sinks continue to drain fine. I've noticed ads for toilets with power flush designs. Do these systems work, and is there a power flushing kit that will convert my existing toilet to a power flush design? I'd rather not replace the toilet, since the fixture color has been discontinued.

You're referring to the power flush design on pressure-assisted toilets, which use regular water pressure to compress air in a tank to increase flushing power. The bowls and trap on these toilets are specially designed for these mechanisms and can't be retrofitted to another toilet.

Besides, your slow-draining problem sounds like a clogging issue, so changing the flush wouldn't help. You probably have a hard object (like a kid's toy)

lodged in the trap of the toilet or in the drain line.

Use a closet auger ($10 to $20 at a hardware store or home center), which is specifically designed for toilets, to remove the clog. If that doesn't work, unbolt and remove the toilet from the flange and check the passageways as far as you can to see if anything is stuck in the opening or the drainpipe.

If the toilet still flushes poorly, call a drain cleaning service.

READER MYSTERY PHOTO

FLECKS IN WATER

For years, our bathroom faucet has spewed out black flecks when we run the hot water. We replaced the faucet, but it didn't help. Our water heater is only two years old. Do we have to replace the copper pipes?

The solution is probably much simpler than that. Just change the stop (shutoff) valve under the sink. You've already replaced the faucet. And since the flecks only show up in the bathroom sink, the valve is the only possibility left. Chances are that it has a black rubber washer that's deteriorating.

To replace the supply stop, turn off the main water supply and disconnect the entire valve from the water pipe and the supply tube. Install a new supply stop ($5 at plumbing stores and home centers). Turn the water back on and check for leaks. Then run water into the sink to clear the black flecks remaining in the supply tube. Also unscrew and rinse the screen at the end of the faucet. It may take a few days for the black flecks to completely disappear.

NOISY OUTDOOR FAUCET

I have an outdoor faucet that makes a loud vibrating noise when I open or shut it. How can I fix it? I have another outdoor faucet that works fine.

The faucet washer is probably worn out. You can easily replace it without removing the entire faucet. First, turn off the water to the faucet. Then use a wrench to remove the retaining nut that's attached to the sill cock (**top photo**).

Slide the handle and stem assembly out of the sill cock. Remove the screw at the end of the stem (**bottom photo**) and remove the washer. Buy a new washer that matches the old one at any hardware store. Then reassemble the faucet. Occasionally the washer is fine but the screw holding it is loose. If so, put a drop of Loctite Threadlocker ($4 at hardware stores) on the threads and tighten it. Some faucets have a spring-loaded sleeve near the washer. If you have this type, replace the entire faucet.

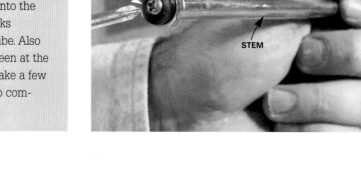

THE REAL DEAL ON TANKLESS WATER HEATERS

I'm willing to make an investment in a tankless water heater, but not until someone convinces me that I'll save on my energy bills and have adequate hot water. What's the real scoop on these?

Tankless water heaters use 30 to 50 percent less energy than units with tanks, saving a typical family about $100 or more per year, depending on water usage. Tankless units (also called "on demand" units) heat water only when you turn on the faucet. They usually operate on natural gas or propane. The main advantage is that they eliminate the extra cost of keeping 40 to 50 gallons of water hot in a storage tank, so you waste less energy. They also offer a continuous supply of hot water, which is ideal for filling a big hot tub or a whirlpool. They're more compact than a standard water heater and mount on a wall.

ARTWORK AND PHOTOS COURTESY OF BOSCH WATER HEATING

The primary disadvantage is the upfront cost. The smaller units ($500) that you often see won't produce enough hot water to serve most households. They'll only serve one faucet at a time—a problem if you want to shower while the dishwasher is running. Larger units that can handle the demand of a whole family run $1,000 and up. (Regular tank water heaters cost $300 to $500, and they last 10 to 12 years, compared with 20 years for a tankless unit.)

But because tankless units have high-powered burners, they also have special venting requirements (a dedicated, sealed vent system, which requires professional installation). Natural gas burners often need a larger diameter gas pipe, which could easily add $500 to $1,000 to the initial installation cost.

The bottom line: When you're pricing a unit, be sure to get an estimate or firm bid on installation costs. This is not a do-it-yourself project unless you have pro-level skills. You can find tankless water heaters at many home centers and plumbing specialty stores. Ask if the unit qualifies for a $300 federal tax credit.

**Figure A
Tankless Water
Heater Details**

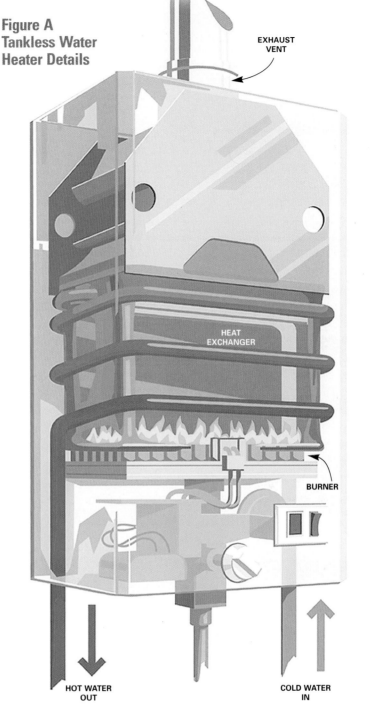

EXHAUST VENT

HEAT EXCHANGER

BURNER

HOT WATER OUT

COLD WATER IN

When a hot water tap is opened, the heating elements turn on. Water is heated as it flows through the heat exchanger.

CLOGGED SEPTIC SYSTEM

The septic tank for my four-year-old home has a 24-in.-long by 3-in.-diameter device that filters the liquid going out to the drainage field. I have to dig up the yard every six months to clean it. Do I have to keep this filter? Can I simply remove it?

Keep it. Septic tanks work by allowing waste to separate into three layers: solids, effluent and scum (**see illustration**). The solids settle to the bottom, where microorganisms decompose them. The scum, composed of waste that's lighter than water, floats on top. The middle layer of effluent exits the tank and travels through underground perforated pipes into the drainage field. There, gravel and soil act as biological filters to purify the wastewater as it sinks into the ground (**see illustration**).

Your state health code requires an effluent filter, so keep it in place. (Not all regional codes require this filter.) Besides, removing the filter could create a far worse (and expensive) problem. Without the filter, waste particles could pass into the perforated pipes and clog them. It would require extensive digging to clean and unclog the system.

However, your filter should not need semiannual cleaning. Most filters don't have to be cleaned until the tank is pumped, which is typically every two to five years. Chances are you're putting filter-clogging materials down your drain, such as grease, fat or food scraps.

The use of a food disposer is a common mistake. A disposer won't break down food particles enough to allow them to pass through the septic tank filter. It can increase the amount of solids in the septic tank by as much as 50 percent. Flushing plastic materials, disposable diapers, paper towels, nonbiodegradable products and tobacco will also clog the system.

For more details on what not to put down your drain, call your state health department.

SEPTIC TANK FILTER

INSPECTION PORT

MANHOLE COVER

OUTLET TO DRAINAGE FIELD

DRAINFIELD

INTAKE FROM HOUSE

SCUM

EFFLUENT

SOLIDS

FOOLPROOF FAUCET INSTALLATION

Pro tricks to help you avoid those frustrating snags that aren't covered in the directions

by **Lucie B. Amundsen**

A stylish new faucet may promise a quick, refreshing new look to your bathroom, but no one promises a trouble-free installation. In fact, the more expensive and fancy the faucet, the harder the install usually is. The printed directions supply you with the bare basics, but a horde of potential snags makes almost every job a complex one. The following tips will get you through the tough spots and save the $150 to $400 a plumber would charge for a house call like this.

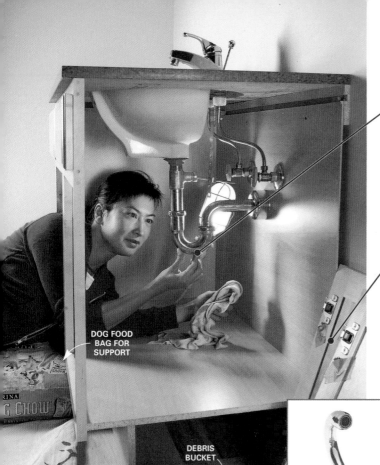

DOG FOOD BAG FOR SUPPORT

DEBRIS BUCKET

Before you dive in

Examine the underside of your sink for unsuspected leaks

Run water through the drain and check for any cracks or leaks that need to be repaired before you start your job. Also test the old P-trap by pushing a thumb on the underside as shown. If it's soft, it's high time to change it out—with plastic if it's not in the public eye or with chrome if it's exposed.

Take off the vanity doors and lay a drop cloth

The cloth will save your flooring from tool scratches and contact with the disgusting debris that comes out of old pipes. It's also worth taking a few minutes to unscrew the vanity doors and remove them for easier access. Tape the loose hinge screws to the doors so you don't lose them.

Pull out your new faucet and check the supply line connector

Supply lines usually won't come with your new faucet. Take your new faucet with you when you buy supply lines to make sure you get the right connector size. Don't trust the labels on the shelf; the supply lines tend to get mixed up. Pros prefer no-burst water supply lines (about $6) made from flexible, braided stainless steel (**photo**, p. 110).

Loosen nuts to free stuck shutoffs

Water shutoffs are notorious for seizing up. Instead of bullying them loose, use a wrench to loosen the packing nuts behind the handles about a quarter turn (you'll get a drip of water). That usually frees them. Turn on the sink faucet to be sure the water is completely off. If you still get drips, replace both shutoff valves ($4 each).

Make a complete shopping list before heading to the store

Avoid numerous trips to the hardware store. The plumbing department should not be the place where everybody knows your name! Your shopping list should include two new supply lines (measure the length!), a small tube of 100 percent silicone caulk (clear), Teflon tape, a basin wrench (**top photo**, p. 109) and a P-trap if needed.

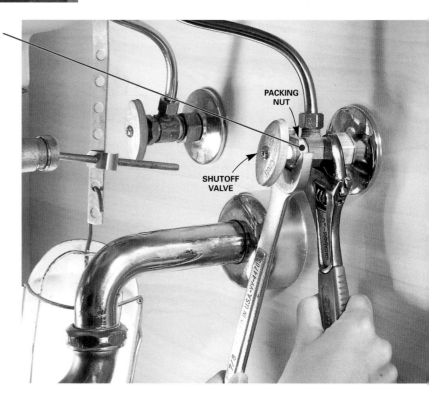

PACKING NUT

SHUTOFF VALVE

Out with the old!

Clear the clutter to get at the basin nut

The instructions for your new faucet won't include how to get the old faucet out, so you're on your own with that. Start by removing the supply lines to clear out the clutter.

Your faucet will be held in place under the sink by some sort of nut. If you're lucky, you can reach it with an adjustable wrench. (Remember that you'll be working upside down, so take a moment to make sure you're turning the nut in the correct direction—counterclockwise.) Or if you're really lucky, you can hand-loosen a plastic nut.

Get at inaccessible faucet nuts with a basin wrench

But chances are that you won't have enough space to get the wrench in. Next reach for a basin wrench as shown. A basin wrench has an extension that allows you to reach up into tight spots that you can't get to with a regular wrench. Use your hand to guide the wrench teeth onto the nut while you twist the handle counterclockwise from below. Using this tool can be an awkward and humbling experience, so don't worry if you fumble around a bit. This tool really works!

As a last resort, buy a nut splitter

If the nut seizes up completely, as corroded "pot metal" ones often do, you'll have to use a nut splitter to break it off (**photo right**). Get one at a plumbing or auto parts store for about $30. Buy the size that fits the faucet threads (**photo above**). A length of pipe will help you apply extra torque. Screw the splitter onto the threaded section of faucet with the teeth pointing upward. Using the ratchet, drive the cutting teeth into the nut. This will split the nut in half and it'll pop apart.

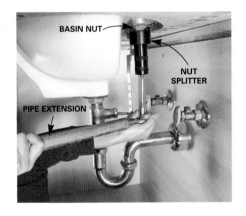

When the pop-up won't pop out

The pop-up assembly consists of a flange (the part you see in the sink) that screws into a body (the part below the sink as shown). If you're lucky, you can simply grab the body (you left the rod on for extra torque) and turn it counterclockwise to unscrew it. Unfortunately, most of the time the flange in the basin also turns, so it won't come apart. At other times it simply won't turn.

Cut a stuck pop-up assembly with a hacksaw

If you're alone, the best solution is to cut off the pop-up body from below. Unscrew the locknut, if possible, and cut the stuck pipe above the nut with a hacksaw. This is difficult work, but be persistent. Once the pipe is cut, you can pry out the flange.

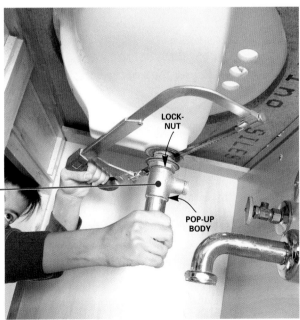

Installation can be challenging

Dry-fit the new faucet

The new faucet directions are primarily written for new construction, where you install the faucet before the sink goes in and you have plenty of work (wrench) space. In your home, you'll run into tight spots where the instructions, followed to the letter, simply won't work.

Remove the handles and spout and set the faucet body into the sink holes to see if it will go in exactly according to the directions. Check the connection methods and adjustment features, tool access for tightening various nuts, and handle and spout seating on the sink top. They should fit flat without rocking.

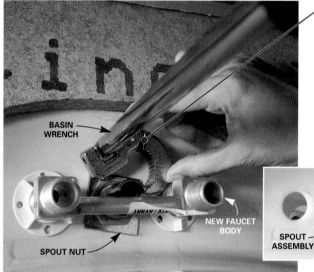

BASIN
WRENCH

NEW FAUCET
BODY

SPOUT NUT

SPOUT
ASSEMBLY

Be prepared to improvise

In our case, there was no way to fit the basin wrench, or any other tightening tool, onto the spout nut. The faucet body was in the way (**photo left**). We ended up disassembling parts of the faucet body to give us an easy shot with a wrench to tighten up the spout assembly (**inset photo below left**). Aligning the spout and faucet assembly washer was also critical after tightening the spout. We had to square up the washer by holding a screwdriver on it and tapping with a hammer.

Study the directions and don't hesitate to call the manufacturer for help. Even the pros do it, especially on high-priced (complicated) faucets. Try to find a way around the problem before tossing it all back into the box.

Check your work at the end

Check for leaks with toilet tissue

When you've finished the entire installation, wipe the valve stem/packing nut zone completely dry and wrap with toilet tissue. Turn on the water and check for obvious leaks at all the connection points. After 10 minutes, check the tissue. If the tissue is damp, tighten the packing nuts or replace the packing or entire valve.

Switch to a plastic P-trap

If your chrome P-trap is in good shape, you can reuse it, but replace the rubber washers. If the trap is out of sight, we recommend switching to a plastic P-trap. They're inexpensive and less likely to leak. Also install new flexible supply lines. Once you've finished the steps shown on p. 111, you're ready to turn the water back on. Remember to retighten the packing nuts behind the oval handles on the shutoff valves if you loosened them earlier.

NEW
SUPPLY
LINE

TOILET
PAPER

Getting the new pop-up perfect

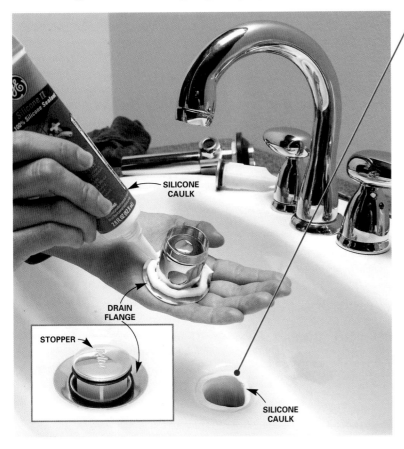

"Overflow" the flange with silicone

The flange at the bottom of the sink is a common leak point. During the manufacturing process, the sink drain hole may be overbuffed or cast more in the shape of an egg than of a flat circle. The leak-free solution is to overflow the flange and the area beneath it in the sink with a bead of 100 percent silicone caulk as shown. This will fill in any factory irregularities in the basin. Press the flange into the drain hole and screw the pop-up body on from below. Then tighten the nut (**bottom photo**). For a white basin, white silicone will look best. Otherwise use clear. Quickly wipe off the excess before it dries and becomes a hassle to clean up.

> **Tip** The pop-up stopper will be in the raised position most of the time, so with the stopper "up," choose the best-looking position for the handle and tape it there.

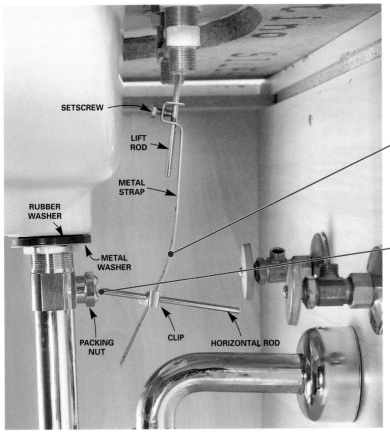

Bend the metal strap so you can clip it farther up the horizontal rod

This will shorten the stroke to raise and lower the stopper.

Tinker with the pivot arm for a smooth operating pop-up

Insert the horizontal arm and stopper into the pop-up body and hand-tighten the packing nut. Slide the metal strap onto the lift rod (handle) and then clip it onto the horizontal rod. Tighten the lift rod setscrew and test the pop-up action. Tighten the packing nut. There's a fine line between a leaky packing nut and a too-stiff pop-up. You'll have to experiment.

HomeCare&Repair

TIPS, FIXES & GEAR FOR A TROUBLE-FREE HOME

RESTORE FREE FLOW TO A CLOGGED FAUCET

If the flow from your kitchen or bathroom faucet isn't what it used to be, the aerator is probably plugged. An aerator can clog slowly as mineral deposits build up, or quickly after plumbing work loosens debris inside pipes. Usually, a quick cleaning solves the problem. Remove the aerator (**Photo 1**) and disassemble it. You may need a small screwdriver or knife to pry the components apart. Scrub away any tough buildup with an old toothbrush (**Photo 2**) and rinse each part thoroughly. Gunk can also build up inside the faucet neck, so ream it out with your finger and flush out the loosened debris.

If the mineral buildup resists scrubbing and you have a standard cylinder-shaped aerator, you can replace it (about $5). Take your old aerator along to the home center or hardware store to find a match. If your aerator has a fancy shape (like the one shown here), finding a match

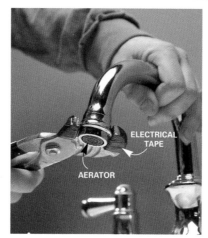

1 WRAP the jaws of a pliers with electrical tape and unscrew the aerator. Close the stopper so the small parts can't fall down the drain.

2 DISASSEMBLE the aerator and lay out the parts in the order you remove them to make reassembly foolproof. Scrub the parts and reassemble them.

won't be as simple. So try this first: Soak the aerator parts in vinegar overnight to soften mineral buildup. If that doesn't work, go to any online search engine and type in the brand

of your faucet followed by "faucet parts." With a little searching, you can find diagrams of your faucet and order a new aerator. Expect to spend $10 or more for a nonstandard aerator.

IMPROVED SHUTOFF VALVES WON'T FAIL WHEN YOU NEED THEM

If you're remodeling your kitchen or adding a bathroom, here's some advice you'll thank us for later: Choose ball-type shutoff valves instead of standard stop valves. Shutoff valves go unused for years. Standard valves have rubber washers that harden with time and other fussy parts that become caked with mineral deposits. Then—when the time comes to replace the faucet or fix the toilet—the valve won't seal off the water flow.

Ball valves are simpler inside. A ball with a hole through it opens and closes with a quarter turn. Fewer complex parts, fewer things to go wrong. Ball valves almost never let you down. This reliability costs you about $6 per valve, vs. $4 for standard valves. Ball valves are sometimes labeled "quarter turn" valves. If you don't find them at a home center or a hardware store, call a plumbing supply store (in the yellow pages under "Plumbing, Fixtures, Parts & Supplies").

GOOD: STANDARD VALVE

BETTER: BALL VALVE

BALL

CUT ENERGY BILLS WITH A PROGRAMMABLE THERMOSTAT

When it comes to energy savings, few upgrades pay off as quickly as a programmable thermostat. If you turn down the heat 5 degrees at night and 10 degrees during the day when no one is home, you'll cut your energy bill by 5 to 20 percent. If you raise the temperature the same amount during the cooling season, your savings will be similar. You can do this with a manual thermostat, but a programmable model never forgets to turn down the heat at night and it can raise the temperature before you get out of bed in the morning.

Home centers carry several programmable models ranging from $25 to $100. Generally, more money means more programming options. Standard programmable thermostats sold in stores work with most heating/cooling systems, new or old. But there are exceptions: Electric baseboard heat systems require a "line voltage" thermostat that's connected to much larger wires than we show here. Heat pumps often require special thermostats, too. If you can't find the one you need at a store, try thermostatshop.com. Before you shop, measure the "footprint" of the old thermostat. If you buy a new one that's at least as large, you won't be left with wallpaper gaps or paint to touch up.

Your old thermostat may look different from the one we show, but removing it will require similar steps. Turn off the power at the main electrical panel by switching off the furnace breaker. If the furnace circuit isn't labeled, switch on the heat (not the air conditioning) and turn off breakers until the furnace stops. Next, remove the old thermostat (**Photo 1**). Chances are, it has a small glass tube containing mercury, which is toxic. Call your city or state environmental or health department for disposal instructions.

You'll find anywhere from two to six wires connected to the old thermostat. If any of them aren't connected to the screw terminals, you won't connect them to the new thermostat either. The terminals are labeled with letters. As you remove each wire, label it to match the terminal using the tags included with the new thermostat (**Photo 2**). Disregard the color of the wires. When you remove the last wire, clip a clothespin to the cable so it can't slip inside the wall.

Mount the wall plate (**Photo 3**). In most cases, you'll simply connect the wires by matching labels to the letters on the new wall plate, but check the manufacturer's instructions to be sure. Program and install the thermostat (**Photo 4**). Don't forget to turn the power back on at the main panel.

1 PULL off the cover ring and remove the screws that fasten the thermostat to the wall plate.

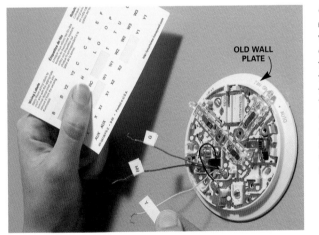

OLD WALL PLATE

2 LABEL the wires as you disconnect them from the screw terminals. Then remove the mounting screws that fasten the wall plate.

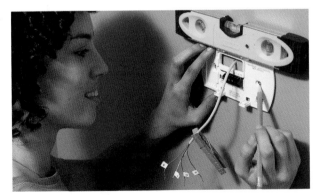

3 MARK the new screw locations, drive in wall anchors and screw the mounting plate to the wall. Connect the wires.

NEW WALL PLATE

4 INSTALL the batteries, program the thermostat and snap it onto the wall plate.

REMOVE A STUBBORN OLD TOILET SEAT
(without heavy equipment or explosives)

Installing a new toilet seat is an easy two-minute job: Just set the seat in place and tighten the nuts. Removing the old seat, on the other hand, can be a frustrating ordeal. Often, the bolts that fasten the seat are so corroded that you simply can't unscrew the nuts. But there's no need to explode—we have the solution.

First, take a look at the bolts that secure the seat. If the bolts or nuts are plastic, they can't corrode and will come off easily. Simply pry open the cover behind the seat to expose the bolt's head. Unscrew the bolt with a pliers or a screwdriver while you hold the nut underneath with the pliers.

OPTION 1

DEEP-WELL SOCKET

Unscrew nuts on metal toilet seat bolts with a deep-well socket. Apply penetrating lubricant to help free corroded nuts.

OPTION 2

Drill a 1/16-in. hole into bolt. Enlarge the hole to weaken the bolt and break it off.

If the bolts are metal, you might be able to unscrew the nuts with a pliers, but the best tool for this job is a socket wrench equipped with a deep-well socket (**Option 1**). Most toilet seats require a 1/2-in. socket ($5). The deep socket fits over the long bolt and grips the nut tightly. Most metal bolts aren't covered by a flip-open cover; all you have to do is turn the nut counterclockwise. Go ahead and twist as hard as you can. If the bolt is brass or badly corroded steel, you might break it off, which is just fine.

If the nut won't budge, douse it with a penetrating spray lubricant such as WD-40. Hold a rag behind the nut to catch the overspray. Give the lubricant 15 minutes to penetrate, then try again. If the bolt spins as you turn the nut and doesn't loosen, or the bolt just spins, go to **Option 2**.

If lubricant won't free the nut, grab your drill, drill bit collection and safety glasses. Using a 1/16-in. bit, drill into the bolt where it meets the nut (**Option 2**). Drill 1/4 in. into the bolt. Next, enlarge the hole with a 1/8-in. bit, followed by a 3/16-in. bit. Then try the socket wrench again. Your goal now isn't to unscrew the nut but to break off the bolt as you turn the nut. If the bolt won't break, keep enlarging the hole. Eventually you'll weaken the bolt enough to break it.

TIGHTEN A FLOPPY FAUCET HANDLE

If you have a loose valve handle—on a shower, bathroom or kitchen faucet—tighten the screw that holds the handle in place. With some faucets, you'll have to pry off the metal button at the center of the handle. With others, you'll find a setscrew near the base of the handle. Setscrews usually require a hex (or Allen) wrench. If tightening doesn't work, the stem inside the handle may be worn, especially if it's plastic. Here's a trick to tighten worn stems on most types of faucets: Wrap the stem tightly with pipe-thread tape and slip the handle back over the stem. In most cases, a single wrap creates a snug fit.

WORN VALVE STEM

PIPE-THREAD TAPE

HomeCare & Repair

EXTEND THE LIFE OF YOUR WATER HEATER

Water heaters often work perfectly for a decade or more without any care, so they're easy to neglect. But a few minutes of TLC once a year pays off by extending the tank's life span and maintaining your water heater's efficiency and safety.

Before you do any maintenance, close the shutoff valve on the cold water supply pipe that feeds the water heater. Then turn on the hot water at any faucet to release the pressure inside the heater's tank. Leave the faucet on until you finish your work. If you have an electric water heater, turn off the power at the main panel. With a gas model, turn the gas control dial to "Off."

First, test the pressure-relief valve located on the top or side of the water heater (**Photo 1**). This safety valve opens automatically if the pressure inside the tank gets too high. (Excess pressure can actually cause the tank to explode.) If the valve doesn't release water when you lift the lever, replace the valve ($12 at home centers and hardware stores). Replacement is simple; unscrew the discharge pipe and then unscrew the old valve. Wrap the

threads of the new valve with pipe-thread tape and screw it into the tank. If your valve is several years old and has never been tested, it might leak after you test it. In that case, replace the valve.

Next, drain the tank to flush out sediments that have settled to the bottom of the tank. Sediment buildup shortens the life of your water heater and adds to your energy bill by reducing its efficiency. Draining 2 or 3 gallons of water is usually enough to flush out sediments, but always let the water flow until you no longer see particles in the bucket.

CAUTION: The water is scalding hot.

Don't worry about any gurgling or groaning noises coming from the heater; it's just air entering the system as water drains out. If the drain valve won't close tightly when you're done, drain the tank completely, unscrew the old valve and screw in a new one ($8). To restart the water heater, open the shutoff valve and let the hot water run at any faucet to purge air from the system. Then turn on the power or relight the pilot.

> **Tip**
> Set your water heater's dial to 120 degrees F. If the dial doesn't have numbers, check the water temperature with a cooking thermometer. Higher temperatures increase sediment buildup and the risk of scalding injuries.

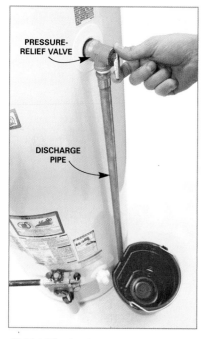

1 PLACE a bucket below the discharge pipe and gently lift the lever on the pressure-relief valve to test it.

2 OPEN the drain valve slowly and let the water run until it's clear and free of sediments. CAUTION: THE WATER IS HOT!

FASTER FLOW FOR A SLOW-FILLING WASHER

If your washing machine fills with a slow trickle, you might need a fill/inlet valve. But chances are you have a simpler problem: plugged inlet screens. These screens catch debris in the water supply and protect a washer's internal parts. Often, screens clog after a remodeling project or after work by city crews on water mains. Any work on water lines can loosen sediment in pipes and lead to plugged screens.

Cleaning the screens is a simple job. The only tricky part is removing the screens without wrecking them (**Photo 1**). Don't just yank them out. Gently squeeze and twist as you pull. You'll distort the screens a little, but you can mold them back into shape with your fingers.

If your screens are cemented in place by mineral deposits, you may not be able to remove them without damage. A new pair of screens will cost about $5 at an appliance parts store.

HOSE SCREEN

Clean the screens with running water or blow out debris with an air compressor. You may have to pick and scrape away stubborn particles with a utility knife.

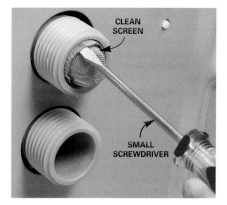

SCREEN

1 TURN OFF the hot and cold water supplies and disconnect the hoses. Use a pair of needle-nose pliers to gently remove the screens for cleaning.

CLEAN SCREEN

SMALL SCREWDRIVER

2 WORK the clean screen back into the inlet by pressing around the rim of the screen with a small screwdriver. Reconnect the hoses, turn on the water and check for leaks.

> **Tip**
> Check your washer supply hoses, too. Some contain screens that can be removed and cleaned just like inlet screens.

TWIST THE FINS TO SILENCE A WHISTLING GRILLE

If you have a grille or register that hums or howls, all you have to do is twist the fins and open them a little. A pliers alone will scratch and kink the delicate fins, so apply electrical tape to a hinge that's about the same length as the fins. Then grab each fin between the hinge leaves and twist slightly.

CURE A DRIPPY SINK SPRAYER

If you find mysterious puddles under your kitchen sink, the most likely suspects are the water supply lines, the drain lines or the seal between the sink and the countertop. But don't forget about the pullout sprayer. Sprayer leaks can fool you because they usually occur only when the faucet is running. There are only two fixes: Either replace the spray head or both the spray head and the hose.

First, check the spray head for leaks. Turn on the faucet and pull out the spray head. Make sure the slide nut is tightly screwed into the spray head (**see left**). Check for leaks, then push the trigger and check again. If water leaks

SPRAY HEAD

WASHER

C-CLIP

SLIDE NUT

HOSE STEM

CRIMP SLEEVE

HOLDER

HOLDER NUT

out from under the slide nut, remove the spray head and slide nut. Turn on the faucet and look for leaks around the crimp sleeve. If you find leaks around the crimp, you'll have to replace the hose and the head. If the crimp doesn't leak, simply replace the head (**Photo 1**). A replacement costs $7 to $20 at home centers and hardware stores.

If the spray head doesn't leak, grab a flash-light, turn on the faucet and check under the sink. Give the hose a quick inspection, then examine the connection under the faucet. If you find a leak at the crimp, replace the hose. If the leak is coming from the stem connection, try to tighten it. You might be able to tighten it with a small pliers, but it's tight quarters under there. The best tool for this job is a basin wrench ($10 at home centers and hardware stores). If tightening doesn't solve the problem, replace the hose (**Photo 2**).

Hoses usually aren't sold separately, so you'll get a new spray head, too. Some hoses have a female fitting that fits over the faucet stem. Others screw into the faucet stem. Many spray head/hose kits include an adapter so the hose can connect to male or female threads. Also pick up a roll of pipe-thread tape ($2) and wrap the male threads before you connect the new hose. You don't have to turn off the water supply to replace the hose, but make sure no one turns on the faucet while the hose is disconnected! Once the new hose is installed, turn on the faucet and check for leaks.

Most spray heads and hoses are interchangeable parts. But some spray heads and hoses connect differently. Home centers and hardware stores usually carry only the standard type shown here. If you have a different type, call a plumbing supplier (in the yellow pages under "Plumbing, Fixtures") or go to any online search engine and type in the manufacturer of your faucet followed by "replacement parts."

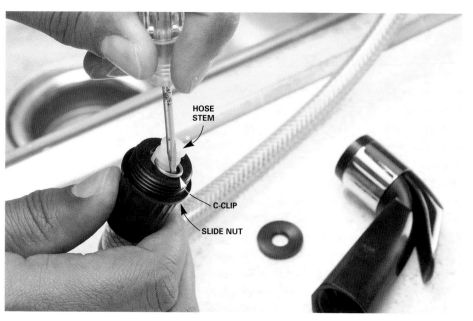

HOSE STEM

C-CLIP

SLIDE NUT

1 REPLACE THE SPRAY HEAD ONLY
UNSCREW the spray head from the slide nut. Remove the washer and pry off the C-clip with a small screwdriver or pocketknife. To install the new head, reverse these steps.

FIX AN ERRATIC SINK SPRAYER

Inside your faucet, there's a diverter valve, which stops the water flow to the spout and sends it to the sprayer when you press the spray head's trigger. Here are the symptoms of diverter trouble:

■ Very little water, or none at all, comes out of the sprayer when you press the trigger. A bad sprayer head can cause this, but more often the diverter is the culprit. To check this, remove the spray head and turn on the faucet. If the water flow out of the hose is weak, the diverter is to blame.

■ The sprayer pulsates like a machine gun.

■ Water continues to flow out of the faucet spout when you're using the sprayer.

Often, a misbehaving diverter needs only light scrubbing with a toothbrush and a good rinse. But since removing a diverter usually requires major faucet disassembly, it's best to simply replace the diverter rather than risk taking it apart again.

Diverter styles and removal procedures differ widely. Some are small valves like the one shown here. Others are larger cylinders that don't look like valves at all. Some newer diverters aren't inside the faucet, but are instead connected to the sprayer hose below. So the first step in diverter repair is finding a diagram of your faucet. If you can't find your owner's manual, do an online search. Type in the manufacturer of your faucet followed by "faucet parts diagram."

DIVERTER VALVE

Disassemble the faucet to access the diverter. Clean or replace the diverter and reassemble the faucet.

With a little searching, you'll find an illustration showing your faucet's internal parts. You'll also find several sources for replacement parts online. To find a local supplier, check the yellow pages under "Plumbing, Fixtures." Diverters cost from $7 to $20.

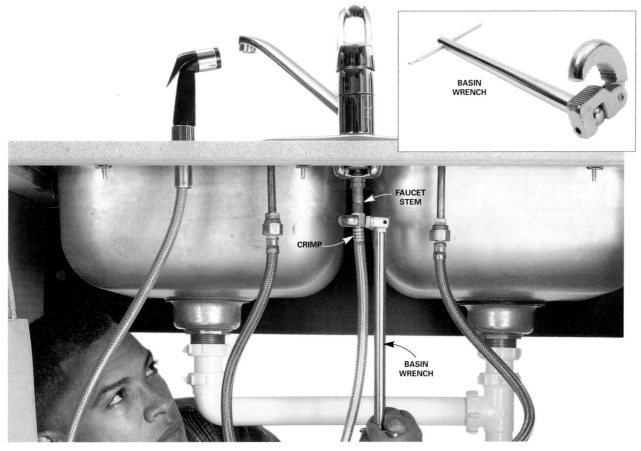

BASIN WRENCH

FAUCET STEM

CRIMP

BASIN WRENCH

2 REPLACE THE SPRAY HEAD AND HOSE

UNSCREW the hose with a basin wrench. Feed the new hose through the holder. Wrap male threads with pipe thread tape. Screw the hose to the faucet stem by hand. Then tighten the connection with the basin wrench.

GreatGoofs®

Super-charged blower

One December Sunday, we returned from church and found the house cold. I checked our old furnace and discovered that the electric blower motor was shot. I removed the motor, examined the mounting bracket and noticed that the motor from my table saw could be hooked up as a temporary substitute. Then I could get someone out the next day to replace the motor. After exchanging the motor, I turned the switch on. The motor roared as it started and I soon noticed dust everywhere in the house—so much that I could write my name on the kitchen table. I then shut off the furnace and realized that the table saw motor was 3,600 rpm—twice as fast as the old motor. The squirrel cage fan had gone into high gear and blown out all the accumulated dust in our ductwork. We kept ourselves warm the rest of the day cleaning every square inch of the house!

Constipated pipes

We had a chronically slow drain that resisted all the common drain cleaners. One day my wife came across an old container of Metamucil and had a brainstorm: If it cleans out people's "pipes," it should clear out plumbing, too. She dumped the whole container down the drain. The Metamucil absorbed water and expanded into a solid 10-ft.-long clog.

We tried liquid drain openers, a drain snake and even a big drill-powered snake, but none of them could penetrate the monster clog. Finally, I duct-taped a spoon to a pole and scooped the gelatinous mass out through the cleanout opening, spoonful by spoonful. It was like getting cranberry sauce out of a 10-ft.-long can.

Hot pants!

As I was installing a basement water softener, my family started to complain about the water being shut off. Well, I tried to hurry.

I was holding a propane torch with one hand while trying to join the pipes with the other. No go—I needed both hands, so I tucked the flaming torch between my knees to free up my other one.

As I reached upward, the torch flipped downward and set my pants on fire! I swatted the fire out and did a fancy two-step to get my pants off. I spent the next hour in the tub soaking off the melted polyester that had stuck fast to my skin.

Luckily, I didn't have a serious burn. I have learned not to rush jobs—or at least to wear flame-retardant work duds when I do.

Quick on the thaw!

It was time to defrost the workshop refrigerator before winter set in. We had already received a dose of cold weather, so my kerosene "bullet" heater was up and running.

In a moment of genius, I decided to speed up the thawing process. I was in a hurry to meet my father-in-law (who had purchased the refrigerator as a gift for me a few years ago), so I moved the heater closer to the refrigerator and continued to tidy up the garage.

Well, the bullet heater sure did the job. When I returned just a few minutes later, it had not only thawed all the ice clinging to the fridge but also melted the plastic liner and shelving!

I know my father-in-law won't let me forget it for years to come.

Hold on!

We wanted to move our washer and dryer down to the basement. Although my wife was due home shortly to help, I decided to get a start on it. I loaded the dryer onto a dolly and rolled it toward the steep, narrow staircase.

I was in trouble immediately. The dryer began to pull me forward, so I dropped to the floor and lodged my feet against both sides of the doorjamb.

Ten minutes later my wife arrived home to find me sprawled at the head of the stairs, sweating and holding on to the dolly with all I had. She began giggling uncontrollably.

One of us had to get below the dryer, but the staircase was too narrow to squeeze past. Luckily, there's an exterior door leading to our basement. While my wife held the dolly, I rushed outside and frantically cut a hole in the locked door.

The two of us were able to lower the dryer down safely. The basement door still has a big cutout in it; it reminds me to ask for help.

Dismantled dryer

When I tossed a load of wet towels into our clothes dryer and pushed the start button, the dryer made an unbearably shrill squealing noise. "Sounds like it's just a belt slipping," said my husband, Eric, pleased with his budding home repair skills.

Hours later, however, he still couldn't find a way into the dryer to remove the screaming belt. In fact, he was doubly embarrassed because he couldn't reassemble the large number of small parts strewn around him on the floor. He declared defeat.

A pro came out the next day and made no comment when I handed him the bag of dryer parts.

Then he demonstrated how easily anyone could open the large, hinged panel on the front of the dryer with a simple tug!

PUSH A BUTTON, SAVE $50

Appliance not working? Try one of these simple fixes before you call the repair service

by **Lucie B. Amundsen**

Few things will make you feel more foolish than calling in a repair pro to come up with a no-brainer solution—such as pushing a button or flipping a circuit breaker. Yet it happens all the time. I had one of these "expensive lessons" when the dryer repair guy handed me a wad of lint caught in my outside vent—and an $80 bill. Pros admit that 25 percent of their calls require just a simple two-minute task.

This article will focus on 11 simple fixes that you often miss. They cost virtually nothing if you do them yourself, saving you big money . . . and your pride.

RESET BUTTON

Disposer

If your disposer won't start, push the reset button and give it a spin

All disposers have an overload feature that automatically shuts off the power when the motor becomes overloaded and gets too hot. Once the motor cools, simply push the reset button on the side of or under the unit (**photo left**).

ALLEN WRENCH

On the other hand, if it hums but doesn't spin, it may have something stuck in it. Switch the disposer off, then try working through it by turning the blades with a special disposer wrench ($10 at home centers) or by turning a bottom bolt (**photo above**). Many disposers have an Allen wrench for that purpose, inset on the bottom of the machine.

> **Pro Tip:**
> "Don't put tea bags or too many potato peels all at once into your disposer. That's a sure way to clog it."

RESET BUTTON

Lights

If the circuit breaker hasn't tripped, look for a GFCI

When a light goes out or a switch doesn't work, you should first check the main electrical panel for a tripped circuit breaker. But don't stop there. Before you change out lightbulbs and switches, see if a GFCI outlet (which may be upstream from the troubled light or outlet) has tripped. Sometimes all the bathrooms or the outside lights are powered through a single GFCI located in one bathroom or elsewhere, such as in a basement. Simply push the reset button on the GFCI and you could be back in business.

Refrigerator

Clean the coils if your refrigerator isn't cooling or conks out

If your refrigerator conks out on a hot day and you have a cat or a dog, immediately check the coils for pet hair. Service pros find this problem on half of their refrigerator calls. The coils are the black tube-and-wire grid that cools the fluid in the compressor. A buildup of hair will cause the compressor to overheat and trigger the overload switch. On many fridges, you get to the coils by opening the grille at the bottom of the refrigerator. Then push a coil cleaning brush ($4 at home centers) into the coils, pull it back and vacuum it clean.

If the coils are located on the back, pull out your fridge (it's often on rollers) and brush them off. Bonus: The clean coils will cool more efficiently and save you as much as $10 a month!

COIL CLEANING BRUSH

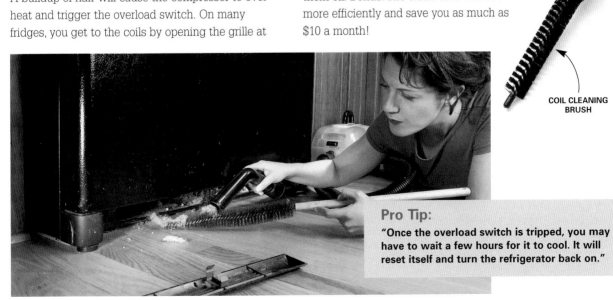

Pro Tip:
"Once the overload switch is tripped, you may have to wait a few hours for it to cool. It will reset itself and turn the refrigerator back on."

Washer

Quiet a noisy washer by leveling it

When a washing machine cabinet rocks, it makes a horrible racket during the spin cycle. The solution is to simply readjust the legs. Screw the front legs up or down until the cabinet is level. When both legs are solid on the floor, tighten each leg's locking nut. In most washers, to adjust the rear legs, gently tilt the machine forward and gently lower it down. The movement will self-adjust the rear legs.

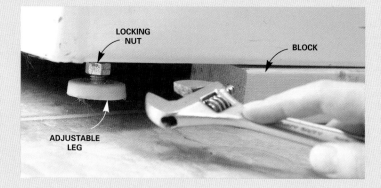

Dryer

If your clothes are still damp after a normal cycle, check the setting and the filter

Our expert repairman responds to many "dryer-not-heating calls" only to find that the machine is set to "fluff air"—a non-heat setting. Avoid the embarrassment. Check the settings first.

Another common cause of poor drying is a clogged lint filter. The filter may look clean, but it may actually be covered by a nearly invisible film caused by dryer sheets. This film reduces airflow and forces

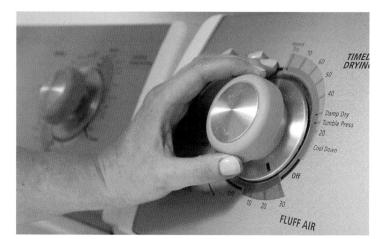

> **Pro Tip:**
> "Test your filter by pouring water into it. If the filter holds water, it's past time to clean it."

the thermostat to shut off the heat before your clothes are dry. Pull out the filter and scrub it in hot water with a little laundry detergent and a stiff kitchen brush.

Also check the outside dryer vent for any lint that may have built up there. The louver door–style vent covers are notorious for lint buildup, which traps heat and turns the heat off in the dryer. Pull the cover completely off to get to these clogs.

Ranges

If the burner won't light, try cleaning the igniter

BURNER PRONG

Gas stove

If your stove burner won't come on, the likely culprit is the spaghetti sauce that boiled over a few days ago. Use a toothbrush to clean off food spills from the igniter. On an electronic ignition stove, it's a little ceramic nub located either on the stovetop or under the ceramic seal strike plate. Also make sure that the round ceramic seal strike plate is properly seated on the burner.

IGNITER

> **Pro Tip:**
> "Dirty igniters are the most common problem. It takes only a minute to clean them."

Electric range

If your electric stove burner won't heat, turn the burner off and pull it out from its socket. Then plug it in again and wiggle it around. If it feels loose, remove the burner again and gently bend the burner prongs slightly outward for a tighter connection. Easy does it. You could end up pushing the whole socket out of its bracket.

Oven won't heat? Check the clock

Blame it on the technology. It so happens that if you set the "time cook" function, the oven, much like a programmed VCR, won't turn on until the appointed time. You may have done this inadvertently, but if your digital display reads "hold," "delay" or "time cook," then the timer is engaged. You'll have to clear it first by pushing the "off" button. On ovens with dials, be sure the knob is turned to "manual."

> **Pro Tip:**
> "I usually tell the callers right on the phone to check the timer setting. I really don't want to charge them $80 to come out and tell them exactly what's in their owner's manual."

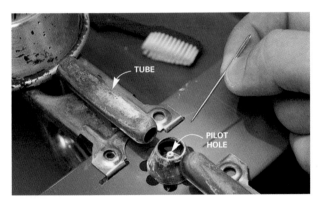

TUBE

PILOT HOLE

Standing pilot gas range

To access the ignition system in an older-style standard gas range, pop the lid. It's usually hinged on the back side. If the pilot flame is out, poke a needle into the pilot hole to clean out soot (be careful not to ream it wider). Brush off any debris and clean the tube that leads from the pilot to the burner. Then relight the pilot.

Air conditioner

If your AC won't come on, the thermostat may be saying no

FUSE BLOCK

AIR CONDITIONER SHUTOFF BOX

CONDENSING UNIT (INCLUDES COMPRESSOR)

RUUD

If you turn your central air conditioner on, off and then on again in rapid order, chances are you'll blow a fuse or shut off a circuit breaker or the air conditioner simply won't respond. That's because the compressor (in the outdoor condensing unit) may have stopped in a high compression mode,

> **Pro Tip:**
> "Another common air conditioner problem is a clogged furnace (blower) filter. A new filter only costs $3."

making it difficult to start until the compression releases. Older condensing units may switch the compressor on anyway, which causes the circuit to overload and blow a fuse. Newer, "smarter" condensing units will prevent this blunder by delaying the AC's "on" function for a few minutes.

It's easy to mistake this delay with a faulty air conditioner. Be patient and give the air conditioner about five minutes to come back on.

To determine if you have a blown fuse, locate the special fuse block near the outside unit. Pull out the block and take the whole thing to the hardware store. A salesperson can test the cartridge fuses and tell you if you need to replace them.

Another simple reason your AC might not come on: You've signed up for a cost discount with your electric company in exchange for limited air conditioning

FUSE BLOCK

CARTRIDGE FUSE

during high-demand periods, and you're in an "off" period. If you can't remember, call your electric company to find out. You don't want to pay the repair technician to drive out and explain this program to you!

Dishwasher

Clean the filter and float switch if the dishes don't come out clean

When your dishwasher no longer gets your dishes clean, a food-filled filter is most often to blame. If it's clogged, water can't make it to the spray arms to clean the dishes in the top rack. The fix takes

> **Pro Tip:**
> "If you can't find the float switch cover, check the toy chest. Kids love to toddle off with it."

two minutes. Simply pull out the lower rack and remove the filter cover inside the dishwasher. (Check your owner's manual if you can't spot the filter.) Then use a wet vacuum to clean off the screen.

While you're there, slide the nearby float switch up and down. If it's jammed with mac and cheese, you won't get any water. If the cover sticks, jiggle it up and down and clean it with water.

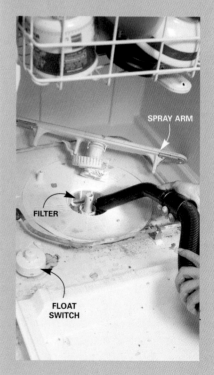

SPRAY ARM

FILTER

FLOAT SWITCH

4 Woodworking & Furniture Projects Tools & Tips

SMART/FAST
WORKSHOP STORAGE
GLUE-GO-ROUND

Here are four good reasons to build this glue caddy for your shop. First, no more hunting for the right type of glue; they'll all be right at your fingertips. Second, you can store the containers upside down. That keeps the glue near the spout—no more shaking down half-filled bottles. Third, upside-down storage helps polyurethane glues last longer without hardening because it keeps the air out. Last, the caddy is so doggone handsome.

Here's how to make yours:

First, arrange all your glue bottles in a circle with 1-in. spacing between the bottles. Add 2 in. to the circle diameter and cut out two 3/4-in. plywood discs. Drill 7/8-in. holes in the center of each one. Measure the various bottle diameters and drill storage holes around the top disc a smidgen larger than the bottles. Glue the discs on a 12-in.-long, 7/8-in. dowel, with a 5-in. space between the discs.

Add a knob of your choice, load up your glue, and you've got an instant grip on every type of sticky problem that comes your way.

HALF OF AN
EXTENSION
LADDER

STORE
SHEET GOODS
ON A LADDER

Got a decade's worth of leftover pieces of plywood, drywall and plastic laminate and spare boards? Here's how to round them up and protect them from moisture, dirt and dings. If you have an old extension ladder lying around, take the sections apart and lay one on the floor near a wall to use as a sheet goods rack. The rail will keep stuff from sliding off. It'll hold everything high and dry off the floor and ready to sort when that next project comes along.

HARDWARE HONEYCOMB

Looking for the right fastener will be like a bee going to nectar with this multi-pocket storage bucket. To make one, round up a plastic 5-gallon bucket ($3 at a home center) and scrap plywood for partitions and floors. Use 3/4-in. plywood for the partitions and 1/4-in. plywood for the floors to match the bucket cutout dimensions shown.

Cut the bucket holes with a saber saw as shown, then saw the crisscrossing bottom partitions with slightly angled ends to fit snugly against the bucket

sides. Saw notches halfway down the center of the partitions so they interlock. Next, cut the round floor to fit the bucket on top of the partition, then drop it in. Cut the next set of partitions, drop those in and then add the next floor. Create the egg carton partition to fit on top and screw or nail it to the upper floor. Then load your bucket. Our system is designed for miscellaneous screws and nails; feel free to try your own configuration to fit your needs.

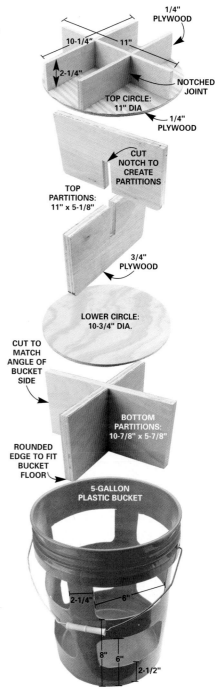

SCRAP BIN ON A ROLL

Here's a low-rolling wood scrap bin that'll capture all the cutoffs while you work on your next project. Bolt swivel casters to the base of a storage bin ($6 at discount stores) and it'll scoot right where you need it. Sure, you can take extra time to beef up the casters-to-bin connection by bolting plywood on before attaching the casters, but it's easier to bolt them right through the thicker, reinforced area of the bin's bottom.

PEGBOARD
CUBBYHOLES

Here's a tool storage technique for all those slender tools and shop accessories. Cut short lengths of PVC pipe (1-1/2- and 2-in.-diameter pipes work well for most items) and slide them over pegboard hooks. Then load them up with files, hacksaw blades, zip ties, pencils, stir sticks . . . you get the skinny.

HARDWARE CLOTH
TOOL ROOST

Store just about every hand tool you need on a strip of vinyl-coated 1/2-in. wire mesh hardware cloth. Make a frame from a scrap of plywood and a couple of 5-in.-long 2x4s. Span the 2x4s with the mesh and staple it on, then bend over the front of the mesh to cover the 2x4 ends. Now have fun filling the mesh with any tool that has a shaft that'll fit through the holes. Or for chisels, pliers and larger-handled tools, just snip out wider openings in the mesh with a wire cutter. For a wrench roost, snip and bend up wires along the front edge of the mesh to make little hanging hooks.

12- OR 14-GAUGE INSULATED WIRE

HARDWARE
LASSOS

To keep your hardware neat and accessible, thread nuts, washers, sockets and other items on short pieces of 12- or 14-gauge electrical wire, then hang them on a toolbox handle or a pegboard hook. Twist the ends of the wire into hook shapes that interlock for easy closing and opening.

PIE PLATE **STORAGE POCKETS**

Screw cut-in-half pie tins and heavy-duty paper plates to a shop wall and you've got space-saving storage for the sanding discs, circular saw blades and abrasive discs that like to hide in a drawer. Be sure to tape the sharp edges on the cut pie plates to protect your fingers!

MINI HARDWARE **HOLDERS**

Store your itty-bitty screws, nails and driver bits in an easily accessible spot on your toolbox. Tack or screw a looped strip of 3/4-in. braided elastic ($1.29 at a fabric store) to a convenient place and slide in loaded and labeled film canisters. They'll ride along snugly and within easy reach for all your jobs.

FILM CANISTER

ELASTIC STRIP

UPHOLSTERY NAIL

HIJACKED **TACKLE BOX**

When the fishing urge stops biting, put that old tackle box to use as a portable hardware and tool tote. Load the nifty fold-out compartments with screws, nails, bolts, tape, electrical connectors—what have you. Stash your pliers, screwdriver, wrenches, hammer, tape measure and other frequently used tools on the bottom level. When chores and repairs start nibbling at your conscience, you'll have the right tackle handy for the job.

8 TABLE SAW **TIPS**

Make cleaner, straighter and safer cuts with these easy-to-make accessories

by **Eric Smith**

1 USE **FEATHERBOARDS** FOR AN EXTRA SET OF HANDS

When it's tough to keep a board aligned with the fence, pull out a featherboard for smooth, straight cuts. Featherboards have a series of wooden "fingers" that hold wood tightly against the saw fence. The fingers are slightly flexible and cut at an angle, so they allow you to push the wood through while maintaining firm, even pressure. They also dig in and hold wood in place if it starts to kick back. They're a great "third hand" when you want the perfect rip. Just push the featherboard firmly against the piece of wood 1 to 3 in. before the saw blade, then clamp it tightly to the saw table. It should be fairly easy to push the wood forward but hard to pull it back. And when you're ripping large boards, add a second clamp for extra-firm pressure.

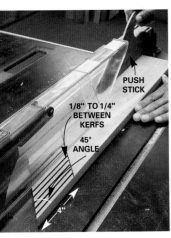

PUSH STICK

1/8" TO 1/4" BETWEEN KERFS

45° ANGLE

CLAMP

PRESSURE AGAINST BOARD

FEATHERBOARD

Make your own featherboards from a 2-ft. length of knot-free 1x4. Cut one end at 45 degrees. Then cut a series of 4-in.-long kerfs every 1/8 to 1/4 in. (narrower on stiff hardwoods, wider on softwoods)—thin enough so the long fingers flex slightly.

2 USE A **HALF FENCE** FOR COMPLICATED GRAIN

Wood with knots or wavy grain and wood that has been dried unevenly will often warp badly as you rip it. If the halves bend outward, one will push against the fence and cause burn marks, a kickback or an uneven cut. If this begins to happen, clamp a smooth, straight length of 3/4-in. wood against the fence, ending at the center of the saw blade. This half fence gives the trapped piece (the section between the

HALF FENCE

BIESEMEYER

CENTER OF SAW BLADE

SEVERE WARP

blade and the fence) room to bend without pushing back against the blade. Keep several push sticks at hand so you can work around the clamps and complete the cut smoothly.

If the two halves bend toward each other as they're being cut—pinching the splitter at the end of the blade guard—turn the saw off and wedge a shim between the two pieces. Then complete the cut.

3 SET UP SIMPLE OUTFEED SUPPORT

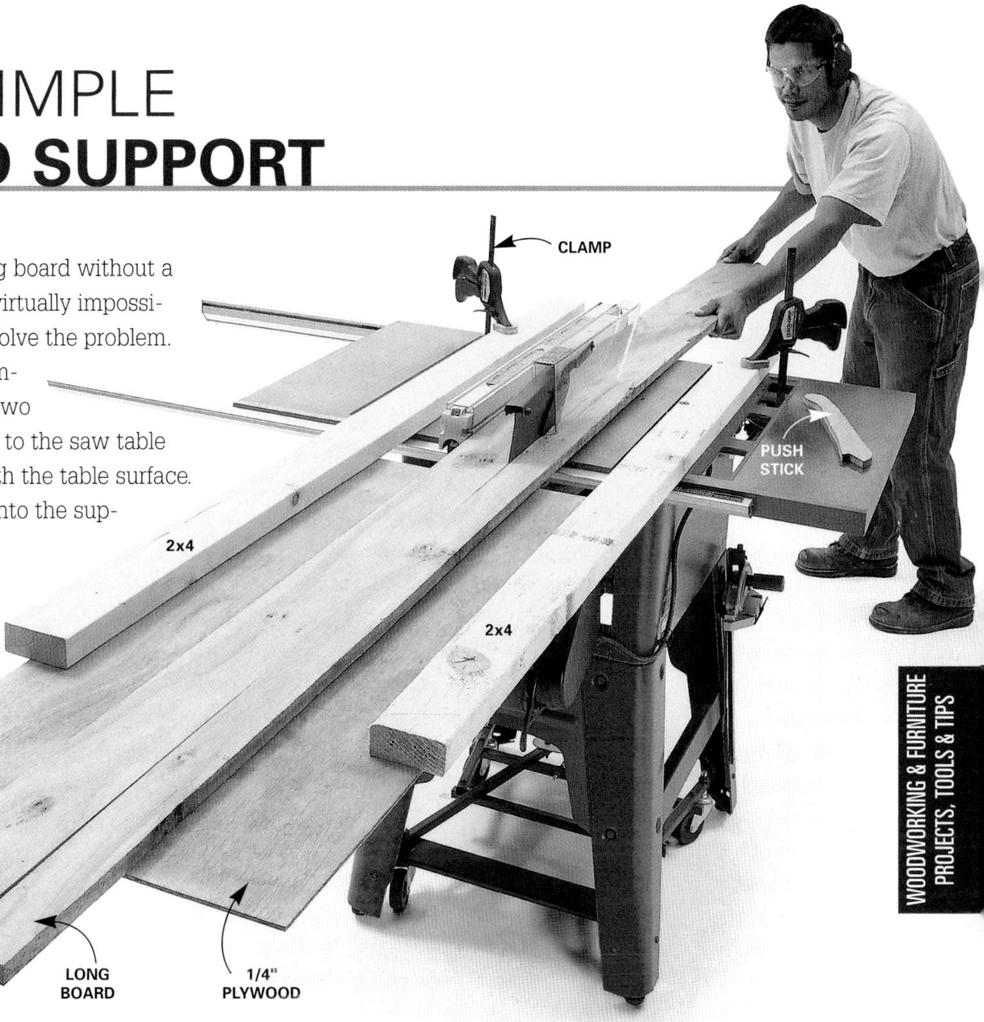

Trying to rip the last few feet of a long board without a helper or support at the other end is virtually impossible. An expensive roller support can solve the problem. But if you don't have one, set up a temporary outfeed support with clamps, two 2x4s and plywood. The 2x4s clamped to the saw table keep the plywood perfectly in line with the table surface. The boards you're cutting will slide onto the support without getting stuck.

To construct a temporary outfeed table, clamp two 8-ft.-long 2x4s to the saw table, cantilevering them approximately 5 ft. over the outfeed side. Then screw or clamp 1/4-in. plywood to the underside of the 2x4s. Keep in mind that this works only with contractor-size and larger table saws with heavy steel or iron tables. It could cause lighter bench-top saws to tip or bend.

CLAMP

2x4

2x4

PUSH STICK

LONG BOARD

1/4" PLYWOOD

4 ADD A FENCE TO THE MITER GAUGE FOR SMOOTHER CROSSCUTS

The narrow width of most miter gauges offers poor support when you're crosscutting, especially when you're cutting at an angle. For better support, screw a wood fence to the miter gauge. (Most gauges have holes for this purpose.) Use a straight 1x3 or 1x4, and make it high enough so that the blade won't cut it completely off. Then it's easy to add a removable stop block for making multiple cuts or change

the angle and make miter cuts with the same fence. However, always double-check the accuracy of the miter gauge with a square or protractor before making any cuts.

To avoid binding and kickbacks when you're cutting, always push the workpiece and fence completely past the blade. Then turn the saw off before pulling the fence back and removing newly cut pieces.

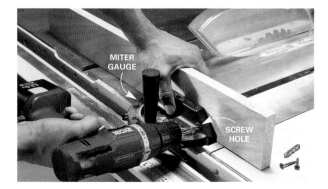

MITER GAUGE

SCREW HOLE

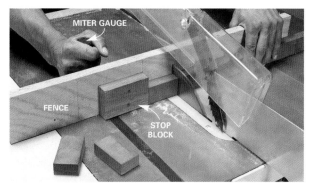

MITER GAUGE

FENCE

STOP BLOCK

5 SAVE YOUR FINGERS WITH **PUSH STICKS**

If you find your hand within a foot of the table saw blade, it's time to reach for a push stick. This essential table saw accessory is notched to hook solidly over the end of the board. You can then push it on through and hold it down firmly at the same time. It allows you to complete a perfectly straight cut while keeping your hands well away from the blade.

It's best to keep at least these two styles handy (**see photo**). Use the long, narrow push stick for smaller, lighter boards and for narrower cuts. And use the broad, flat push

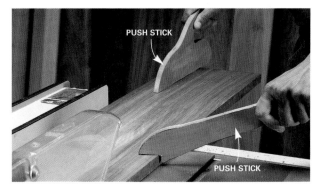

PUSH STICK

PUSH STICK

stick for wider, heavier boards when you need to apply more downward pressure.

As a rule, use 1/2-in. plywood for general-purpose push sticks. It's light and tough and won't split as easily as most solid wood. But don't hesitate to make several different thicknesses and styles to use in special situations. Customize your push sticks with different handles, shallower notches (for 1/4-in. plywood, for instance), or strips of rubber or sandpaper for better grab.

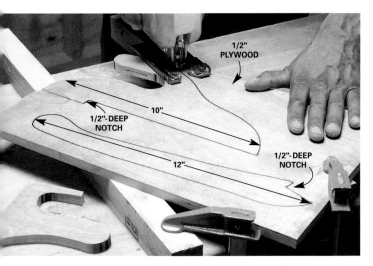

1/2" PLYWOOD

10"

1/2"-DEEP NOTCH

12"

1/2"-DEEP NOTCH

6 CLAMP ON A LONG FENCE FOR **LONG BOARDS**

Keeping a long, heavy board or a full sheet of plywood tight against a short fence is a challenge, especially when you work alone. It's all too easy for the wood to wander away from the fence, ruining the cut or causing the blade to bind and leave burn marks along the edge. To avoid these problems, clamp a long level or a long, straight board to the fence. The longer the fence, the easier it is to keep the wood firmly against it.

TABLE SAW FENCE

4' LEVEL

7 CUT **NARROW STRIPS** WITH A SLIDING JIG

To make a series of identical narrow strips for shelf edging, you don't need to remove the blade guard or move the fence for every cut. Just attach a short strip of wood slightly thinner than the width of the rip cut to the end of a 4-ft. 1x6. Then hold the board against it and push the jig through. The jig keeps your hands well away from the blade, and you can rip as many pieces as you need without ever moving the fence.

To make the jig, attach a 5-in.-long strip of wood, 1/16 in. narrower than the width of the desired rip, to the end of a 1x6 as shown. Basically you're cre-ating a horizontal push stick. Add a handle near the end of the jig to give yourself better control as you run the jig through the saw.

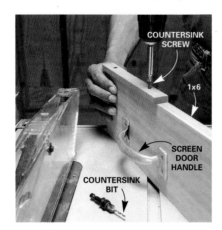

COUNTERSINK SCREW

1x6

SCREEN DOOR HANDLE

COUNTERSINK BIT

IDENTICAL STRIPS

3/8" STRIP

5/16"

SLIDING JIG

8 TRIM **CROOKED BOARDS** WITH A PLYWOOD STRAIGHTEDGE

The prettiest pieces of wood at the lumberyard aren't always straight and smooth. But cleaning up those rough edges isn't difficult. To straighten out a crooked board (with minimum waste), simply screw it solidly to a straight strip of plywood. Then run the board through the saw with the ply-wood against the fence. Your board will now have a straight, smooth side to hold against the fence when you're ripping it to width.

Plywood straightedges are also handy for ripping tapers. Simply mark the desired taper on your board, align it with the edge of the plywood, screw it in place, and cut.

Make the sliding plywood straight-edge from a 1-ft. x 8-ft. strip of 3/4-in. plywood. Attach the rough board to the plywood with screws driven (predrilled) through a waste section. If there's not enough waste area, screw up through the plywood into the rough board and fill the small holes later. Or consider using special sur-face-mounted hold-down clamps, available from woodworking stores.

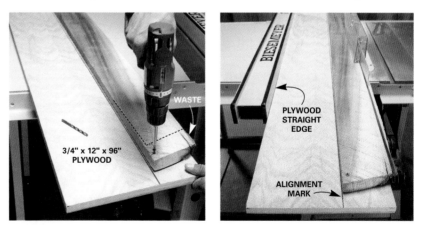

3/4" x 12" x 96" PLYWOOD

WASTE

PLYWOOD STRAIGHT EDGE

ALIGNMENT MARK

Editor's Note: A word about blade guards

Get together with any group of woodworkers and carpenters and invariably you'll hear gruesome stories about table saw injuries. All the accidents have one thing in common: The blade guard was removed. There is a persistent myth in the carpentry world that blade guards are difficult to work with, but in our experience, it's simply not true. They slide up easily as the wood goes through, and the blade is clearly visible through the plastic. And they save fingers. — Eric

NO-TANGLE CORD COILING

I've seen contractors store very long cords by doubling them up and somehow coiling them into a series of loops that come apart without tangling when it's time to use the cord again. We'd like to know how to do that.

If you're vexed by tangled cords, here's a great trick to learn. Start by holding both ends of the cord in your left hand. Grab the doubled cord with your right hand and fully extend both arms (**Photo 1**).

Make a loop with the doubled cord, then hold the loop in your left hand. Continue making loops until you're almost out of cord (**Photo 2**). If the cord isn't badly twisted or stiff, you shouldn't get any figure eights.

What you have left after making the loops will be the exact middle of the cord. Wrap this once or twice around the loops to secure them (**Photo 3**). Feed the middle back through the wrap to make a handle for easy carrying (**Photo 4**).

1 HOLD the plug ends in your left hand and stretch the cord with your right hand.

2 MAKE a series of loops until you're almost out of cord.

3 WRAP the middle of the cord around the loops.

4 INSERT the cord into the small loop that you just made. Pull the middle of the cord through the loop to make a handle.

PIPING FOR COMPRESSED AIR

What is the best material for piping compressed air to different areas in my shop and garage: PVC or copper?

Don't use PVC pipe. If it breaks under pressure, the plastic will shatter and send pieces flying like shrapnel. Use copper instead. It's available at most hardware stores and home centers. Solder it using the same fittings as you would for water supply lines.

If you don't want to solder, use galvanized or black steel pipe. Measure the pipe runs and buy exact lengths; otherwise you'll have to cut and thread the ends yourself. Unlike gas and water lines, air compression lines don't require perfect joints, so don't worry if they leak a tiny bit.

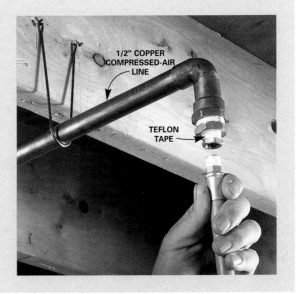

1/2" COPPER COMPRESSED-AIR LINE

TEFLON TAPE

UTILITY
WARDROBE

A day's work and $250 of materials yield this sturdy storage cabinet for off-season clothing

by **Brett Martin**

This simple wardrobe is the perfect spot to store those heavy jackets, boots, hats and gloves until winter rolls around and it's time to store your summer things. Or you could add shelves and make it the permanent storage cabinet for backpacks, tents, life preservers or any other seasonal items that stack up in your garage.

In this article, we'll show you how to build this practical, sturdy cabinet out of low-cost materials. We'll also show you how to make simple, strong joints using pocket screws. The only specialty tool you'll need is a pocket screw jig ($22 to $100). A miter saw, a table saw and an air compressor with a brad gun will make the job a lot easier, but you can get by without them. Allow about a day to build the cabinet, plus a half day for painting.

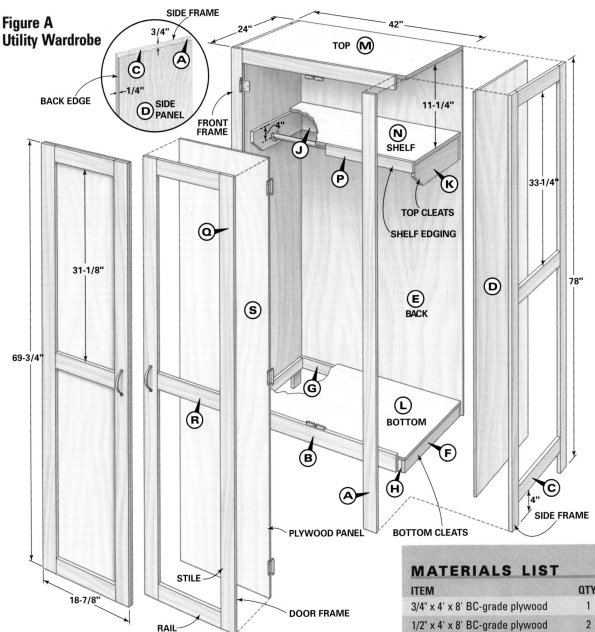

**Figure A
Utility Wardrobe**

SIDE FRAME

3/4"

C · A

BACK EDGE

1/4"

D · SIDE PANEL

24"

42"

TOP (M)

11-1/4"

4"

J

(N) SHELF

(P)

(K)

TOP CLEATS

SHELF EDGING

33-1/4"

(D)

78"

31-1/8"

(Q)

(S)

(E) BACK

69-3/4"

(R)

(G)

(L) BOTTOM

(B)

(H)

(F)

(A)

(C)

4"

SIDE FRAME

PLYWOOD PANEL

BOTTOM CLEATS

STILE

DOOR FRAME

RAIL

18-7/8"

Materials and costs

To keep costs low (about $250, including hardware), we made the wardrobe from BC-grade plywood and knot-free 1x3s. If you want to make the cabinet even more utilitarian, you can use lower grades of wood and cut the cost in half. However, the doors might twist a bit and not shut evenly. BC plywood has a smooth sanded face that's nice for painting. The knot-free poplar 1x3s (available from a local home center) are stable and easy to cut and join. Be sure to choose straight ones!

Build the frame

Start by cutting the 1x3 rails and stiles for the frames to length (A, B and C), following the Cutting List. Then use a pocket screw jig and the "step bit" that comes with it to drill two holes at both ends of each rail (**Photo** 1). You'll cover these holes with plywood later, so begin your holes on the less attractive side. We used a jig that's fastened to the end of the rail by a

MATERIALS LIST	
ITEM	**QTY.**
3/4" x 4' x 8' BC-grade plywood	1
1/2" x 4' x 8' BC-grade plywood	2
1/4" x 4' x 8' BC-grade plywood	1
1x6 x 8' poplar	1
1x3 x 8' poplar	12
1x2 x 8' poplar	2
1x2 x 6' poplar	1
6' chrome closet pole	1
Closet pole brackets	2
Self-closing flush door hinges	6
Door handles	2
Threaded metal base glides	4
Magnetic catches	4
1-1/2" brad nails	1 box
1" brad nails	1 box
1-1/2" pocket screws	1 bag

CUTTING LIST

KEY	QTY.	SIZE & DESCRIPTION	KEY	QTY.	SIZE & DESCRIPTION
A	6	3/4" x 2-1/2" x 78" poplar stiles	K	2	3/4" x 5-1/2" x 19-1/4" poplar top cleats (side)
B	2	3/4" x 2-1/2" x 37" poplar front rails	L	1	3/4" x 23" x 39-1/2" plywood floor
C	6	3/4" x 2-1/2" x 18-1/4" poplar side rails	M	1	3/4" x 23-1/4" x 40-1/2" plywood top
D	2	1/2" x 23" x 73-1/4" plywood side panels	N	2	3/4" x 20" x 39-1/2" plywood shelf
E	1	1/4" x 40-1/2" x 73-1/4" plywood back panel	P	1	3/4" x 1-1/2" x 39-1/2" shelf nosing
F	2	3/4" x 1-1/2" x 22-1/4" poplar bottom cleats (side)	Q	4	3/4" x 2-1/2" x 69-3/4" poplar door stiles
G	1	3/4" x 1-1/2" x 39-1/2" poplar bottom cleat (back)	R	6	3/4" x 2-1/2" x 13-7/8" poplar door rails
H	1	3/4" x 1-1/2" x 38" poplar bottom cleat (front)	S	2	1/2" x 18-7/8" x 69-3/4" plywood door panels
J	1	3/4" x 5-1/2" x 39-1/2" poplar top cleat (back)			

face clamp, although other types are available (see Buyer's Guide, p. 142).

To create solid, smooth joints, apply a bead of wood glue along the end of a rail (B), then butt it against the top of a stile (A) so the top edges are flush (**Photo 2**). With the joint overhanging your work surface, clamp the rail and stile together with a "face" clamp (part of the pocket screw kit) to keep them aligned. Also clamp your stile to the work surface. The key is to make sure the edges and the faces of the two boards are flush before you drive the screws. Then, using the special pocket screw drive bit, fasten the joint with 1-1/2-in. pocket screws. If you're a pocket screw rookie, practice on scrap wood first to get the hang of it.

Assemble the two side frames, the front and the two door frames in this manner, using **Figure A** as a guide. If your end cuts are perfectly square, your frame should also be square, but check them with a framing square anyway.

With the frames built, apply glue along the edge of a side frame, clamp it to the front frame so the edges are flush (make sure the pocket screw holes face inside), then fasten them with 1-1/2-in. nails (**Photo 3**). Do the same for the other side frame. Wipe away any glue that oozes out. The glue provides the primary holding power. The nails simply hold everything in place until the glue dries.

Add the sides and back

We added 1/2-in. plywood to the side frames for stability. We held it 3/4 in. short of the top and 1/4 in. from the back to provide convenient grooves for inserting and nailing the top and back panels (**Figure A**).

Cut the side and back panels (D and E) accurately. If they're not square, the cabinet won't be square. Building a support spacer with two 2x4s and 1/2-in. plywood simplifies the side panel installation (**Photo 4**). Set the spacer under the bottom rail on a side frame. Apply a generous bead of glue to the side frame, then set the side panel in place (the good side facing out), resting it on the spacer. Butt the panel against the front frame. The frame

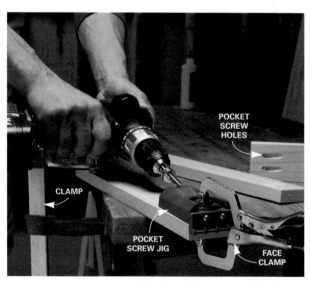

1 CUT the 1x3 rails and stiles to size for all the frames, following the Cutting List above. Drill pairs of pocket screw holes in each end of the rails.

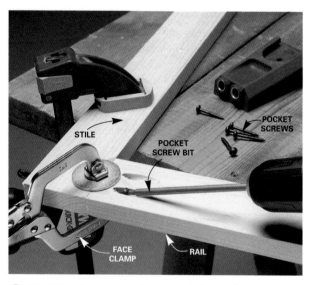

2 SPREAD glue on the rail ends and fasten them to the stiles with pocket screws. Clamp the boards as you fasten them to hold the board edges even.

3 SPREAD glue on the leading edge of the side frames and clamp them to the front frame so the top and sides are flush. Nail the frames together with 1-1/2-in. brads.

4 CUT the side panels to size. Apply glue to the inside face of the frame, set the side panels in place, clamp them, then nail them with 1-in. brads.

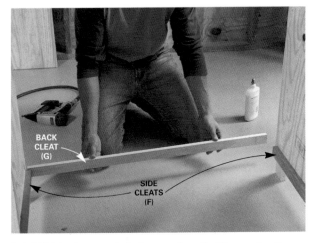

5 CUT the bottom 1x2 cleats to length. Glue and nail the side cleats first. Then glue and nail the front and back cleats.

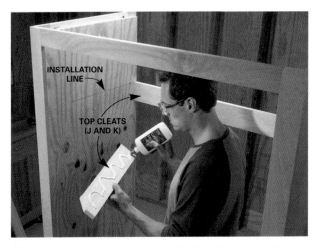

6 CUT the top cleats to length. Nail the back cleat into place. Then glue and nail the side cleats.

may not be exactly square, so flex the frame if necessary to align it with the panel.

Clamp the panel to the framing. Use several clamps to keep the panel tight against the rails and stiles. Nails won't close any gaps between the plywood and the framing—that's the clamps' job. Anchor the panel with 1-in. nails. Install the panel on the other side the same way.

Now cut the 1x2 bottom cleats and 1x6 top (shelf) cleats to length (see the Cutting List, p. 139). Glue and nail the 1x2 side cleats first (F). Align them with the bottom of the plywood panels, and butt them against the front frame. Clamp them before nailing them. Glue and install the front and back cleats as well (G and H; Photo 5).

Measure down 12 in. from the top of the side panels

and install the 1x6 top back cleat (J) so the back is aligned with the edge of the plywood side panels (toenail the cleat into the plywood). Then glue and install the top side cleats (K; Photo 6). Drive 1-1/2-in. nails through the cleats into the stiles and drive 1-in. nails through the plywood panels into the cleats from the outside.

Now place the wardrobe face down on the floor. Apply glue along the back edges of the side panels and cleats. Install the back panel (E) and tack it into place with 1-in. brads (Photo 7).

Install the top, bottom and shelf

We used 3/4-in. plywood for the floor, ceiling and shelf to add stiffness and strength to the cabinet. Cut the floor, top

7 LAY the wardrobe face down. Spread glue and nail the back panel (E) into place with 1-in. brads spaced every 8 to 10 in.

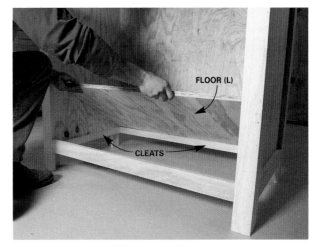

FLOOR (L)

CLEATS

8 CUT the floor, top and shelf to size. Glue the top and nail it into place. Stand the wardrobe upright, then glue and nail the floor and shelf to the cleats.

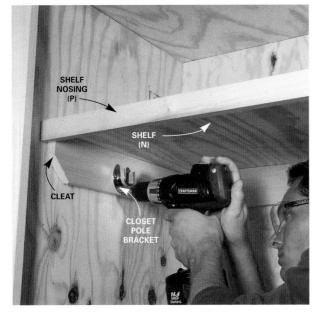

SHELF NOSING (P)

SHELF (N)

CLEAT

CLOSET POLE BRACKET

9 POSITION the closet pole brackets 4 in. below the shelf and 10-3/4 in. from the back cleat. Screw them into place. Measure and cut the closet pole to length.

DOOR PANEL

DOOR FRAME

10 CUT the door panels to size, then glue and nail them to the door frames. All edges should be flush.

and shelf (L, M and N) to size. With the wardrobe still on its face, apply glue along the top of the side and back panels. Fasten the top into place using 1-1/2-in. brads.

Then stand the wardrobe back up and install the floor (**Photo 8**). Cut the 1x2 nosing (P) to length. Glue and nail it along the front of the shelf, then install the shelf. The nosing will stiffen the shelf and keep it from bowing.

Mark the side cleats under the shelf 10-3/4 in. from the back cleat (the halfway point inside the wardrobe) and install closet pole brackets. Fasten the brackets into place with screws (Photo 9).

Cut the closet pole to length and install it. We recommend a chrome pole rather than wood, since chrome can hold a heavier load without sagging.

Paint the wardrobe, and build and attach the doors

Follow the Cutting List to cut the door panels (S) to size. Apply glue to the back of a door frame, set a panel over it, aligning it with the top and sides of the frame, then tack it into place (**Photo 10**). Do the same for the second door.

We don't show it, but it's easiest to prime and paint the wardrobe and doors at this point. We used an exterior latex paint, since we planned to keep the wardrobe in a garage. For a smoother finish, lightly sand the first coat with 120-grit paper before applying the second coat. Once the paint is dry, fasten the door hinges. You have some flexibility where you place the hinges, but keep the location the same on both doors. We installed our hinges

11 LAY the wardrobe on its back. Screw the hinges to the doors, then center the doors over the opening. Insert a 1/8-in. spacer between the doors.

1/8" SHIM

VIX BIT

DOOR HINGE

12 PREDRILL holes in the front stiles and screw on the hinges. Stand the wardrobe upright, then install the magnetic catches and door handles.

2 in. from the top and bottom, and at the middle.

Installing the doors can be tricky. You want the doors to open and close without banging together, yet you want the gap between them kept to a minimum. To do this, place the wardrobe on its back and make a tiny mark on the rails at the midpoint of the door opening. Center the doors over the opening, overhanging the sides, top and bottom by 3/8 in. Insert a shim between the doors at the top and bottom to create a 1/8-in. gap (**Photo 11**). Use the midpoint marks to keep the doors centered.

Predrill the hinge holes on the stiles using a 3/32-in. bit. We used a special Vix bit ($10; **Photo 12**), which precisely centers the holes. Standard drill bits may shift slightly, off-setting the hole. Even this slight movement may keep the doors from closing properly.

Stand the wardrobe upright to attach the remaining hardware. Installing metal magnetic catches at the top and bottom of the doors will hold them firmly closed and help keep them from warping.

The wardrobe is designed for function, but you can still have fun with its appearance. We gave ours three coats of "red pepper" latex paint, then spot-sanded it for a weathered, rustic look. To complete the theme, we used galvanized pipe for the closet pole instead of chrome and complementary hinges and door handles.

3/8"
SELF-CLOSING
INSET HINGE

Editor's Note: Leveling feet

Since most garages and some basement floors are not level, we installed adjustable "feet." A package of four threaded metal base glides costs $3 at home centers and hardware stores. Drill a 1/4-in. hole in the bottom of the stiles, stick in the inserts, then place the glides inside the inserts. When you move the wardrobe to the garage or basement, adjust the glides until level.

If you live in a hot, humid climate, consider adding two 4-in. round vents to the top to allow for better air circulation.
— Brett

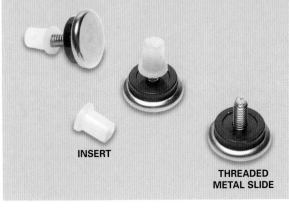

INSERT

THREADED
METAL SLIDE

STAINING
BLOTCH-PRONE
WOOD

Get a perfect finish on even hard-to-stain woods like cherry and pine

by **Jeff Gorton**

Some types of wood, like pine, cherry, birch and maple, are notoriously difficult to stain. A board that has a nice, attractive grain pattern can end up with dark, splotchy areas after you apply the stain. But there's a simple way you can prevent most stain blotches. In this article, we'll show you how.

Dark splotches show up when stain pigments become lodged in areas of grain that are more open. Unfortunately, it's not easy to tell which boards this will affect. One test is to wipe your board with mineral spirits. Spots that are prone to blotching show up darker. But the best test is to apply stain to a sample of the wood you're using. If the stain appears uneven or has unsightly dark areas, run the additional tests we show here to determine the best staining process.

STEP 1: SEAL THE WOOD BEFORE APPLYING STAIN

Most stain manufacturers make prestain conditioners, but you'll get better results with the method we show here. We're using a wipe-on oil finish (Zar Tung Oil Wipe-On Finish) as the sealer. The key is to apply a thin base coat to partially seal the wood before staining. Sanding sealers, dewaxed shellac and wipe-on finishes will all do the trick.

Some types of stain perform better than others on blotch-prone wood. In general, gel or heavy-bodied stains (we're using Zar Oil-Based Wood Stain) work best. Since these types of stain tend to have a high concentration of pigments, they also work better if you have to add several layers for a darker color (**Step 2**, p. 145). Just make sure the sealer and stain you're using are compatible. Using products from the same manufacturer is the safest bet.

Photo 1 shows how to make a test board with different concentrations of sealer. The concept is simple. The percentage of solids in the sealer determines how completely the pores in the wood are sealed. If the wood was sealed completely, it would be difficult to get any stain to stick. Diluting the sealer with mineral spirits allows you to experiment with different degrees of sealing. When you apply the stain (**Photo 2**), you'll see the results. Then you can choose the dilution rate that delivers the best results for your project.

Let the sealer dry for a few hours. Then sand the wood lightly with 220-grit paper before applying stain.

An inexpensive turkey baster is a great tool for measuring small amounts of finish and mineral spirits. Mark the baster with a permanent marker. Just draw out equal amounts of sealer and solvent to make a 50 percent solution. We used disposable plastic cups as mixing containers.

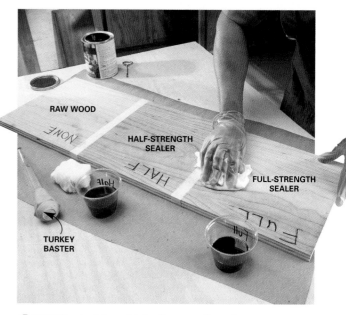

1 DIVIDE a test board into three sections. Leave one section raw, wipe full-strength sealer on one section, and wipe half-strength sealer on the third section. Let it dry for about an hour and sand lightly with 220-grit paper.

2 RUB stain over all three sections with a rag. Wipe it off to leave an even layer. Decide which amount of sealer gives you the desired look.

Tip End grain can look great and complement the board's surface, but it often ends up too dark. The solution is simple, though. Use the same prestain sealing method we show here to seal the end grain. You can also use this method on woods like oak that don't require a prestain sealer. Just be careful to sand off any sealer that gets on the face of the board before you stain.

STEP 2: APPLY SEVERAL COATS OF STAIN TO GET THE DESIRED SHADE

Start by making a test board with your chosen sealer concentration. Then stain the entire board. Let it dry and add a second layer of stain to all but one section. Repeat this process until you get to the desired color depth.

However, applying multiple coats of stain isn't always the best way to achieve a deeper color. For one thing, it'll take a long time to finish the project. You have to wait for each layer of stain to completely dry before adding the next. Otherwise, the new coat will dissolve the previous coat and you'll have a real mess on your hands. In fact, some stains will dissolve the stain below even if it is dry. (That's why testing is critical for a nice finish.) Another problem with multiple coats is that the stain will begin to obscure the natural grain. One solution is to opt for a less concentrated sealer. You'll get a bit more blotchy appearance, but the grain will show up better—a fair compromise.

ONE COAT OF STAIN

TWO COATS OF STAIN

THREE COATS OF STAIN

FOUR COATS OF STAIN

STEP 3: FINISH YOUR TEST BOARD TO GET THE TRUE EFFECT

Treating your test board just like the finished project will give you a true representation of the final color and depth of the finish. Make sure you sand the test board with the same grit as you intend to use on your project. After you arrive at the desired degree of sealing and number of stain coats, apply the final clear finish to see how it looks (**photo below**). This is also a good time to test the effect of different sheens. Most finishes are available in sheens ranging from almost flat to high gloss. You'll be surprised at how much richer the stain looks after a coat of finish.

NATURAL-BRISTLE BRUSH

OIL-BASED FINISH

ONE COAT OF STAIN

TWO COATS

THREE COATS

FOUR COATS

Seal pine before staining

Dark stains on pine can look horrible. In addition to blotchiness, the softer areas between the grain lines soak up stain like a sponge, creating an unnatural look. The photo below shows the dramatic difference between the raw and sealed areas of pine using the same stain color. Experiment with sealing the wood on your next pine project. You'll be amazed at the results.

STAINED WITHOUT SEALER

SEALED AND STAINED

WorkshopTips™

DIAL-A-CURVE

All you need to trace an exact arc is a thin strip of metal, a threaded rod and a couple of wing nuts and washers. Drill holes in the ends of the metal bar or strip, then bend the ends in a vise. Slide in a threaded rod and tighten the wing nuts to create the desired curve for tracing. Because of its density, the metal maintains a nearly uniform radius when pressed into a curve.

We experimented with various thicknesses, lengths and types of metal and got the best results for large-radius curves with a 1/8-in. x 1-in. x 4-ft. aluminum bar ($8.99 at Ace Hardware). For smaller-radius arcs, a 12-in. x 1-in. .032 brass strip ($2 at Ace Hardware) works great. Use 1/4-in. threaded rod ($3) for the aluminum bar and 6-32 threaded rod ($1) for the brass strip.

1/8" x 1" x 4' ALUMINUM BAR — BIG CURVES — 12" BRASS STRIP — SMALL CURVES — THREADED ROD

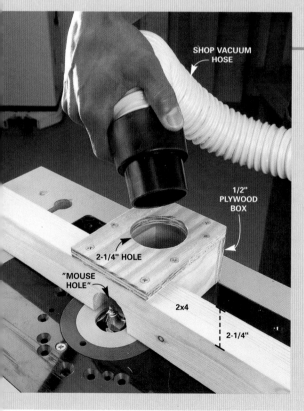

CLAMP

CHIP-SWALLOWING ROUTER FENCE

This made-from-scraps router fence—along with your shop vacuum—collects wood chips while you work.

On a table saw, cut a straight piece of 2x4 to 2-1/4 in. wide for the fence's height, being sure the vertical face and bottom edge of the fence form a 90-degree angle.

Saw a "mouse hole" in the center of the fence to fit over the router bit, then screw together a plywood box with a hole in the top to fit your shop vacuum hose (1-1/4 in. or 2-1/4 in. diameter).

It's noisy to run a router and vacuum at the same time, so wear hearing protection!

SHOP VACUUM HOSE — 1/2" PLYWOOD BOX — 2-1/4" HOLE — "MOUSE HOLE" — 2x4 — 2-1/4"

EASY-TO-READ MARKS ON YOUR PROJECTS

Have you ever used a pencil to mark dark wood and then been unable to find your mark? Or made indents that took extra time to sand away? Use white chalk to mark parts instead. This technique comes in handy when you're marking parts from a cutting list or marking grain matches for a glue-up project. The chalk sands away easily in seconds without leaving an indentation. But don't use colored chalk or you may have trouble getting the pigment out of the pores.

CUTTING THREADED ROD

When you're shortening a bolt or threaded rod with a hacksaw, you always mangle the threads at the sawn end, making it difficult to get a nut threaded onto it. This tip produces a much better ending. Thread two nuts onto the bolt at the cutoff spot, tighten them against each other, then saw against the shoulder to create a clean right-angled cut. Next, loosen the nuts and file a slight bevel around the end to clear burrs created by sawing. Then spin off the nuts to clean and realign the threads. Your shorter bolt will work just like a new one from the box.

1 Cut against nuts

2 File cut edge

3 Remove the nuts

MULTI-SKILLED SKEWERS

Pick up a pack of wood skewers ($2 at a grocery store) for barbecuing and keep them handy in your shop. Here are great uses for them:

- Puncture that pesky seal in caulk tubes.
- Apply glue in dowel holes or biscuit slots.
- Scrape gunk out of crevices on furniture you're refinishing.
- Plug stripped-out screw holes on antique furniture so the screws will grip tightly.

You get the point!

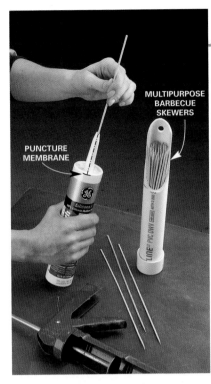

PUNCTURE MEMBRANE

MULTIPURPOSE BARBECUE SKEWERS

MEASURE AND MIX ON THE CHEAP

Need small containers for mixing and dispensing stain, paint and epoxy? Save and reuse Jell-O and Crystal Light plastic cups. Customize the larger Jell-O cups with ounce markings for precise measurements when you're mixing two-part formulas. Just borrow the kitchen measuring cup, pour water—an ounce at a time—into the disposable cups and trace each level with a fine-tip permanent marker.

VIBRATION MITIGATION

If vibrating tools leave you with aching joints, try on a pair of cycling gloves. The gel-filled palms are designed to absorb vibration. A pair costs about $15 at discount stores.

WorkshopTips™

ACCURATE ANGLES FOR SAWS

For precise cuts, don't trust the sloppy angle gauge that's supplied with your table saw. Instead, use an 8-in. adjustable drafting triangle (about $14 at a drafting supplies store or online at www.gsdirect.net). Hairline gradations on the scale are easy to see for setting the angle you need. Then just hold the adjusted triangle against the blade or fence and your project parts will be cut precisely. P.S. As always, make the first cut on a scrap board to be doubly certain you've set your angle correctly.

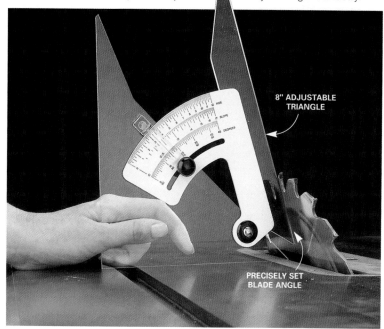

8" ADJUSTABLE TRIANGLE

PRECISELY SET BLADE ANGLE

ONBOARD GLUE SPREADER

For years I used my finger to spread glue beads on the edges of boards. Then, in sweaty haste, I'd wipe my fingers on my pants and another pair of nice jeans would become "work-only" attire.

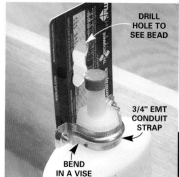

DRILL HOLE TO SEE BEAD

3/4" EMT CONDUIT STRAP

BEND IN A VISE

To make the job less messy, all you need is an old credit card (or new, your choice), a 3/4-in. two-hole EMT conduit strap (50¢ at a home center) and two 1/8-in. nuts and bolts. Crook the conduit strap in a vise to level the conduit strap wings with the bottle cap. This way the credit card stays flat when you bolt it on. Drill a couple of window holes in the middle of the credit card so you can monitor the size of the glue bead, then drill bolt holes in the end of the card, snap the conduit strap onto the bottle cap and bolt on the card.

Practice applying glue on a scrap board and in a few minutes you'll get it down (pun intended). Be sure to use fresh glue—the lightly bending card will spread it like butter.

JIFFY JUNK SORTING

It'll only take a second to nab the perfect-size nuts or washers from that big can loaded with 20 years' worth of leftover hardware. Pour the cargo onto a rubber car mat ($2 at discount stores), rake through the pile until you find the right what-ever, then use the mat as a chute to pour the heap back into the can.

POUR OUT TO SORT

CAR MAT

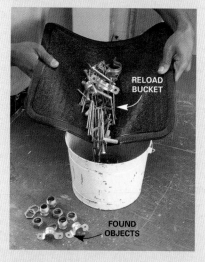

RELOAD BUCKET

FOUND OBJECTS

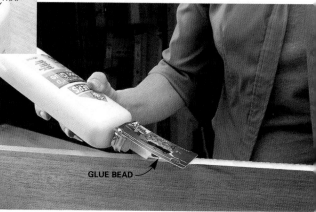

GLUE BEAD

5" CORNER BRACE

JOIN CURTAINS AT CORNER

HOOK-AND-LOOP STRIPS

EYE BOLT HOLE

1-1/4" CAP

5" CORNER MOUNTING STRAP

3/16" EYE BOLT

1-1/4" PVC

TENSION NUT

USE DRILL TO WIND UP CURTAIN

4-MIL POLY

HIGH-ROLLING SPRAY BOOTH

Seal off paint or dust particles in your shop with this low-cost roll-down shield.

1. Center and drill 3/16-in. holes in the PVC caps for the eye bolt axles. With a hacksaw, cut one of the corner braces in half to create two metal straps. Assemble the eye bolts, caps, straps, nuts and washers as shown. Snug the nuts against the caps.
2. Screw the assembled caps and braces to the ceiling joists so a corner is created when the poly unrolls.
3. Measure the distance from cap to cap and cut the PVC pipe to fit, then apply poly to the pipe with carpet tape.
4. Unscrew one of the braces, stick the pipe into the caps (a "press fit" is all you need) and reattach the braces. Roll down the poly and apply short lengths of hook-and-loop strips along the edges to help seal the corner.

You'll need the following parts, which are available at hardware stores and home centers:

- 4-mil poly ($6 for a 10-ft. x 20-ft. sheet)
- One 1-1/4-in. PVC pipe ($2.50 for 10-ft. length)
- Four 1-1/4-in. PVC caps ($1 each)
- Carpet tape ($6)
- Four 3/16-in. x 3-in. eye bolts, nuts and washers
- Three 5-in. corner braces ($5)

GETTING AN EDGE ON PAINT STRIPPING

And now, a nomination for the messiest job in everyone's shop: paint stripping. Here's an idea for making the job faster and easier.

Cut two slots directly across from each other in the rim of a 3-lb. coffee can (a Dremel rotary tool with a cutoff wheel works great to cut the slots). Drop a 1/16-in.-thick metal strip ($1 at a hardware store) in the slots, folding and bolting the metal strip to the can.

Now you can work swiftly and cleanly while stripping, loading up a 4-in.-wide drywall knife and scraping it against the metal edge to clean the sludge off the blade for another pass.

METAL STRIP

BEND AND BOLT ON END

Gallery of Ideas

ROCK-SOLID WORKBENCH

This workbench has all the features of a professional unit. It features a 3-1/4-in.-thick, rock-solid flat top, plenty of storage and robust vises that will hold your work for any woodworking task. It's mounted on casters, so you can wheel it away from the wall and get the sawdust flying in minutes. Simple joinery and cut-to-fit trim make this project fairly easy, even if you've done only rudimentary cabinet building.

Project Facts

Cost: Around $600
Skill level: Intermediate
Time: 3 days or more

FROM DEC/JAN, 2006, p. 56

STACKABLE SHELVING

These shelves are easy to build, stylish enough to display your collection of favorite things, yet strong enough to hold plenty of books. In addition, you can easily customize the versatile system to fit around windows, doors, desks and other features and make every inch of space count. It's all built from 3/4-in. plywood, oak 1x2s, iron-on veneer tape and readily available hardware.

Project Facts

Cost: Around $150
Skill level: Advanced beginner
Time: 2 days to build; 1-2 days to stain and finish

FROM OCTOBER, 2006, p. 64

GRAND BOOKCASE

FROM DEC/JAN, 2006, p. 34

This classic-looking cherry bookcase was designed with paneled doors, crown molding and tall, open shelves. It has two depths of shelves to hold books and treasures and three large cabinets to hide an assortment of stuff. The modular construction makes it buildable in a small workshop and easy to disassemble and reassemble in your living room or great room. There are lots of steps involved in building it, but there are no interlocking parts or complex joinery.

Project Facts

Cost: Around $1,200
Skill level: Intermediate to advanced
Time: 20 hours to build; 10 hours to stain and finish

WALL-HUNG WORKBENCH

FROM NOVEMBER, 2006, p. 60

This wall-mounted, modular workbench is adaptable to nearly any size work space. It has built-in lighting above the workbench and dust collection ports for portable tools. Another slick feature is the bench dog system, which clamps long pieces with the assistance of the end vise. Generous drawers are great for organizing small parts and bits, and underneath the worktop you'll find shelf space for larger bench-top and power tools.

Project Facts

Cost: Around $650, plus extra for hardware and vise
Skill level: Intermediate
Time: 4 days to build; 1-2 days to apply finish

To order photocopies of complete articles for the projects shown here, call (715) 246-4521, email familyhandyman@nrmsinc.com or write to: Copies, The Family Handyman, P.O. Box 83695, Stillwater, MN 55083-0695. Many public libraries also carry back issues of *The Family Handyman* magazine.

WOODWORKING & FURNITURE PROJECTS, TOOLS & TIPS

ALL-WEATHER
UMBRELLA TABLE

It's solid and stable and you can build it in a weekend!

by **Eric Smith**

An umbrella table doesn't have to look like an industrial chunk of metal or plastic. We designed ours with a cedar top and sides not only for longevity and stability, but because it will look handsome with minimal upkeep for years. The sides cloak a heavy concrete weight that anchors the umbrella.

In this article we'll show you how to build this umbrella table step-by-step. The tapered base may look like the work of a skilled craftsman, but the entire project—including the angled parts—is super simple. If you've tackled a few woodworking projects in the past, you can complete this one in a weekend. If you have only a little experience with woodworking tools and techniques, this is a good learning project.

Tools, money and materials

You'll need a miter saw, a circular saw, a drill and a pocket hole jig ($60 to $150; **Photo 7**). You can rip boards with a circular saw, but a table saw will give you better results.

With its knot-free cedar top, our table costs about $150. If you use less expensive lumber, yours could cost less than $100. You can, for example, use 5/4 cedar or pressure-treated deck boards for the top (if you select good pieces). Other good choices include teak, redwood, cypress and white oak. For the base, we used plywood and No. 2 cedar. Our cedar boards were 7/8 in. thick, but 3/4-in.-thick boards would also work. Patio umbrellas are available starting at about $100 at home centers.

A Note on Wood
Home centers often sell boards with a high moisture content, and they can shrink noticeably as they dry out. For a furniture project like this, it's a good idea to store your wood flat, up off the ground, in a dry location for a few weeks before you use it.

GRAIN DIRECTION

SIDE PANEL (A)

1 CUT all four sides (A) from a 4 x 4-ft. sheet of plywood (**Figure B**). Your cuts don't have to be perfect—they'll be hidden behind the rails and stiles.

1-1/4" SCREWS

CLEATS (B)

2x4 STOP

2 SCREW the corner cleats (B) to two of the side panels with four screws along each edge. Screw the other two side panels to the cleats to form the table base.

Build the base

The umbrella stand's base is simply a tapered plywood box with trim (**Figure A**). Cut four side panels (A) from a 4 x 4-ft. piece of 5/16-in. T1-11 plywood (**Photo 1**). T1-11 is a common type of rough-sawn exterior-grade plywood available at most lumberyards. **Figure B** shows how to lay out the cuts. Then use corner cleats (B) to join the panels (**Photo 2**).

The corner stiles, which act as the legs of the base, come next. Four of the stiles (D) are full-width 1x4s (3-1/2 in. wide) and four (C) are ripped to 2-5/8 in. wide. Cut the stiles to length (**Photo 3**), then glue and clamp them together. Let the glue set for an hour before you attach the stiles to the corners of the base with glue and 1-in. screws (**Photo 4**). Use plenty of glue to ensure a strong bond with the rough plywood.

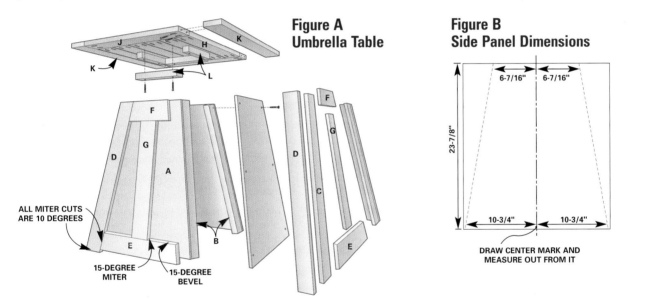

Figure A
Umbrella Table

ALL MITER CUTS ARE 10 DEGREES

15-DEGREE MITER

15-DEGREE BEVEL

Figure B
Side Panel Dimensions

6-7/16" 6-7/16"

23-7/8"

10-3/4" 10-3/4"

DRAW CENTER MARK AND MEASURE OUT FROM IT

SHOPPING LIST

ITEM	QTY.
T1-11 5/16" rough-sawn plywood (no grooves) (A)	1
Pressure-treated 2x2 x 8' (B, L)	2
Rough-sawn cedar 1x4 x 8' (C, D, E, F, G)	6
Clear (grade D or better) cedar 5/4 x 4 x 8' (H, J)	3
1-1/4" exterior screws	1 lb.
1" exterior screws	1 lb.
2" exterior screws	12
2-1/2" exterior screws	4
1-1/2" coarse-thread pocket screws	1 lb.
Exterior wood glue	
Exterior finish	
Concrete mix	

CUTTING LIST

KEY	PCS.	SIZE & DESCRIPTION
A	4	21-1/2" base x 12-7/8" top x 23-7/8"-tall plywood side panel
B	4	1-1/2" x 1-1/2" x 23-1/2" pressure-treated inside corner cleats
C	4	7/8" x 2-5/8" x 26-3/4" corner stiles
D	4	7/8" x 3-1/2" x 26-3/4" corner stiles
E	4	7/8" x 3-1/2" x approx. 17-1/2" lower rails
F	4	7/8" x 3-1/2" x approx. 9-1/2" upper rails
G	4	7/8" x 3-1/2" x 19-3/8" center stiles
H	6	1" x 3-1/2" x 22" top slats
J	2	1" x 3-1/2" x approx. 22" short frame sides
K	2	1" x 3-1/2" x 29" long frame sides
L	4	1-1/2" x 1-1/2" x 10" inside top cleats

WOODWORKING & FURNITURE PROJECTS, TOOLS & TIPS

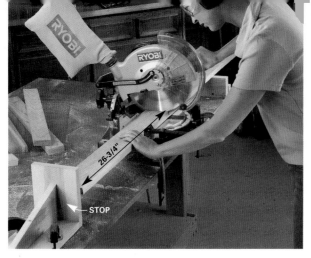

3 CLAMP your miter saw and a stop to your workbench. Set your saw to 10 degrees and cut the stiles (C and D).

4 SET the base on a pair of 2x4s. Glue and clamp the stiles (C and D) to each other. Then spread glue on the stiles and screw them to each corner from inside.

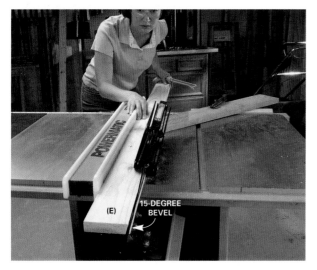

5 TILT your table saw 15 degrees and rip a bevel along the top edge of the lower rails (E) so water will drain off.

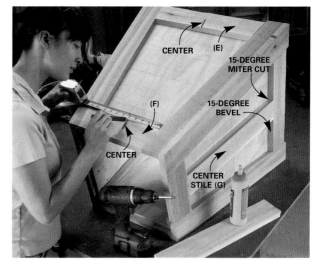

6 ATTACH the rails (E and F) with glue and screws driven from inside. Then mark their centers, position the center stiles (G) and fasten them.

Add decorative rails and stiles

Bevel the top edges of the lower rails (E; **Photo 5**). Then cut the upper and lower rails to length, mitering the ends of the rails at 10 degrees. Test-fit them, then glue and fasten them to the plywood with screws driven from inside.

To complete the base, add the center stiles (G). Cut a 15-degree bevel on one end of each center stile and make a square cut on the other end. Make each stile about 1/8 in. too long, check the fit and shave off a smidgen with your miter saw until it fits perfectly. Center the stiles when you glue and screw them into place (**Photo 6**).

Assemble the top with pocket screws

The slats (H) must be precisely the same length, so cut them using the stop you used to cut the corner stiles (**Photo 3**). When you cut the short frame sides (J), don't rely on the measurement (22 in.) given in the Cutting List. Slight variations in the widths of the slats can change this measurement. Instead, lay out the six slats with 1/8-in. spacers between them, measure the total width of the row of slats and add 1/4 in. Then cut the short frame sides, lay them in place and take a measurement for the long frame sides (K). With all the parts laid out, drill pocket holes (**Photo 7**). Start assembly by joining two frame sides at one corner, then add the slats before attaching the other two frame sides (**Photo 8**).

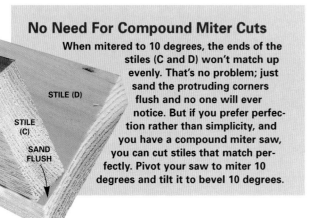

No Need For Compound Miter Cuts

When mitered to 10 degrees, the ends of the stiles (C and D) won't match up evenly. That's no problem; just sand the protruding corners flush and no one will ever notice. But if you prefer perfection rather than simplicity, and you have a compound miter saw, you can cut stiles that match perfectly. Pivot your saw to miter 10 degrees and tilt it to bevel 10 degrees.

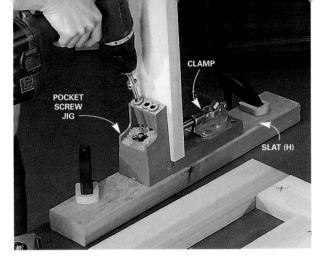

7 CUT and lay out the tabletop (Figure A) with the best side of each part face down. Mark the pocket hole side, then drill two holes per end with a pocket hole jig.

Labels in image: CLAMP, POCKET SCREW JIG, SLAT (H)

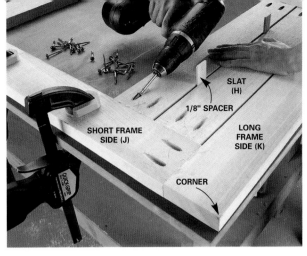

8 JOIN one corner with glue and pocket screws. Position the slats (H) with 1/8-in. spacers and fasten them. For flush joints, clamp the piece you're screwing into.

Labels in image: SLAT (H), 1/8" SPACER, SHORT FRAME SIDE (J), LONG FRAME SIDE (K), CORNER

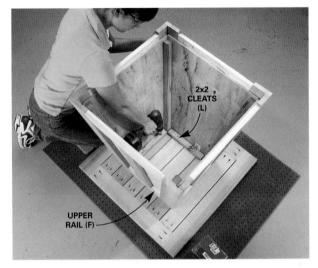

9 CENTER the base on the tabletop and screw 2x2 cleats (L) to the tabletop with 2-in. screws. Don't overdrive the screws or they'll poke through the top. Drive screws through the upper rails (F) into the cleats.

Labels in image: 2x2 CLEATS (L), UPPER RAIL (F)

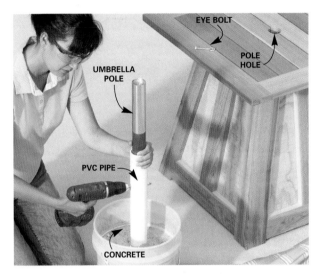

10 SET the lower end of the umbrella pole in the base. Drill a 3/8-in. hole through the pipe and pole. Secure the pole by running a 1/4-in. eye bolt through the hole.

Labels in image: EYE BOLT, POLE HOLE, UMBRELLA POLE, PVC PIPE, CONCRETE

Next, fasten 2x2 cleats (L) to the underside of the top (Photo 9). Then drill a 3/16-in. hole through each upper rail (F) and drive a 2-in. screw into each cleat. You can remove the tabletop simply by removing these four screws; this makes finishing, moving and storing the table easier. Drill a hole through the center of the top with a hole saw. Our umbrella pole required a 2-in. hole.

Before finishing, dab exterior wood glue on the end grain at the bottom of the legs. Then apply exterior oil finish to the inside and outside of the table. We used exterior teak oil.

Anchor the umbrella with a heavy base

You don't have to spend $50 or more on a fancy umbrella base. You can easily make a simple-but-stable base with a 5-gallon bucket, a 60-lb. bag of concrete mix and 2 ft. of PVC pipe. You'll need 1-1/2- or 2-in. pipe, depending on the diameter of your umbrella pole.

Mix the concrete and water in the bucket. Cover the bottom end of the pipe with duct tape to keep the concrete out. Set the pipe into the concrete and push it all the way to the bottom of the bucket. Hold a level against the pipe to make sure it's standing straight up. After the concrete hardens, drill a hole so you can fasten the pole to the pipe (Photo 10). Also drill a hole through the bucket at the level of the concrete so rainwater can drain. 🏠

Master Pocket Screw Joinery In Minutes

Don't be intimidated by pocket screw joinery. The pocket screw jig may look complicated, but after about 10 minutes of practice you can create tight, strong joints. A good-quality pocket screw kit (containing a jig, clamp, drill bit and driver) costs from $60 to $150, depending on the features. It's well worth the investment. One source is www.kregtool.com.

RE-COVER A CHAIR SEAT

If you have upholstered chair seats that are stained, worn out or just plain ugly, there's no need to call a pro. You can do a first-class upholstery job yourself, even if you have zero experience. Don't worry about making mistakes; you can correct them by prying out staples and starting over.

If the chair is fairly new, you can simply cover the existing fabric with new material. But it usually makes sense to tear off the old fabric and replace the foam padding, since most foam has a life span of only five to 10 years. Many fabric stores carry foam and upholstery fabric, but for the best selection and advice, start with an upholstery store (under "Upholstery Fabrics" in the yellow pages). For a small chair like the one shown here, expect to spend at least $10 on foam, batting and fabric. You'll also need a can of spray adhesive ($6), a scissors, a stapler and 5/16-in. staples.

Turn the chair upside down and remove the screws that fasten the seat to the chair frame. Then tear off the old fabric with a pliers and pry out the staples with a small screwdriver. If the seat is made from particleboard, you might find that it's warped, crumbling or even broken. Making a new seat is easy: Just lay the old seat on a piece of 1/2-in. plywood, trace around it and cut a new seat with a jigsaw.

Cut the foam to size with a scissors. Take the wood seat outside and give the topside a light coat of spray adhesive. Position the seat carefully when you set it on the foam; the adhesive grabs instantly and you may not be able to pull it off. Cut the batting and fabric (**Photo 1**). Stretch the batting slightly as you staple it into place (**Photo 2**). Staple the fabric at the middle of all four sides and flip the seat over to make sure the pattern is centered. Tug the fabric toward the corners as you staple the first side. Go to the opposite side and stretch the fabric across the seat as you staple it. Repeat this process for the other two sides.

If your seat has rounded corners, you can wrap them so that no folds or creases are visible from above (**Photo 3**). If the seat has square corners, crease and fold the fabric as you would when you gift-wrap a box (**Photo 4**). It's usually helpful to trim away excess fabric as you work on corners. Before you screw the seat onto the chair, consider treating the fabric with a stain repellent if it wasn't treated at the factory.

oops!

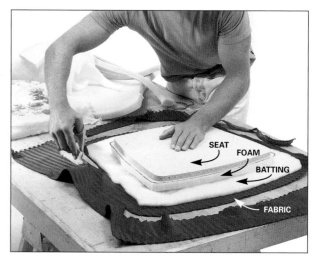

1 CUT the foam about 1/2 in. larger than the wood seat. Cut the batting at least 2 in. larger and the fabric at least 3 in. larger.

RESCUE RUSTY TOOLS

It happens. You leave a handsaw, a framing square or a hammer lying in the yard overnight (or longer). By the time you discover it, it looks like something retrieved from the Titanic. You can rescue those rusty tools. Empire Manufacturing has two products to handle rust on hand tools, as well as on bigger surfaces like table saw and jointer tables.

First in the lineup is the TopSaver kit ($22). Spritz a little TopSaver on the rusty surface and let it sit a couple of minutes. Then use an abrasive pad to scour the surface. You'll be amazed at how little elbow grease it takes to remove the rust and how quickly it rolls off. If there's a little rust left, repeat the process. The saw pictured here required just one application. The TopSaver kit includes an 8-oz. bottle of TopSaver, coarse and ultra-fine abrasive pads, disposable gloves and four cloths for cleaning up when you're done.

Once the rust is gone, protect the tool against future rust. An extra spritz of TopSaver can provide a layer of protection, but Empire's Table-Top Lubricant, $15 for 8 oz., will do an even better job. Spritz this on and it will help prevent rust and provide an oil-free lubrication to allow a tool, such as your handsaw, to slide more easily past the wood. On a table saw, you'll instantly notice that it's easier to feed wood on a lubricated surface than on a non-lubricated one.

There are no oils or silicones in the Empire products, so there's nothing to harm your glue joints or finish. These products are available at hardware stores and online.

① Spray

② Scour

③ Wipe "TOPSAVER" "TABLE-TOP LUBRICANT"

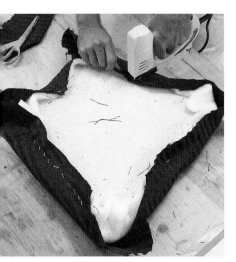

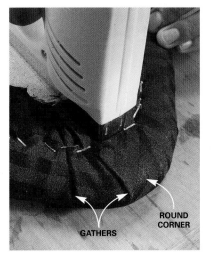
GATHERS ROUND CORNER

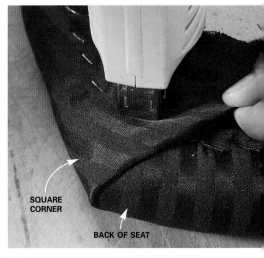
SQUARE CORNER BACK OF SEAT

2 STAPLE the fabric at the middle of each side and work toward the corners, stretching the fabric as you go. Stop about 2 in. from corners and leave the corners for last.

3 CREATE gathers in the fabric to form a smooth curve around curved corners. Work toward the corner from alternating sides. Then pull back the "ear" of fabric and staple it.

4 FOLD fabric around square corners. If your seat has square corners toward the rear, fold the fabric against the back edge of the seat, where the crease will be hidden by the chair's back.

ADVANCED
ROUTER
TECHNIQUES

Go beyond the basics: Use your router to make strong joints, plane edges, cut smooth curves and more

by **Gary Wentz**

SMOOTH CUTS ON COMPLEX SHAPES

Cutting shapes with a pattern bit has two advantages over cutting with a jigsaw, band saw or scroll saw: Because you perfect the pattern first, you won't make mistakes when you cut the workpiece. And when you're making several identical parts, a pattern saves time, since you do the fussy shaping work only once.

PATTERN BIT

To make the bracket pattern shown here, we cut 1/2-in. MDF with a jigsaw and perfected the shape with a belt sander. We traced the pattern onto boards and rough-cut each bracket, leaving about 1/8 in. excess to be removed by the router. We made the pattern and each rough bracket about an inch too long so we could drive screws through them rather than use clamps, which often get in the way of the router. The screw holes were cut off when we cut the brackets to their final length. As with straight-guide cuts, you may have to make several shallow passes and then a final pass after you remove the pattern (see p. 160).

FINISHED
BRACKET

SCREW

ROUGH
CUT

PATTERN

Create a smooth pattern from 1/2-in. MDF. Clamp or screw the pattern to a rough-cut workpiece and cut the final smooth shape with a pattern bit.

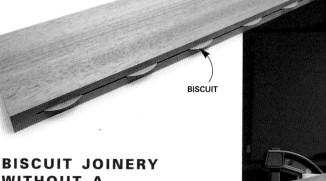

Cut slots for biscuits with a slot cutter mounted on an arbor that's equipped with a bearing. Cut a continuous slot on boards thicker than 3/4 in.

BISCUIT JOINERY WITHOUT A BISCUIT JOINER

If you want to make biscuit joints, you don't have to shell out $100 or more to buy a biscuit joiner. In most cases, a router equipped with a 5/32-in. slot bit ($30) can cut perfect slots to fit the biscuits. Mark the biscuit positions on both adjoining boards as you would with a biscuit joiner. Then cut a slot that's about 1/2 in. longer than the biscuit. On thick boards, you don't even have to mark out anything; just cut one quick, continuous slot on each board. Add glue and biscuits and then clamp it to create a strong joint.

There are two situations where a router can't substitute for a biscuit joiner: A router can cut slots only along the edges of a board, not across its face; and it can only cut along square edges, not beveled ones. Most slot cutters cut slots about 1/2 in. deep, which suits No. 20 biscuits. If you want to use smaller biscuits, buy a kit ($40) that includes three bearing sizes for No. 0, No. 10 and No. 20 biscuits. Item No. P10-4601 at www.pricecutter.com, (888) 288-2487.

WOODWORKING & FURNITURE PROJECTS, TOOLS & TIPS

Editor's Note: Homemade base plates add versatility

When I get a new router, the first thing I do is explain to my wife why I need yet another power tool. The second thing I do is remove the plastic base plate. Then I make a plate that's a few inches larger than the original from 1/4-in.-thick acrylic ($15 for an 18 x 24-in. sheet at home centers). I use the original plate as a template to position the screw holes and the center hole. Acrylic has sharp edges, so I round them slightly with sandpaper. In about five minutes,

I have an oversized plate that I can fasten to a trammel (top photo, p. 162), stretchers (bottom photo, p. 160) or any other jigs I dream up. One of my routers is mounted on a 12 x 12-in. piece of 3/8-in.-thick acrylic and does double duty. Although it's a bit big and clumsy, I can use it as a handheld router. Or I can screw it to a pair of sawhorses, attach a primitive fence, and use it as a portable job-site router table.

— Gary

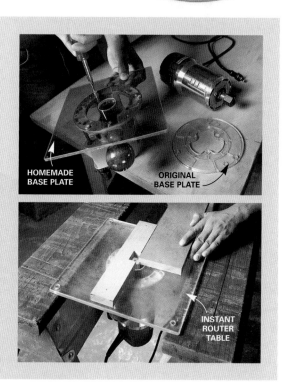

PLANE A STRAIGHT EDGE

When you have a crooked board, the best tool for creating a straight, smooth edge is a "jointer" ($250 or more). When you want to shave down a door just a little—more than a sander can handle, but not enough for a saw—a handheld power planer ($100 or more) is best.

If you don't have these tools, try the second-best solution for either of these jobs: a router with a "pattern" bit (a straight bit guided by a bearing). Just clamp or screw a straight guide to the workpiece. The router's bearing rolls along the guide, and the bit cuts a straight, smooth edge. Use plywood, MDF or a perfectly straight board as your guide. Inspect the edge of the guide before you rout; any bump or

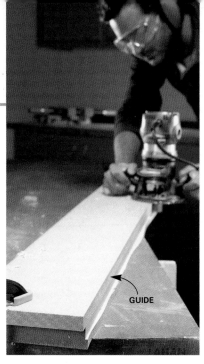

TOP BEARING

PATTERN BIT

GUIDE

FIRST CUT

1 RUN a pattern bit along a guide to cut a straight edge. For thick boards, remove the guide after the first pass.

2 USE the first cut to guide the second pass. Make a third pass if necessary.

crater in the guide will transfer to the workpiece. If you're shaving off more than 1/8 in. of wood, make multiple passes no more than 1/4 in. deep. Choose a pattern bit that's at least

1/2 in. in diameter ($25). The larger the diameter, the less risk there is of chipped, splintered cuts. "Top bearing" bits are more versatile than versions that have a bearing below the cutter.

FLATTEN A BOWED SURFACE

Whether it's a cupped board or a panel that was misaligned during glue-up, the best way to flatten wood is to run it through a planer. But even if you have a planer, you've probably encountered situations where it's not wide enough to handle the job. Here's how you can use your router with a straight bit to plane wide material: Mount an oversized base plate on your router (see the Editor's Note, p. 159) and screw the base plate to a pair of stiff, straight "stretchers." Make your stretchers at least twice as long as the width of the workpiece, plus 8 in. Make a pair of rails at least 8 in. longer than the workpiece. The height of your rails depends on the length of your router bit. Plane

STRAIGHT BIT

STRETCHER

RAIL

BASE PLATE

BLOCK

Plane boards or panels flat with a straight bit. To keep the cutting depth uniform, screw your router base to stretchers that ride on rails. Blocks hold the workpiece.

the "crowned" side of the workpiece first. To do this, slide the stretchers back and forth across the rails. This is a slow process; you may have to make several passes, lowering the bit

about 1/8 in. after each pass. When the crowned side is flat, flip the workpiece over and flatten the "dished" side. Routers leave a rough surface, so both sides will need sanding.

MILL TRIM IN A PINCH

If you need to replace a piece of trim but can't find a match for the wood species or profile at a home center, walk over to the tool aisle and check out the router bits. Sometimes a router bit—or a combination of two bits—can reproduce a trim profile. Rounded edges and coves are the easiest to match. A 1/2-in. round-over bit, for example, produces perfect base shoe molding.

Finding the right router bit

Most home centers and hardware stores carry only common bits. For slot cutters or pattern bits, visit a supplier that caters to woodworkers. To buy online, type "router bits" into any search engine and you'll find dozens of sources. To request a catalog of router bits, call pricecutter.com at (888) 288-2487.

ROUND-OVER BIT

Duplicate thin trim by first routing the profile on a wide board. Then sand the profile smooth and cut off the finished piece with a table saw.

REPAIR AND REINFORCE CRACKS

When a table top or chair seat splits, you might be able glue the crack back together. But often the crack is too dirty and splintered to form a strong glue joint. And even with a good glue joint, the stresses that caused the split in the first place may crack it open again.

Here's how to make a stronger repair: Cut a recess in the back side of the wood with a 1/2- or 3/4-in. straight bit and glue in a plywood "scab." Make the recess deep enough to accept plywood that's about half the thickness of the wooden part. When cutting the recess, start at the crack and work outward, gradually enlarging the recess. If you have to deepen the recess with a second pass, you may have to make a homemade base plate large enough to span the recess (see Editor's Note, p. 159).

STRAIGHT BIT

PLYWOOD

CRACK

RECESS

Cut a recess on the underside of cracked furniture parts. Force glue into the crack, clamp it together and glue plywood into the recess to strengthen the repair.

CUT PERFECT ARCS AND CIRCLES

Often, you can create a curve that's "good enough" using a jigsaw followed by a belt sander. But when an arc or a circle has to be flawless, a router is the perfect tool. Some careful setup is required, but the results are worth it. Mount an oversized base plate on your router (see Editor's Note, p. 159) so you can screw it to a 1x4 trammel. Before you start cutting the arc, raise the bit just above the wood. Then position it at the top of the arc and at both ends to make sure the cutting path is correct. When you cut, make shallow passes no more than 1/4 in. deep. Keep the router moving to avoid burn marks. You can use a 1/2-in. or smaller straight bit or a spiral bit to cut arcs. Spiral bits cut faster with less chipping, but they cost about twice as much as standard straight bits ($55 for a 1/2-in. spiral bit). Don't use a spiral bit that's smaller than 3/8 in. diameter. Small spiral bits break easily when you're making deep cuts.

Connect your router to a trammel and screw the trammel to a block. Cut the arc by making repeated shallow passes with a straight or spiral bit.

EASE SHARP EDGES WITH A ROUND-OVER BIT

Whether you're building furniture or installing trim, avoid leaving sharp edges on wood. They're more likely to chip, splinter or dent with everyday use. Sharp edges also create weak spots in paint and other finishes, leading to cracking and peeling, especially outdoors. Fussy carpenters often ease sharp edges with sandpaper or a file. But a 1/16- or 1/8-in. round-over bit ($15) does the job more consistently and neatly. These small-profile bits are difficult to set at the correct cutting depth, so always test the cut on scrap wood first. 🏠

Round sharp wood edges with a small round-over bit. Run a 1/8-in. round-over bit along door bottoms to prevent splinters and snags on carpet.

WorkshopTips™

GLUING PEDESTAL

Ever scratched your head over how to position clamps on a project that requires clamping from all four sides? This gluing pedestal makes the job a breeze. Buy a 12-in. pipe nipple with pipe flanges on both ends and screw it to a couple of scraps of 3/4-in. plywood. Cut the pedestal top an inch or so bigger than the project to make clamping easier. Now, with the base of the pedestal clamped on your workbench, you can crank on the clamps from every angle—up, down and sideways. (Be sure to cover the top with plastic sheeting or wax paper, or the top will become a permanent part of the project.)

3/4" PIPE FLANGE

3/4" x 12" PIPE NIPPLE

ROCK-SOLID FEATHERBOARD

The problem with most featherboards is that they're nearly impossible to clamp so they stay put. But here's an improved version that stays right where you clamp it on a table saw or router table. And it's simple to build from a couple of scrap boards. Here's how:

Cut a 45-degree angle on the end of a 4-in.-wide hardwood board and saw the "feathers" 3 in. long into the angled end. Attach a second board at a right angle midway along the first board with pocket screws, biscuits or dowels. Presto, you're done! You've created a featherboard with two clamping points. Adjust and clamp it right where you want it, and it'll maintain uniform pressure on workpiece after workpiece without slipping.

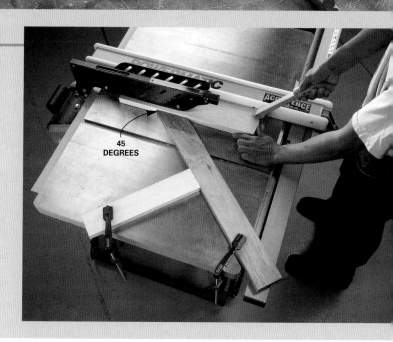

45 DEGREES

WorkshopTips™

MINI PUTTY KNIFE

Is your putty knife too wide to fit into that little can of wood filler? Snip a 6-in. segment from an old hacksaw blade, grind the snipped end to resemble a low-angled chisel and then wrap the blade with electrical tape for a makeshift handle. You'll like how your home-made flexible knife spreads putty in a narrow path, minimizing cleanup. (And the built-in hanging hole is a putty nice feature.)

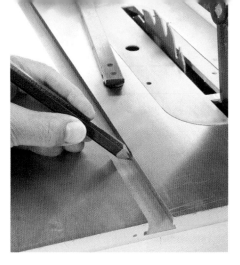

PENCIL LUBE FOR MITER SLOTS

When the miter gauge on your saw or sander starts to stick, grab a pencil and lubricate the miter slot with a few quick strokes of the pencil lead (which is really graphite, a great dry lubricant that won't attract dust). You'll find this lube job helpful for any sliding metal parts that get tacky from lack of use.

REALLY COOL HOLE-SAWING

SAWDUST CLEARANCE HOLES

SAWDUST

I've always dreaded using a hole saw. The friction heats up the blade to the point where it dulls the blade, burns the wood and actually heat-bonds the plug inside the hole saw.

Today, a cooler head prevails when I'm hole-sawing. Before sawing the hole, run the saw lightly on the wood to scribe the hole's circumference, then drill two 3/8-in. holes just inside the circle. As you saw, sawdust falls through the holes rather than binding, clogging and burning against the cutting teeth. The saw runs cooler and cuts faster, and the sawn plug pulls out much easier.

P.S. If you saw the hole until the pilot bit just breaks through the wood, then flip the board over and saw from the other side, the plug will practically fall out on its own.

SCRATCH-FREE SAWING

Here's how to cut an inch off a nicely finished door or workpiece when you don't want to risk dinging up the surface with that scratched-up shoe on your circular saw. Apply painter's masking tape to the shoe and you'll saw scratch-free every time.

SNIP 'N' GRIP WIRE CUTTERS

Here's a time-saving tool modification. Fill the concave section of a wire cutter with silicone caulk, let it dry overnight, then slit the silicone with a razor blade to create a soft-jaw section on the wire cutter. Now when you cut off nails or pieces of wire, the cut pieces will stay in the cutter and not fly across the room. No more getting out the reading glasses and flashlight to hunt down cut-offs on your shop floor!

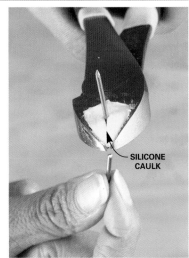

SILICONE CAULK

CHAIN COMPASS

Project running you in circles? Trace perfect arcs or circles in an instant with a ballpoint pen, an awl or a nail, and a short length of plumber's chain (60¢ a foot at home centers). The pen pokes through the chain's smaller links just enough to create an exact radius when you keep the chain taut while tracing. As a bonus, each link provides a 1/2-in. increase or decrease in radius for quick adjustments without measuring.

AWL

PLUMBER'S CHAIN

WorkshopTips™

INSTANT WORKBENCH

Go on, take an hour to build this sturdy, simple workbench from a single sheet of 3/4-in. plywood. Then spend only a couple of seconds tapping it together whenever you need it. It can hold heavy power tools, large project assemblies or even that old outboard motor you're overhauling.

Cutting list:

- Two 38-in. x 8-in. stretchers
- Two 27-1/2-in. x 23-in. legs
- One 48-in. x 30-in. top
- Two 26-in. x 3/4-in. x 3/4-in. side cleats
- Two 12-in. x 3/4-in. x 3/4-in. end cleats

Saw 4-in. x 3/4-in. notches in the legs and stretchers, spacing them 3 in. in from the edge on the legs and 4 in. in from the ends on the stretchers. Tap them together to create an interlocked base. Lay the top upside down on the floor, then position the base so the top overhangs all four sides equally. Screw cleats on the top so they will fit just inside the base. Position them slightly away from the base to make assembly easy. Stand everything right side up and put your instant workbench to work!

8"

4"

4"

STRETCHER
(38" x 8")

4"   3"

"LEG"
(27-1/2" x 23")

3/4" THICKNESS

TOP
(48" x 30")

CLEATS

NEW ANGLES ON TOOL SHARPENING

Here's a better way to hold tools securely while you're grinding them—and take the guesswork out of creating the right bevel angle. It's a short piece of 2x4 with an angled end and a 1-1/4-in. hole for a clamp. I made one for chisels and plane blades, and a few more with different angles for wood-turning tools. Large labels with the tool's name tell you which blocks are for which tools.

For a Delta grinder with a 6-in.-diameter wheel, a 5-1/2-in.-long piece of 2x4 aligns the tool to the wheel just right. For other grinders you may need to adjust this length. **Note:** The angle you cut on the block is not the same as the tool's bevel angle. But let's skip the math. To determine the block angle, turn off the grinder and hold the tool's bevel flush against the wheel. The angle of the tool shaft to the workbench is the angle to cut on the 2x4.

STRETCHY PIPE CLAMPS

Moaning again that your pipe clamps aren't long enough to assemble your new "monsterpiece"? Pipe down and quit whining! A few extra 2- and 4-ft. pipe segments plus a handful of pipe couplings are all you need for the extra-long or extra-wide job. Screw couplings and extra pipes to those too-short pipes to create the needed lengths. If the clamps are under the wood, add spacers slightly higher than the couplings perpendicular to the pipes. When you're finished, unscrew and store the extra pipes with couplings and you'll be ready for the next jumbo project that comes down the pipeline.

PIPE COUPLINGS

PIPE CLAMPS

DVD
WALL CABINET

Got an open Saturday morning? Pull out your table saw and build this simple, sturdy cabinet

by **Travis Larson**

Build this project from three boards, a little plywood and 12 ft. of trim.

Do you have DVDs scattered all over the room? We offer this handsome cabinet as one solution to the clutter. As shown, the cabinet is 42 in. wide and holds about 60 DVD cases. Go ahead and expand or shrink the width to better hold your collection or to fit a particular spot on the wall. The construction techniques will be the same no matter the width. In this story, we'll show you simple cutting and joining techniques that'll deliver fine cabinet-quality results. We'll show you how to make clean and accurate crosscuts, rabbets (grooves on edges), and miters so you'll wind up with a spectacular finished product.

You don't need any special woodworking skills to complete this project, but you will need a table saw. To get good, true, splinter-free results, buy a 40-tooth carbide blade. If you have a pneumatic nailer, use it with 1-1/2-in. brads to fasten the cabinet parts and 1-in. brads to nail the cornice. This will speed up the assembly and give better results than hand nailing. All told, the actual cutting and assembly only take a few hours, plus time spent finishing. Expect to spend about $65 for all the hardwood you'll need.

Choose the wood to match your decor

Our cabinet is made of oak and finished with oil stain (Minwax "Golden Oak") and shellac. Make your cabinet from whatever wood best matches your room's decor. But be aware that if you choose wood other than poplar, oak or pine, the home center probably won't stock matching molding for the top and

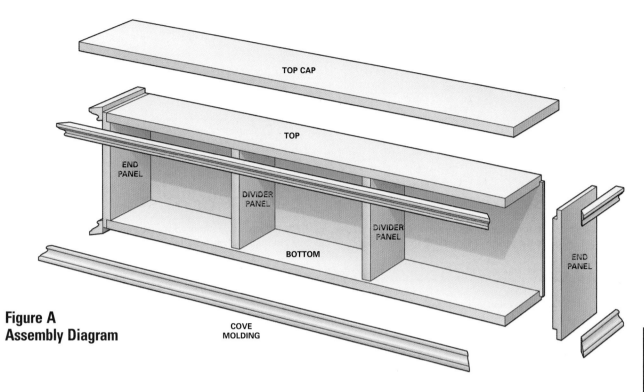

Figure A
Assembly Diagram

Labels in figure: TOP CAP, TOP, END PANEL, DIVIDER PANEL, DIVIDER PANEL, BOTTOM, END PANEL, COVE MOLDING

bottom. If you choose paint for the finish, select poplar boards and clear pine molding.

Rip the parts to width first, then to length

Begin by ripping the two 6-ft.-long 1x8s to 6 in. wide, then crosscut the end and top and bottom boards to length as we show (**Figure B**). Go ahead and rip the divider panels to the final 5-in. width, but hold off on cutting the dividers and top cap to length for now. Cut those when you assemble the cabinet frame so you can measure and cut for perfect fits (**Photo 9**).

The key to clean tight joints is to make matching pairs of parts exactly the same length. We used our table saw, but you could use a miter box instead.

The small fence that comes with your miter gauge isn't much good for holding wood square to make accurate cuts. Extend it by screwing a 24-in.-long fence extension to the miter gauge, with the right side hanging a bit past the blade (**Photo 1**). (There are holes in the miter gauge just for this task.) One of the leftover pieces from your previous rips will work great for the extension fence. Choose screw lengths that penetrate the wood about 5/8 in. after allowing for the miter gauge wall thickness.

Don't trust the angle indicators on your miter gauge;

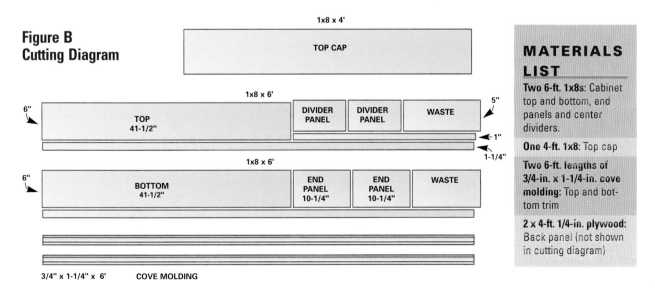

Figure B
Cutting Diagram

Labels: 1x8 x 4', TOP CAP, 1x8 x 6', TOP 41-1/2", DIVIDER PANEL, DIVIDER PANEL, WASTE, 5", 6", 1", 1-1/4", 1x8 x 6', BOTTOM 41-1/2", END PANEL 10-1/4", END PANEL 10-1/4", WASTE, 6", 3/4" x 1-1/4" x 6' COVE MOLDING

MATERIALS LIST

Two 6-ft. 1x8s: Cabinet top and bottom, end panels and center dividers

One 4-ft. 1x8: Top cap

Two 6-ft. lengths of 3/4-in. x 1-1/4-in. cove molding: Top and bottom trim

2 x 4-ft. 1/4-in. plywood: Back panel (not shown in cutting diagram)

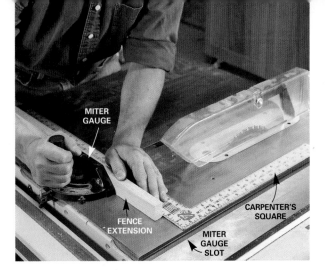

1 SCREW a 2-ft.-long extension fence to the miter gauge. Square the miter gauge with the miter gauge slot.

2 RIP the boards to width (use Figure B for cutting dimensions), then cut the top, bottom and sides to length.

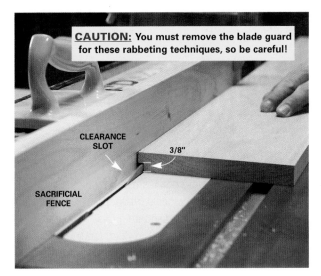

3 SET the blade to cut 3/8 in. deep. Make a series of passes along the back edge of each board, moving the fence away from the blade with each pass until the width is 1/4 in.

4 SET the fence 3/4 in. from the far edge of the blade and make a series of 3/8-in.-deep overlapping saw kerfs to rabbet the top and bottom of the end panels.

they're bound to be inaccurate. Instead, square the miter gauge to one of the miter gauge slots with a carpenter's square (**Photo 1**). When it's square, tighten up the locking handle. Raise the blade and cut off the end of the fence and you're ready to crosscut. The end of the fence perfectly marks the saw blade's path. Line up measurement marks with that end and you'll know exactly where to place the board for cutting.

Nest the wood against the miter gauge clear of the blade, start up the saw, and push the wood all the way past the blade. To be safe, shut off the saw before removing both parts.

Cut the rabbets

Now cut the 3/8-in.-deep, 1/4-in.-wide rabbets on the back of the bottom, top and sides to create a recess for the 1/4-in.-thick plywood back (**Photo 3**). First lower the blade below the throat plate and clamp a straight 3/4-in.-thick sacrificial board to the saw fence. Position the clamps at

least an inch above the table so the 3/4-in. boards can slide under them. Move the fence over the blade so it will cut about 1/8 in. into the sacrificial board, then lock the fence, turn on the saw and slowly raise the blade into the board until it's about 1 in. above the table to cut a clearance slot (**Photo 3**). Lower the blade to 3/8 in. above the table to start cutting the rabbets.

Nudge the fence about 1/16 in. away from the blade and make cuts on all four boards (**Photo 3**). Be sure to hold the boards tight to the fence and the table for smooth, complete cuts. And keep your hands well away from the blade, because you have to remove the guard to make this cut. Continue moving the fence in 1/16-in. increments and making cuts until you approach the final 1/4-in. depth of the rabbet. Then check the depth with 1/4-in. plywood and make fine adjustments in the fence to make a final cut. The plywood should fit flush with the back edge of the board.

Leave the depth setting on the blade and use the miter gauge to cut the rabbets on the end panels. Set the fence

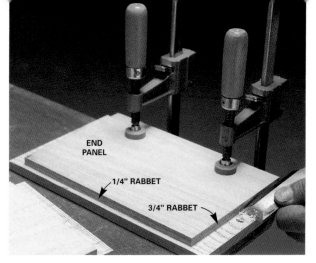

5 SMOOTH the saw marks by shaving the rabbets flat with a sharp chisel.

6 COVER the rabbets with masking tape and apply stain to all the cabinet parts.

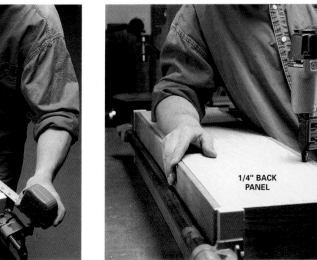

7 GLUE AND NAIL the end panels to the top and bottom. Then clamp the assembly and check for square.

8 CUT the back panel to fit, then glue and nail it into the rabbets with 1-in. brads.

to cut 3/4 in. wide (measured to the far edge of the blade). Make a series of cuts at each end (**Photo 4**). Push the wood completely through and stop the saw before pulling the miter gauge back. The more and the narrower passes you make, the less you'll need to clean up the saw kerfs later. Smooth any saw marks with a sharp chisel for a cleaner-looking, tighter-fitting joint (**Photo 5**).

Sand all the surfaces up to 120 grit for open-grain woods like oak, pine, cherry and walnut. And sand to 220 grit for closed-grain woods like maple and birch.

Stain before assembly

If you're staining, we recommend staining the parts at this point because it's tough to get into inside corners after you assemble the cabinet. For stronger glue joints, cover the surfaces of the rabbets with masking tape to keep stain off (**Photo 6**). Cut the plywood back about 1/2 in. larger than the opening, prefinish it at the same time and cut it to exact size later along with the center dividers.

This step will give you better finishing results, but it will add to the project completion time because it means letting stains dry before assembly. If you're wild to complete the cabinet in one shop visit, go ahead and assemble it, then stain and finish it afterward.

Assemble the sides, dividers and back

Glue and nail each end panel to the top and bottom boards. Four 1-in. brads, two at the top and two at the bottom, are plenty. Then clamp the assembly together to pull the joints tight (**Photo 7**). Check for square right away before the glue sets. You'll need clamps that are at least 5 ft. long for this. Use blocks to spread the pressure over the whole joint. If one of the diagonal measurements is longer than the other, gently squeeze another clamp across those corners to pull the frame square. If you don't have long clamps, just glue and clamp the joints together with a few extra brads. (The joints might not be as tightly fit as clamped ones, but you can plug slim gaps with wood filler

9 MEASURE and cut the center dividers to fit. Then space them equally and nail them with 1-1/2-in. brads.

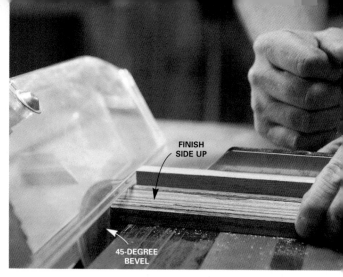

10 CUT the moldings to length using the miter gauge with the saw blade set at a 45-degree bevel.

11 USE a scrap of cove molding to test-fit lengths. Glue and nail the molding with 1-in. brads.

12 CUT the top cap to length so that the end overhangs match the front. Then glue and nail it to the molding with 1-1/2-in. brads.

later.) Measure and cut the back to fit, then glue and nail it in place with 1-in. brads spaced every 6 in. (Photo 8).

Save the dividers for last. Measure and cut them to fit, then space them equally in the cabinet and nail them through the top and bottom with 1-1/2-in. brads (Photo 9). No glue is needed.

Add the cove trim and top cap

Cut and install the cove molding starting at one end, then the long front piece, then the other end. To get perfect final lengths (Photo 11), cut 45-degree bevels on a short piece of molding to use as a test block when you're fitting and cutting. Use your miter gauge to cut the bevels. The technique is the same as crosscutting, only with the saw blade set to 45 degrees (Photo 10). Leave 3/16 in. of "reveal" (exposed cabinet edge) for a nice look. You can go with a wider or narrower reveal as long as it's consistent. Fasten the molding to the cabinet with glue and 1-in. brads.

Center the top cap on either side of the molding and flush with the back, then glue and pin it to the molding with 1-1/2-in. brads (Photo 12). Place the brads carefully over the thick part of the trim. It's easy to accidentally blow through the narrower, contoured front.

Clear-coat the cabinet with the finish of your choice. It's easier to apply smooth coats of finish with a spray can than with a brush, especially when you're finishing the interior. We used three coats of shellac. It dries quickly so you can completely finish (all three coats) in one day. It's also the least hazardous of all finishes. Do your spraying in a dust-free room and you won't even have to sand between coats.

Hang it on the wall

With a 42-in. cabinet, you should be able to hang it with 2-1/2-in. screws driven through the back and into two studs. But if you can only find one stud, use drywall anchors near the end farthest from the stud.

5 Exterior Maintenance & Repairs

IN THIS CHAPTER

HandyHints®

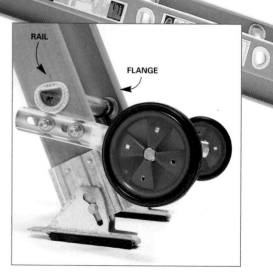

LADDER POUCH

There's no need to load up your tool belt when you're working from a ladder. Any type of hook, pouch or pocket made for a tool belt works just as well when mounted on a ladder.

ROOF GRIPPER

An old foam cushion from a sofa or chair not only saves your knees but also grips asphalt shingles and keeps you from sliding down a steep pitch. It won't prevent falls, though, so it's no substitute for safety equipment like a harness and roof jacks.

BLAST SCREENS CLEAN

If you have an air compressor and an air nozzle, you can clean window and door screens in seconds without removing them. Just turn the air pressure to 60 psi and blow away dust, debris and cobwebs.

DID YOU BUY THE **RIGHT PAINT?**

Don't let these common misconceptions ruin your next paint project.

Misconception:
All paints are basically the same, so buy the cheapest

Truth:

Don't fall for this one. All paints have the same *types* of ingredients, but the quality and performance of those ingredients vary significantly. Better-quality paints have better resins and more of them, so the paint adheres better and lasts longer. They have higher-quality pigments that cover better and are less likely to fade. And they have additives that help you brush them out faster and smoother. All in all, the ingredients in higher-quality paints cost more, and you won't find them in the cheaper paints.

Semi-transparent oil stain, cedar tint

Misconception:
It's best to paint your deck with an opaque stain

Truth:

Solid stains are a good choice for smooth outdoor surfaces like siding and deck rails, but they're not a good choice for decking. The wood won't absorb enough stain to withstand the abrasion of foot traffic and it'll soon show wear. Semi-transparent stains or tinted sealers are better choices because the wood will absorb more stain, giving it better protection. Still, you have to clean the wood and renew the stain every two to three years.

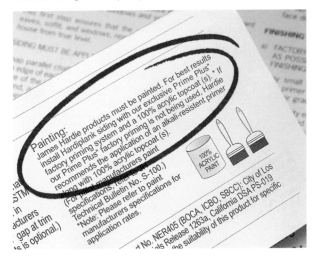

BEADED WATER

SHINY MILL GLAZE

Misconception:
Oil primers are better than latex primers on bare wood

Truth:

In general, both oil and latex primers work well on bare wood. But in some cases one works better than the other. An oil primer will work better than latex on new wood that has a "mill glaze," that is, a polished surface caused by the planer during the smoothing process. You can usually spot the shine if you examine the wood closely (**see above**). Or sprinkle a little water on the surface. If it beads up rather than sinks in, choose an oil primer, since the wood will usually absorb it better than it does latex. If you want to use latex, first sand to dull the shine.

A latex primer will work better than oil to "spot prime" knots and pitch pockets (dried). Choose a special "stain blocking" type for this purpose. Once the spot priming dries, prime the entire surface with an oil or latex primer.

Misconception:
You don't have to reprime factory-primed building materials

Truth:

Beware! Sometimes the manufacturers of siding and other materials prime their products only to protect them in transit and on the job site. The coating isn't always intended to be the base coat for paint. To determine if you have to reprime, read the manufacturer's finishing recommendations for the product you purchase.

Misconception:
Outdoors, oil stains are better than latex stains because they last longer

Truth:

It depends on the surface. Oil stains generally penetrate wood better than latex stains and perform best on rough surfaces like rough-sawn wood and cedar shingles, which will soak up a lot of stain. Semi-transparent oil stains excel here because you can apply several coats and achieve good wood protection without hiding the natural texture and grain. You can expect the stain to last from four to seven years. They're easier to renew, too. You can simply power wash to clean and recoat.

However, latex stains (especially solid ones) excel on smooth wood surfaces. They won't erode as quickly as oil stains. You can expect a solid latex stain on smooth, vertical wood to last four to six years. Keep in mind that no stain will last more than two to three years on horizontal surfaces that are exposed to the sun and rain.

ROUGH-SAWN BOARD

SEMI-TRANSPARENT OIL STAIN

Misconception:
You shouldn't put an oil primer over latex topcoats
Truth:

Generally speaking, applying oil primer over latex isn't a problem. A clean, solid, well-prepared base for the new paint is the most critical issue. However, several situations specifically call for an oil primer.

1. If the old topcoat shows significant chalking, that is, the pigment comes off on your finger when you rub the topcoat, then scrub the surface well using a detergent and brush, rinse and apply an oil primer when the surface thoroughly dries.

2. If the topcoat shows extractive staining (water-soluble substances in cedar and redwood; **photo below**) bleeding through the surface, scrub, let dry and prime with a stain-blocking oil primer.

Misconception:
You can't paint treated wood
Truth:

Actually you can paint treated wood, but you may not like the results. The decay-resistant chemicals won't harm the wood's ability to hold paint. However, treated wood is usually a lower grade. It has knots, cracks and other surface flaws that a paint film tends to highlight (**see photo**). A semitransparent stain is usually a better choice because it emphasizes the natural "rough" character of the wood.

PRESSURE-TREATED WOOD

Extractive bleed — use stain-blocking oil primer!

Misconception:
You can't paint wood once you've applied a water repellent
Truth:

Using a water repellent on bare wood in areas vulnerable to moisture—such as windowsills, trim and siding near the ground, and board ends in exposed locations—is the best thing you can do to prevent peeling and extend the life of your paint job. Unfortunately, *paintable* water repellents can be difficult to find. *Don't paint over a water repellent unless the label specifically says that you can.* The label often specifies that you use an oil primer.

Several common paintable brands include:

- Woodlife Classic Clear Wood Preservative (Wolman; 800-556-7737; www.wolman.com).
- Weatherscreen Clear Wood Preservative (PPG; 412-434-3131; www.ppg.com).
- Penofin Exterior Finishes (800-736-6346; www.penofin.com).

3. If you notice wax bleed on older types of hardboard siding, thoroughly scrub the surface and apply an oil primer. Heat from the sun sometimes causes the wax used as a water repellent to migrate to the surface and create a dark, blotchy appearance. Then apply 100 percent acrylic latex topcoats to yield the best long-term durability.

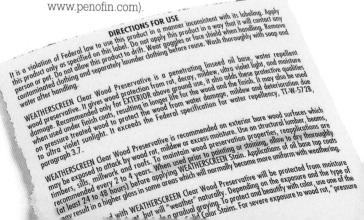

CLEAR OIL FINISH

Misconception:
Varnish is a good finish for outdoor furniture

Truth:

Nope. Choose varnish for outdoor furniture only if you want to refinish wood as your hobby. Varnishes begin to peel within a year or two when exposed to direct sunlight. Then you have to scrape, sand and refinish to keep the furniture looking good, a time-intensive and laborious task. Sailboat owners do this to keep their mahogany and teak looking sharp, but you probably won't want to do it as a routine chore. A wipe-on exterior oil finish won't last as long (perhaps a year), but it's much easier to renew. (One example is Australian Timber Oil from Cabot, 800-877-8246, www.cabotstain.com.) Every year, simply give the surface a light sanding and reapply the oil.

Misconception:
Enamel paints are the best choices for woodwork and trim

Truth:

In general, it's true that enamel is the best choice for trim, but the word enamel can be confusing, and is no longer helpful when you're making paint decisions. Enamel once referred to resin-rich oil paint, that is, paint that contains a high proportion of oils to make it brush out more smoothly and dry to a glossy finish. Now it can also refer to resin-rich latex paints, which have similar qualities.

To avoid confusion, it's better to avoid the word enamel and choose your trim paint based on type (oil or latex) and sheen (gloss or semigloss).

Misconception:
You can't paint vinyl siding

Truth:

Actually, it's no problem to paint vinyl siding. The old color won't peel because the pigments are mostly mixed into the material itself. But it can fade, or you may simply want a color change.

If it's new and you want to alter the color, wash it with a detergent, then rinse. If it's older and somewhat faded, you have to be a bit more aggressive. Scrub it with a brush and detergent and water to remove chalking and mildew as well as dirt. Then apply two coats of a 100-percent acrylic paint. You don't need a primer.

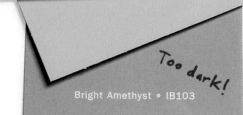

Avoid painting light-colored vinyl with paint darker than the original color. The darker color will absorb more heat on the sunny sides and cause the vinyl to expand and contract more than before. The siding may start to bow or look wavy.

Kayak Yellow • IB74

Too dark!

Bright Amethyst • IB103

RENEW SINGLE-PANE WINDOWS

On older single-pane windows, the glass is usually surrounded by putty called glazing compound, which holds the glass in place and seals out the weather. This putty often lasts decades, but over the years it becomes rock-hard, cracks and even falls off the window. Loose or missing compound lets wind and rain leak in around the glass.

Replacing the putty around one pane of glass will take 15 minutes to an hour, depending on the size of the pane and the stubbornness of the old putty. Replace broken glass while you're at it. This adds only a few minutes and a few dollars to the job. If you call a glass repair service to do the job, it'll cost $50 to $100 (under "Glass" in the yellow pages).

It's possible to replace glass and putty with the window in place, but you'll save time and get better results if you can remove the window and clamp it down on a flat surface. If you have broken glass, get it out of the way before you remove the old putty. Put on heavy gloves and eye protection, place a cloth over the broken pane and tap it with a hammer. With the glass thoroughly broken up, pull the shards out of the frame by hand. Pull out the old glazing points with a pliers. If the old glass is in good shape, leave it in place.

The next step is to get rid of the old putty. If the putty is badly cracked, you can pry away large chunks quickly (**Photo 1**). Putty in good condition takes longer to remove. With a heat gun in one hand and a stiff putty knife in the other, heat the putty to soften it and gouge it out. Wear leather gloves to protect your hands from burns. Keep the heat gun moving to avoid concentrating heat in one spot. Otherwise the heat will crack the glass. If your heat gun doesn't have a heat shield attachment, protect the glass with a scrap of sheet metal. When the putty is removed, prime any bare wood inside the window frame. A shellac-based primer such as BIN is a good choice because it dries in minutes.

If you need new glass, measure the opening, subtract 1/8 in. from your measurements and have the new glass cut to size at a full-service hardware store. Take a shard of the old glass with you to match the thickness. You'll pay from $5 to $30, depending on the size of the pane. Also buy a package of glazing points ($2) to hold the glass in place while the new compound hardens. Glazing compound ($5) is available in oil-based and latex/acrylic versions. The latex products, which usually come in a tube, have a longer life expectancy and you don't have to wait days before painting them as you do with oil-based putty. But they often begin to dry before you

LOOSE PUTTY

HEAT GUN

HEAT SHIELD

1 PRY OUT loose chunks of glazing compound with a putty knife. Soften remaining areas with a heat gun and scrape away the putty.

can tool them smooth. If neat, smooth results are important, choose an oil-based putty (such as DAP 33).

For installation of new glass, the directions on glazing compound may tell you to lay a light bead of compound inside the frame and then set the glass over it. That works well with soft latex compound. But if you're using stiffer oil-based compound, lay in a light bead of acrylic latex caulk instead. Set the glass onto the caulk, then wiggle and press down to firmly embed the glass. Install the

glazing points, then apply new putty as shown in **Photo 3**.

To complete the job, smooth out the new glazing compound (**Photos 4 and 5**). Oil-based putty is easier to work with when it's warm. To heat it, set the can in a bowl of hot water for a few minutes. Remember that oil-based putty remains soft for days, so be careful not to touch it after smoothing. You'll have to wait several days before you can prime and paint oil-based putty; check the label.

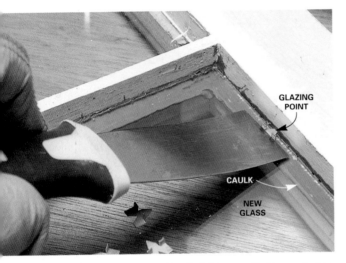

2 SET new glass onto a bead of latex caulk. Press glazing points into the wood every 8 in. Let the excess caulk that oozes out under the glass harden and slice it off with a utility knife later.

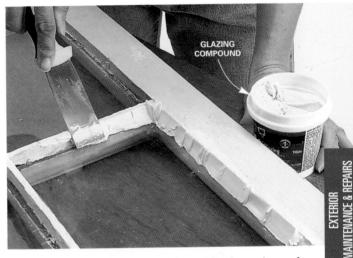

3 COVER the perimeter of the glass with a heavy layer of compound. Be sure to completely fill in the recess; don't leave any gaps or hollow spots.

4 DIP a putty knife in mineral spirits to lubricate it and smooth out the compound. Wet the knife again and run over the compound as many times as it takes to create a smooth surface.

5 DRAG the ridge of excess compound away from the finished joint and scrape it up. Be careful not to touch the smoothed surface.

EXTERIOR MAINTENANCE & REPAIRS

HomeCare&Repair

1 SMEAR lipstick on the latch and stick masking tape to the strike plate. Close the door to determine where the latch contacts the plate.

2 REMOVE the strike plate, place it in a vise and enlarge the hole with a file. You may also have to enlarge the hole in the doorjamb.

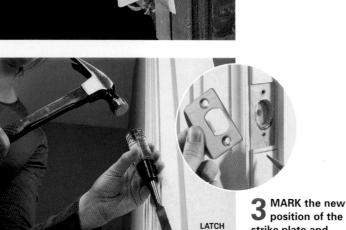

3 MARK the new position of the strike plate and enlarge the mortise with a chisel. You may also have to enlarge the latch hole in the jamb.

FIX A DOOR LATCH THAT WON'T CATCH

When a door latch won't catch, it's because the latch doesn't align with the hole in the strike plate. Sometimes you can clearly see the misalignment. If not, do the "lipstick test" (**Photo 1**).

■ **Tighten the hinges first.** If you find that the latch contacts the strike plate too high or too low, make sure all the door's hinge screws are tight. If that doesn't solve the problem, try this trick: Remove one of the screws on the jamb side of the hinge and drive in a 3-in. screw. The long screw will grab the wall framing and draw in the whole doorjamb slightly. To raise the latch, do this at the top hinge. To lower the latch, do it at the bottom hinge.

■ **Enlarge the strike plate hole.** If long screws don't solve the too-high or too-low problem, measure the misalignment of the lipstick marks on the strike plate. If the latch misses the strike plate hole by 1/8 in. or less, remove the strike plate and enlarge its hole with a file (**Photo 2**). A half-round file ($6 at home centers and hardware stores) matches the curve of the latch hole.

■ **Move the strike plate.** If the latch contacts the strike plate at the correct level but doesn't go in far enough, or if the latch strikes more than 1/8 in. too high or too low, you'll have to reposition the strike plate. You can move it up or down and in or out. Use a sharp chisel to enlarge the strike plate mortise (**Photo 3**). Then hold the strike plate in place and drill new 1/16-in. holes for the screws. Install the strike plate and fill the gap in the mortise with wood filler. Remove the strike plate to paint or finish the patch.

GreatGoofs®

Look out below!

I was afraid of falling off my roof while painting a dormer, so I went to the back of the house, tied a rope around a large pine tree, tied the other end around my waist and climbed to the roof.

Just before I lowered myself toward the dormer, I heard a child saying something in the distance. I paused, walked to the edge of the roof in the back and saw that my 7-year-old son had untied the rope from the tree and wrapped it around his waist. He proudly looked up and said, "I've got you, Dad!"

Luckily, I was able to climb down and explain to him that this arrangement would not work. Then I retied the rope to the tree and asked my wife to guard it—and my safety.

> **Editor's Note:**
> A rope around your waist isn't a safe way to prevent a fall. Always use safety equipment that's designed for the job, such as roof brackets and a personal fall arrest system (aka roof harness).

Between hornets and a hard place

Hornets had built a good-size nest in our porch light, so I rounded up a can of insecticide and a large cloth and waited until dark, when the pests would be in their hive.

That night I quickly wrapped the cloth around the light fixture to keep all the angry, buzzing hornets inside. But when I tried to grab the can of spray at my feet, I realized I couldn't reach down that far without letting go of the cloth—the only thing between me and an irate colony of stingers. Was I stuck!

Fortunately, it was summer and the windows were open. After I gave a few desperate yells, my wife came and rescued me from my potentially painful pickle.

Sticky situation

Eager to cross one more project off my to-do list, I went outside to paint window trim just before dark. Who needs daylight when you have a 500-watt work light?

I finished the first coat and returned an hour later to find an ugly surprise: Stuck to the paint like flypaper were hundreds of tiny insects that had been attracted by the work light!

I waited until the next day to sand off the bugs and apply the final coat of paint—and this time I finished well before dark.

REPLACE A PATIO DOOR

How to install a new smooth-rolling and leakproof sliding door

by **Travis Larson**

I f you've been putting up with a drafty patio door that sticks, fogs up or leaks during a heavy rainstorm, it's time to consider a new, energy-efficient replacement. While a high-quality door isn't cheap, it'll cut down on drafts, require almost no maintenance, and glide smoothly and latch securely. Best of all, you'll save $300-plus if you install it yourself.

At first glance, replacing such a big door may seem intimidating. But if you read through this article, you'll see that it's similar to replacing a window. We'll walk you through each step, including a special section on the critical flashing details that make the new door leakproof.

Manufacturers of higher-quality units have made installation fairly simple and straightforward. If you have experience installing a window or a swinging door, you should have no trouble with a sliding patio door. Other than basic carpentry tools, you'll only need a 4-ft. level and a screw gun. But we also recommend using a reciprocating saw fitted with an 8-in. bimetal blade to hack through shims and nails (**Photo 5**). Unless you're a brawny DIYer, another useful tool is a strong helper for short periods to assist with the heavy, awkward panels and door frames.

In most cases, you can replace that old slider with a smoothly operating, energy-efficient door in about a day. Add a few more hours to retrim the outside and the inside and you're done.

Measure the opening before you buy

Before you run off to buy your slider, pull off the interior trim around the old door and measure the rough opening for width and height. (If you want to reuse the old trim on the new door, pull the nails through the unfinished side.) Make sure you measure to the framing right next to the old doorjamb. You may have to cut away overhanging drywall to get at it (**Photo 1**). To check the height, make sure you're measuring to the subfloor, that is, the wood or concrete that the doorsill actually rests on and not a secondary layer of particleboard or plywood (underlayment). You can check for underlayment by pulling off a nearby heat register and looking at the floor layers bordering the opening. Then select a door that fits your rough opening. The door catalog will list its rough opening requirements. The door dealer will walk you through sizing and door options. (See "Buying a Patio Door," below.)

Once you get your door home, you'll save a lot of time if you finish any exposed wood surfaces on the door before beginning the installation. That'll save you from tricky brushwork cutting in around exterior claddings, weatherstripping and hardware, and keep smelly finishes out of your living quarters.

In our demonstration, we're removing a 6-ft. slider surrounded by wood trim and vinyl siding. Our new door was slightly smaller so we had to deal with a small gap surrounding the new exterior trim. Most new replacement doors will have a similar gap, no matter what exterior siding you have. If your old door has exterior trim fastened to the door frame, remove the trim and follow the installation steps we show. But if the siding comes right up to the door frame (no trim), you'll probably have to remove the siding or cut it back and restore it after installing the door in order to achieve a leak-free installation. And if you have stucco or brick, you'll probably have to add trim to fill the gap and rely partly on high-quality caulk to seal out water. We'll talk more about this later.

You never know how smoothly a patio door tearout and installation will go, so start in the morning to give yourself the best chance to finish up before nightfall. If you're not going to beat the witching hour, cover the opening from the inside with sheets of plywood cut about 6 in. larger than the opening. Run 3-in. screws through the plywood and drywall into the framing where the holes will be covered by the interior trim. If it's chilly out or threatens to rain, also staple plastic over the exterior to keep out drafts and water.

Removing the old door

Sliding patio doors are heavy (60 to 100 lbs. per panel), so it's best to remove the old panels one at a time and then

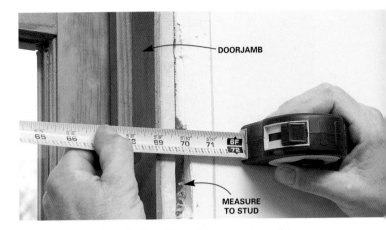

1 PRY the interior trim free. Then chip away drywall to expose framing and measure the rough opening width (distance between studs) and height (floor to beam). Then select a new door that fits that rough opening.

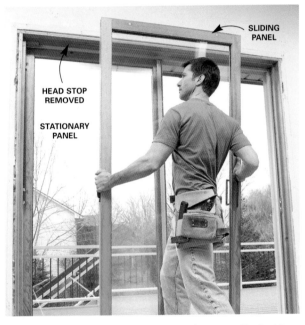

2 LATCH the door, then unscrew and remove the inside head stop. Unlatch the door, tip the top of the sliding panel inward and lift it free of the track.

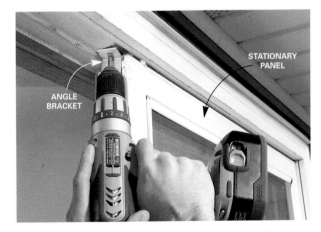

3 UNSCREW and remove any angle brackets at the top and bottom of the stationary panel.

4 PRY the stationary panel free of the frame at the top and bottom, slitting caulk or paint as necessary with a utility knife. Tip it inward and lift it free.

EXTERIOR TRIM

PRY AT TOP AND BOTTOM ONLY

5 PRY OFF the exterior trim, then cut between the door frame and the framing with a reciprocating saw. Pull the entire frame from the opening.

BIMETAL BLADE

6 LAY flexible flashing over the sill, wrapping it up the opening sides at least 2 in. and over any flashing or siding below.

FLEXIBLE FLASHING

DECK LEDGER DRIP CAP

tackle the door frame. Start with prying free any exterior trim pieces and then remove first the sliding and then the stationary panel (**Photos 2 – 4**). Usually the sliding panel wheels rest on the bottom track and the panel is held at the top by a removable strip of wood called the "inside head stop." Unscrew the inside head stop and remove the panel by tipping the top into the room and then lifting the bottom rollers free of the track (**Photo 2**). Some doors may have a channel instead of a head stop at the top, and you may need to lower the door on its rollers using the adjusting screws at the base to gain clearance (**Photo 11**). Then lift the panel straight up until the rollers are clear of the track, and pull the bottom into the room to free the panel.

Removing the stationary panel can be trickier. Generally there'll be an angle bracket at the top and maybe one at the bottom that you unscrew and remove (**Photo 3**). Then slide the panel toward the latch to clear it from the side jamb so you can lift it free. If it won't budge, use a utility knife to cut through any paint or caulk where it touches the frame and try prying the top and bottom again. If it still won't come free, don't beat yourself up. Replace the angle brackets so it won't fall out later and go to the next step of cutting the jambs free from the opening. Cut through insulation, fasteners and shims with a reciprocating saw sporting an 8-in. bimetal blade (**Photo 5**). Most likely, the threshold will be glued to the floor with beads of sealant, and it may take substantial prying with a flat bar to free it. Then get a buddy to help lift out the frame along with the panel. Cut up the frame in chunks for disposal.

Check the floor for level

In rare situations, the floor under the door will be out of level. Sweep the floor free of debris and check it with a straight board and a 4-ft. level. If it's within 1/4 in. of level over the 6-ft. opening, let it be; the door should still slide smoothly. But correct larger variations with two long, tapered shims placed directly under the sill (use treated wood on concrete). Fill any voids with polyurethane caulk to keep out drafts.

Leakproof flashing

In general, the directions that come with the door will be fine for assembly and installation of the new unit. Unfortunately, they assume you're installing the door in a new wall that doesn't yet have exterior siding. Replacing an old door can be a bit more complex.

Begin flashing at the bottom. Apply flexible flashing directly under the doorsill and 2 in. up the sides (**Photo 6**). Flexible flashing comes in 4- to 6-in.-wide rolls ($10) and has a sticky side so it adheres to the underlying surfaces. It's thick and seals around fasteners that are driven through it. It's imperative that the flashing laps well over any deck flashing or weather barrier below the door

(Photo 6). You may have to overlap two rows, as we did, to get the necessary coverage. Pros will usually rest the new doorsill (caulked) directly on the flashing, but for further protection in wet locations (rain will splash against the door bottom from all angles), add a "sill pan" as well (Photo 7). We chose a Jamsill Guard ($40; see Buyer's Guide, p. 188). It comes in three separate parts that glue together with PVC cement. Next apply flashing over any building paper, house wrap or sheathing along the sides and fold it around the door frame opening. We couldn't work the sticky flashing behind the vinyl trim, so we tucked No. 15 roofing felt about 2 in. under it instead.

Our slider was sheltered by a wide, low soffit, so we didn't have to worry about top flashing. But if your slider is unprotected, leave the top fin intact and slip it under the weather barrier (felt, house wrap, etc.) under the siding when you slide the new door frame into the opening. Then slip in a drip cap (usually included with the door) up under the weather barrier as well (Figure A). Follow this basic principle: Keep water flowing toward the exterior surface, just like shingles do.

Figure A
New Door
Flashing Details

The key to making your sliding door leakproof is to carefully follow the proper flashing techniques. The basic principle is to continually keep water flowing downward to the exterior. In most cases, you can follow the details we show here for flashing the sill. The side details will vary depending on the new door frame details and the exterior siding on your home. Most doors have plastic nailing flanges ("fins") that you lay over some type of house wrap (extend the house wrap if necessary). Then lay adhesive-backed flexible flashing over the flange/house wrap joint to seal it. Finish the sides by nailing on the side trim and caulking the gaps. The top details vary slightly. If you need a trim piece at the top, slide a metal drip cap under the house wrap and nail the trim directly below it. If you don't need an extra trim piece, slide the nailing flange under the house wrap, seal it with flexible flashing, and lay the house wrap over it, sealing the corners with small sections of flexible flashing.

DRIP CAP

NAILING FLANGE

FILLER TRIM

DOORJAMB

FLEXIBLE FLASHING

NAILING FLANGE

HOUSE WRAP

SILICONE CAULK

FLEXIBLE FLASHING

PLASTIC SILL PROTECTOR

THRESHOLD SUPPORT BOARD

DRIP CAP

EXTERIOR MAINTENANCE & REPAIRS

Installing the new door

Installing your new slider is usually the easiest part of the job. Be aware that every manufacturer has slightly different weatherstripping systems, handle and lock hardware, and ways to fit the doors into openings, so they may not exactly match the ones shown in our photos. Read and follow the door instructions for those details.

If you have a "knockdown" (not preassembled) door frame, assemble it on the deck, garage floor or other flat surface.

"Dry-fit" the assembled door frame in the opening to make sure everything fits (Photo 8), then rest it flat and put two beads of silicone caulk on the underside of the sill (where the directions call for it). Slip the door frame back into the opening and push the door fins tight against the sheathing (Figure A). (Line the fin groove up flush with the outside of the sheathing if you're not using fins.) Center the door frame in relation to the siding or trim. Otherwise it'll look bad from the outside. Then plumb, shim and screw the door in the opening (Photo 9) following the manufacturer's instructions. Be sure not to bow the jambs in or out when you drive the screws.

7 PREP and lay a special vinyl sill pan over the flashing. Clean the joint overlaps with PVC cleaner, then lay the parts in place and weld the seams with PVC cement.

SILL PAN

PVC CEMENT

8 ASSEMBLE the frame following the manufacturer's instructions. Apply two beads of silicone caulk along the length of the threshold and tip the frame into the opening.

PREDRILLED HOLE

SHIMS

PREDRILLED HOLE

9 CENTER the frame in the opening and screw it into place, using a level and shims to square it. Check the frame for square and make final adjustments when you install the stationary panel.

Follow the instructions to install the stationary panel first and then the slider. Tip the stationary panel into the opening and slide it within about 1/4 in. of the side jamb, and make sure the gap is even top to bottom. If it's more than 1/4 in. out of plumb or the jamb bows, adjust the frame for plumb and straightness and adjust the shims if necessary. Install angle clips, weatherstripping and trim as needed.

Then rest the sliding panel wheels on the tracks and tip the panel into the opening. Have a helper hold it in place while you screw in the head stop. Slide the door about 1/4 in. from the frame and check the gap from top to bottom. Raise or lower the rollers at the bottom. Adjust the rollers until the gap is even and the door rolls freely (**Photo 11**). Finish up by installing the handle and the locking hardware.

Finishing up the inside

Standard slider doorjamb depths are designed to fit standard 4-9/16-in.-thick walls (2x4 studs plus 1/2-in. drywall and sheathing). If your walls are thicker, as in our case, you'll have to add extension jambs (**Photo 12**). Cut the top piece to fit first, then shim it and nail it in place. Then install the side extension jambs. Leave an even 1/8-in. reveal (back-set) between the extension jamb and the doorjamb.

Insulate around the frame with fiberglass packed tightly against the exterior sheathing and more loosely near the drywall. (Foam insulation is a bit more difficult to use because even minimal-expanding types can bow in jambs and affect weatherproofing or door operation.) Add interior trim around the door, leaving another 1/8-in. backset between the trim and the extension jambs.

Finishing up the outside

You'll frequently be installing a door that's smaller than the one you removed. This will leave a wider gap that you'll have to fill with exterior trim. Match the new trim to the existing as much as possible. Whatever trim you choose, rip the trim slightly narrow so you leave 1/8-in. gaps on both sides. Seal these gaps with a high-quality acrylic or silicone caulk.

Finish up your installation by screwing or nailing a 3/4- to 1-in.-thick piece of cedar, treated wood or composite material directly under the overhanging lip of the threshold to support it (**Photo 13**). Some sliding door manufacturers offer a premade aluminum support strip as an alternative. ⌂

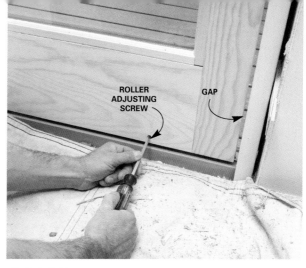

10 TIP the stationary panel into the opening, push it against the door frame and install any angle brackets to anchor it (Photo 3). Tip the operable panel into place and screw the inside head stop to the top of the door frame.

11 SLIDE the door slightly open and adjust the roller heights until the gap between the jamb and the panel is consistent.

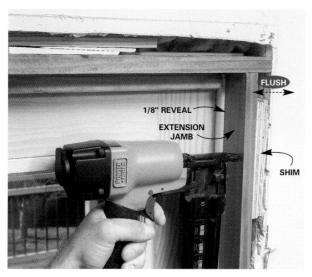

12 IF YOU NEED extension jambs, rip them to width and then shim and nail them into place, leaving a 1/8-in. reveal at the door frame. Then add the casing with another 1/8-in. reveal.

13 CUT filler strips to fit between the door frame and the siding with a 1/8-in. gap on both sides. Fill gaps with silicone caulk. Cut a threshold support block to fit between the deck and siding, then slip it into place and nail it.

NewProducts

Fiberglass doors, but you'll swear they're wood

If you're in search of a door that looks like wood but is more durable and energy efficient, consider fiberglass doors like the ones from JELD-WEN. The doors can be painted or stained, have the realistic wood grain of mahogany and alder, and when finished look so much like wood that you can't tell the difference—even up close.

According to the manufacturer, they have more than twice the amount of fiberglass of other fiberglass doors. Plus, polyurethane is used on the "skin" for increased strength. These features make the doors stronger and heavier (they can withstand hurricane forces).

At $600 to $800, the doors are less expensive than wood but more expensive than steel. They're available at door supply companies, lumberyards and some home centers.

JELD-WEN, (800) 877-9482. www.jeld-wen.com

JELD-WEN WINDOWS® AND DOORS

AUTHENTIC WOOD GRAIN LOOK

5 WALL FRAMING TIPS

by **Jeff Gorton**

Wall framing always looks simple and straight-forward, but a mistake here—a wall that's too short or a window opening slightly too small—wastes lots of time and effort later. In this article, we'll show you simple techniques designed to ensure accurate results. Keep in mind, though, that carpentry practices and jargon vary from region to region and even from one carpenter to the next. So don't be surprised if some of the labels and marks we show aren't exactly what you'd encounter on a local building project. The basic concepts are the same, and with this information your next framing project should go smoothly and error free.

1 SNAP LINES AND SET THE PLATES IN PLACE

STACKED PLATES

TOP PLATE

BOTTOM PLATE

CHALK LINES

Eliminate mistakes by chalking a full-size map of your walls directly on the floor. First mark the inside edge of the wall at each corner and snap chalk lines. Mark the location of interior walls as well and snap chalk lines on both sides of interior wall locations to ensure correct plate positions. Double-check all of your layout lines to make sure the walls are parallel, the corners are at right angles and the dimensions match the plans. Then measure and cut a top and bottom plate for each wall as shown. Double-check lengths by setting the plates in their exact position.

2 MARK WINDOWS AND DOORS FIRST, THEN LAY OUT THE STUDS

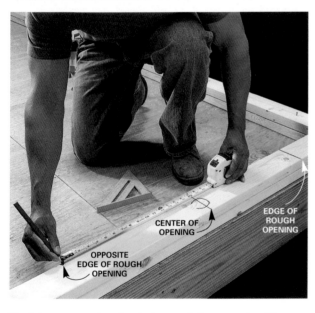

CENTER OF OPENING

EDGE OF ROUGH OPENING

OPPOSITE EDGE OF ROUGH OPENING

15-1/4"

16" MARK

32" MARK

KING STUD MARK

EDGE OF FIRST STUD

TRIMMER MARK

Find the center of each window and door opening. Then divide the "rough opening" (given on your plan or in the window literature) by two and measure out to the left and right of the center mark. Write a "T" to the outside of both marks to indicate trimmer locations. Measure over 1-1/2 in. and draw another line. Mark an "X" outside these marks for the full-height king studs.

With the openings marked, lay out the stud locations (**right photo above**). The goal is to position the studs every 16 or 24 in. so that the edges of 4x8 sheets of plywood align with the centers of studs. Subtract 3/4 in. from the first layout mark. Then hook your tape on a partially driven nail at this mark, and mark at each 16- or 24-in. multiple. Make an "X" on the same side of each layout mark to indicate the stud position. Mark studs that land between window or door trimmers with a "C" to indicate cripples rather than full-height studs.

3 TRANSFER THE LAYOUT MARKS TO THE BOTTOM PLATE

Set the plates side by side and transfer the marks from the top plate to the bottom plate using a square. Some carpenters mark only the edge of the plates. We show marking the wide face, which will help you align twisted studs. Tack the pairs of plates together with 8d nails after marking them so they don't get separated and mixed with other plates. Then set them aside until you're ready to build that wall.

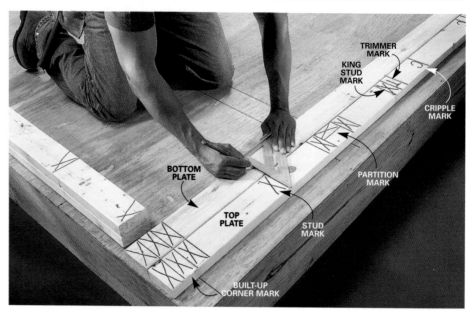

TRIMMER MARK

KING STUD MARK

CRIPPLE MARK

BOTTOM PLATE

PARTITION MARK

TOP PLATE

STUD MARK

BUILT-UP CORNER MARK

4 NAIL FULL-HEIGHT HEADERS TO THE TOP PLATE

TOP PLATE

BUILT-UP HEADER

KING STUD

TRIMMER STUD

KING STUD

TRIMMER STUD

BUILT-UP CORNER ASSEMBLY

BOTTOM PLATE

Calculate header lengths by adding 3 in. to the rough opening width. Add 6 in. to headers that require two trimmers on each side. Cut header parts and nail them together. Label the headers.

In many plans, headers are positioned against the top plate. If yours are, begin wall assembly by positioning and nailing these "full-height" headers to the top plate with 16d nails (**top left photo**). Then lay full-length studs between the plates and nail king studs to the headers and to the top and bottom plates (**bottom left photo**). Nail in all the full-height studs as well as corner assemblies. Note: Sight down each stud before you nail it in and orient any bow (crown) upward. Next install the trimmers (**bottom left**).

5 ADD CRIPPLES ABOVE HEADERS AND UNDER SILLS

In wall plans that have openings with cripples above the header, cut and nail together the king studs and trimmers first. Then position and nail them to the plates. Set the header on the trimmers and nail through the king studs to hold it in place. Then measure, and nail the cripples into place (**top photo**). You have to toenail the bottom of the cripples to the header.

Window openings are just like doors but with the addition of a rough sill. Mark the top of the sill by measuring down from the header. Use the rough opening height for this dimension. Cut the lower cripples and place one under each end of the sill as a temporary support while you toenail the sill to the trimmers with a pair of 8d nails at each end. Align the cripples with the layout marks and nail through the sill and bottom plate to hold them in place. Use pairs of 16d nails. Some carpenters like to double the rough sill, especially on openings wider than about 3 ft. If you do this, remember to allow for the thickness of a double sill when you cut your cripples. 🏠

CRIPPLE LOCATION

HEADER

KING STUD

TRIMMER STUD

PARTITION ASSEMBLY

ROUGH SILL

CRIPPLE

EXTERIOR MAINTENANCE & REPAIRS

WEATHERPROOF
EXTERIOR TRIM

*PVC trim looks and cuts like wood, but there are a few special tricks
to install it successfully.*

by **Travis Larson**

Tired of scraping and repainting your trim? Or disheartened when you find that your trim has rotted and will no longer hold paint? Then step back and consider the advantages of replacing those problem boards with PVC trim—your worries will be over.

Cellular PVC (polyvinyl chloride) trim is a close cousin of the familiar white plastic plumbing pipes. (The "cellular" part just means it's filled with zillions of tiny air bubbles to make the material lighter and less expensive to manufacture.) But unlike its cousin, it's specially formulated to make it resistant to sunlight, hold paint well and easy to work with.

PVC trim looks just like wood (well, flawless wood) and lasts virtually forever. It's impervious to rot and insect attack and doesn't absorb water. It holds paint well because water can't penetrate the material behind the paint. And if you like the look of white trim, you may not have to paint it at all (more on this later). It's an especially good substitute for wood trim in areas that are highly exposed to water, such as corner board and door trim that's near the ground or unprotected by an overhang.

Although you install cellular PVC trim almost like wood, there are a few crucial differences. In this story, we'll show you those special cutting, joining and fastening techniques so your PVC trim will perform flawlessly for the life of your home. Don't worry—there aren't any fancy tools or skills required. If you've cut and installed wood trim before, you have the moxie to work with PVC.

PVC trim is sold in 5/4 (1-in.) and 4/4 (3/4-in.) thicknesses in the common widths found with wood. But the selection may be limited. You'll probably have to special-order some thicknesses and widths. Trim is sometimes only sold in 18-ft. lengths, so you may want to have your order delivered. Most companies offer material that has an embossed wood grain side and a smooth side, so you can choose the look you want. Don't confuse cellular vinyl trim with polyurethane-core, vinyl-coated products. While they too are highly durable low-maintenance products, their installation techniques are different.

PVC trim isn't cheap; expect to pay about the same price you'd pay for clear, knot-free wood. (We paid $41 for an 18-ft. 1x6.) Other PVC products are also available, including preformed outside corners (**Figure A**), tongue-and-groove boards, and sheet goods that you can carve up and work just like plywood. Find PVC trim by contacting lumberyards in your area. Or check the Buyer's Guide, p. 199, to find a supplier.

Figure A
Cellular PVC Profiles

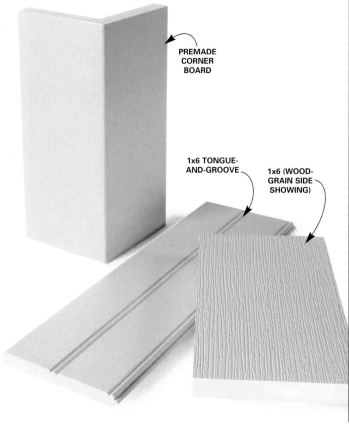

PREMADE CORNER BOARD

1x6 TONGUE-AND-GROOVE

1x6 (WOOD-GRAIN SIDE SHOWING)

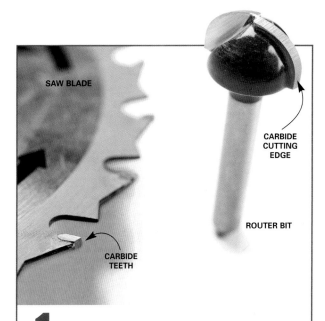

SAW BLADE

CARBIDE CUTTING EDGE

ROUTER BIT

CARBIDE TEETH

1 Cut with carbide-tipped saw blades

Cut PVC trim with the same hand and power tools that you use for wood. But use only carbide-tipped saw blades; plain steel ones will dull quickly. In general, the more teeth a blade has, the smoother the cut edges will be. We recommend standard combination saw blades. You can easily rout decorative edges or grooves with routers or shapers, but use carbide-edged bits as well.

Sawn edges aren't as easy to sand as wood. So if possible, plan your work so that newly cut edges will butt against siding, soffits or other trim, and let the smoother factory edge show wherever possible. Sanding isn't always necessary, especially if you plan to paint. But sand exposed edges that are highly visible, like near the front door. Use a random orbital sander with 100-grit paper. Belt sanding doesn't work well because the friction from the belt melts the plastic rather than smoothing it.

16" O.C.

1/2"

·CEMENT JOINT

3 Cement seams for sturdy, watertight joints

One advantage of PVC is that you can "weld" joints to keep them tight and prevent water from penetrating behind the trim. Manufacturers recommend a special type of PVC cement that has a longer "open time" than the type of cement that plumbers use on plastic pipes. You can buy this cement wherever you buy the trim. You'll have about five minutes of working time to clamp and fasten the joints before the cement sets. Smear a little cement on both surfaces and then clamp or screw the joint together. Wipe off any excess right away with a damp rag; unlike PVC pipe cement, it's water soluble and won't mar finished surfaces if you remove it immediately.

STAINLESS STEEL FINISH SCREWS

2 Fasten with stainless steel screws or hot-dipped siding nails

When it comes to choosing your fasteners, don't scrimp by using fasteners that won't last as long as the vinyl trim. Stainless steel screws with small finish heads are the best choice because they'll never corrode. You can also use hot-dipped galvanized nails, but they may corrode and stain the trim over time. If you want a flawless finish, choose screws, countersink them slightly, and then use an exterior filler to hide the screw heads. In areas that are completely protected from water, like under a soffit, you can use a 15-gauge air nailer with galvanized nails and fill the holes with paintable caulk or filler.

HOT-DIPPED SIDING NAILS

PVC tends to expand and contract with temperature changes, so fasten it well. Drive screws or nails into framing only, never just to the sheathing. Select fastener lengths that will penetrate at least 1-1/2 in. into the framing. No predrilling or countersinking is necessary if the temperature is over 40 degrees F when you install the trim. But lower temperatures call for both drilling and countersinking; otherwise the vinyl may split. Place fasteners every 16 in. at both sides of the trim, spacing them about 1/2 in. from the edges. If you're using 10-in. or wider trim, add another fastener in the middle.

Follow all of the flashing techniques that you would with wood trim. You still want to prevent water from penetrating between the trim and the wall sheathing behind.

LONG-SETTING PVC CEMENT

PREASSEMBLED
WINDOW FRAME

4 Preassemble window and door trim

Prebuild PVC trim assemblies and then install them as a unit rather than a piece at a time as you would with wood. This will take a little longer but will result in perfectly tight joints that won't need caulk. Cement and screw end joints like miters and butt joints. Longer joints like corner boards can be simply cemented and clamped (see below).

Pocket screws are the best method of joining corners when you're cementing window and door trim assemblies (Photos 1 and 2). Use the coarse-threaded version of pocket screws. Cut miters to fit and dry-fit your cuts to check the joints and lengths. Measure carefully when applying trim around vinyl or aluminum-clad windows to leave a 1/8-in. expansion gap between the trim and frame for caulk.

1. Drill

POCKET
SCREW
JIG

WINDOW
FRAME
MITER

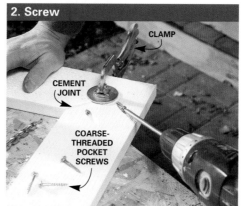

2. Screw

CLAMP

CEMENT
JOINT

COARSE-
THREADED
POCKET
SCREWS

EXTERIOR
MAINTENANCE & REPAIRS

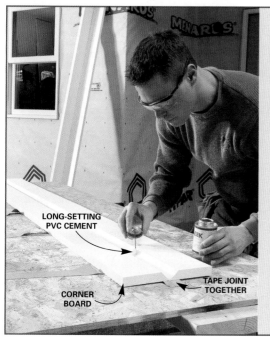

LONG-SETTING
PVC CEMENT

CORNER
BOARD

TAPE JOINT
TOGETHER

TAPE JOINT
CLOSED

MITER

5 Preassemble corner boards

Some manufacturers offer premade trim for outside corners, but it's somewhat pricey. It's easy to make your own. Start by ripping 45-degree bevels on one edge of each board on a table saw. Then push the bevel tips together tightly and tape the boards together with packaging or duct tape. Apply cement to both bevels, then fold the boards together and clamp the joint for about 15 minutes with more strips of tape.

1/8" GAP

6 Leave expansion gaps on long pieces

PVC trim will expand and contract with wide variations in temperature. If you're installing trim in temps higher than 80 degrees F, cut pieces to fit tightly. If it's between 60 and 80 degrees, leave a 1/16-in. gap for every 18 ft. of length. Below 60 degrees, leave a 1/8-in. gap. After installation, cover the gap with acrylic or urethane caulk. Avoid silicone-based caulks; they don't adhere well to vinyl.

7 Fill fastener holes before you paint

Fill small holes with an exterior filler and lightly sand it smooth after it dries. Or use a paintable caulk and smooth it with your finger. Fill larger holes or damaged areas with auto body filler, and again, sand it after it cures.

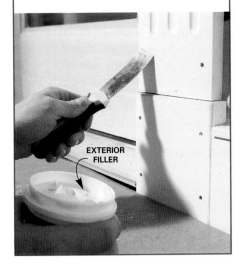

EXTERIOR FILLER

45-DEGREE SCARF JOINT

STUD POSITION

8 Splice long trim pieces with scarf joints

Splice long pieces of trim with "scarf joints," that is, overlapping 45-degree joints. Cut the first piece of trim to fall just short of a stud so the second overlapping trim piece can be fastened to the stud an inch or so from the end to prevent splitting.

9 Paint vinyl trim with 100-percent acrylic exterior paint

Although painting PVC trim isn't necessary, we recommend it. Otherwise your trim will look stark white and you may see filler over holes that's not an exact color match. And the edges and ends (especially ones that you have cut or routed) will collect dirt and begin to look gray over time.

There's no hurry for painting after installation; you can wait as long as you want. PVC won't weather or lose its ability to hold paint. Before you paint, use mild detergent to clean off grime and oils left over from handling and make sure the surfaces are dry. Then finish it with any exterior 100-percent acrylic paint. Use lighter shades rather than darker shades. Dark colors tend to absorb more heat and increase expansion. ⌂

100 PERCENT ACRYLIC PAINT

Buyer's Guide

The following are manufacturers of PVC trim:
- **AZEK:** (877) 275-2935. www.azek.com.
- **Custom Decorative Mouldings:** (800) 543-0553. www.custom-moulding.com.
- **Fypon:** (800) 446-3040. www.fypon.com.
- **Nesco Mfg.:** (480) 756-6675. www.nescomfg.com.
- **Royal Building Products:** (866) 852-2791. www.royalbuildingproducts.com.

NewProducts

Lattice you can use

I never liked using wood lattice. It's flimsy, it looks worn even when new and it's hard to paint. Some vinyl lattice products aren't much better. They look like plastic and scratch easily.

GeoMatrix's SevereWeather plastic lattice has changed my opinion. The color goes all the way through the lattice, so scratches aren't visible. The lattice is solid and offers the maintenance-free benefits of vinyl but looks like wood.

The lattice, available exclusively at Lowe's ($15 to $25 for 4 x 8-ft. sections), comes in five colors to dress up outdoor projects. Vinyl post sleeves ($25 per 8-ft. section) are available to keep your project maintenance free.

GeoMatrix, (248) 643-7764. www.lowes.com

PHOTOS GEOMATRIX

EXTERIOR MAINTENANCE & REPAIRS

The Family Handyman

SPECKLED ALUMINUM SIDING

We have black spots the size of flyspecks on our aluminum siding. The only way to remove them is by scraping with a metal tool, but that scrapes off the paint. I've tried several liquid solutions, but to no avail. How can I remove the spots?

The spots are most likely "artillery fungus," also known as "shotgun fungus," so-called because of its ability to leap up to 20 ft. It's a wood-decay fungus that lives on moist landscape mulch and is especially common in the Eastern United States. The fungus is sensitive to light, so it's often found on white and light-colored surfaces, including siding and cars.

The fungus won't hurt your aluminum siding, nor will it degrade wood siding. The problem is wholly cosmetic. The bad news is the fungus is nearly impossible to remove and can leave a stain. If you own a pressure washer, try that first. Then try a cleaner specially formulated for removing mold and mildew, such as Soft Scrub (available in a 36-oz. bottle for $4.99 at Home Depot). Or make your own cleaner by mixing a solution of 30-percent vinegar and 70-percent

water. Another home remedy is to mix 1/3 cup of powdered laundry detergent (such as Tide or Fab), 2/3 cup of powdered household cleaner (it must be non-ammonia, such as Spic & Span or Soilax), 1 quart of liquid bleach and 1 gallon of water.

Test any solution in a small, inconspicuous area to make sure it doesn't discolor the siding. Apply the cleaner with a soft bristle brush, and rinse well. Start at the bottom and work up to avoid streaks. Be aware that these cleaners may not entirely remove the black spots.

When it comes to prevention, we don't know of any chemical treatment to stop the problem. If you spot the fungus, bag up all of the mulch around the house and take it to a landfill. Then put down a layer of black plastic and cover it with stones.

NO MORE CLOGGED GUTTERS

The small leaves from the locust trees near my house really clog the gutters. Do those newer (and more expensive) types of gutter protectors such as Gutter Pro and Gutter Helmet really work?

Solid guards, which cover all of the gutter except for a narrow crack to let the water through, do work well. The lip on the guards relies on surface tension to draw the water down into the gutter, while the solid covering deflects leaves and other debris that would otherwise drop in (**photo at right**).

Gutter Topper, Gutter Helmut and Gutter Pro are examples of companies that make solid guard covers. Any of these should keep you from having to clean your gutters again. The guards work on every type of gutter, except plastic "C" shapes. Since the guards fit over the gutter rather than inside, they'll cover most standard-size gutters. They're typically attached to the gutter with brackets, with the upper edge slid under the lower shingles.

As you noted, these systems are expensive. You can't buy them at home centers. They're usually professionally installed, which explains part of the higher cost. (Look

under "Gutters" in the yellow pages.) Screened gutter guards, which are much less expensive and available at home centers, don't work as well. They'll keep out most leaves, but you can expect smaller debris, such as seeds and pine needles, to get through. Screens also make gutter cleaning more difficult, because you have to move them aside to get at the debris. However, in some cases they may be all you need.

WATER DOWN THE CHIMNEY

Every time it rains, water drips down the chimney and accumulates inside the fireplace. We had a cap installed, but it didn't help. Do we have to seal the top of the chimney somehow?

You probably have a bad crown. The crown of a masonry chimney is a concrete top that ideally looks something like the one shown. It has an angled top to shed water and it overhangs the brick to keep drips off the chimney sides. It surrounds the clay flues but doesn't encase them. A 1/4-in. gap allows the clay flues to expand and contract from repeated heating and cooling without cracking (or cracking the crown). (The flues "float" inside the brick chimney walls; that is, they're supported by the brick but not attached to it.) A high-quality polyurethane caulk seals the flue/crown gap and prevents water penetration.

In truth, few chimneys built before the mid-1980s have crowns built this well. Many early crowns were simply sloped washes of leftover mortar. Most have cracked and deteriorated, opening gaps around the flues. If you feel safe and confident about walking on your roof, climb up and inspect the crown. If it's sound, caulk cracks and gaps

with polyurethane. Otherwise, hire a chimney builder ("Chimney Builders and Repair" in your yellow pages) or a chimney sweep ("Chimney Cleaning") certified by the Chimney Safety Institute to evaluate the condition of your chimney and fix it.

Flue caps will help reduce water coming down the flue itself, but they won't help much if you have a bad crown.

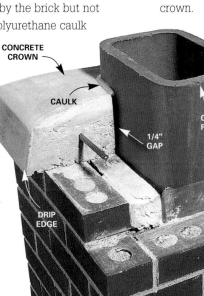

Typical Masonry Chimney

Labels: CONCRETE CROWN, CAULK, 1/4" GAP, CLAY FLUE, FURNACE VENT, DRIP EDGE

THE SEARCH FOR A ROOF LEAK

I've got a small water stain on my ceiling and I can't figure out where the water came from. I went up into the attic and checked the rafters and roof boards, but I can't find any staining or signs of leaks. Any ideas?

FROSTY NAIL

Roof leaks are often tough to locate. Sometimes the water shows up at a spot distant from the leak. If your ceiling has a plastic vapor barrier between the drywall and the attic insulation, push the insulation aside and look for flow stains on the plastic. Often water runs to openings in the vapor barrier, such as at ceiling light fixtures.

If you can't see any telltale flow marks, and since the stain is fairly small, look at the underside of the roof for "shiners." A shiner is a nail that missed the framing member. Moisture that escapes into the cold attic from the rooms below often condenses on cold nails. Sometimes you can spot this if you climb up into your attic on a cold night. The nails will look white because they're frosted. When the attic heats up a bit during the day, the frost melts and drips, then the nails frost up at night again and so on. The solution is to simply clip the nail with a side-cutting pliers.

Problem

PREVENTING ICE DAMS

I'm concerned about ice dams forming on my roof. Will deicing cables prevent ice dams and is there a downside to using them?

Deicing cables should work. Ice dams result from repeated cycles of thawing and freezing, which cause snow and ice to melt, then freeze along the roof edge. This "dam" traps water, allowing it to work under the shingles. Deicing cables heat the roof edge and keep it free of ice.

Install the cables along the roof edge where ice tends to build up (**photo below**). Attach the cables following the manufacturer's directions. Then simply plug them into a ground fault circuit interrupter receptacle after heavy snowfalls or when you see ice dams beginning to form. These cables are available at select hardware stores and home centers, starting at $35. Systems that include sensors that turn on automatically cost $100 and up. One brand is Easy Heat (800-537-4732, www.easyheat.com).

The only downsides are the cost of electricity (which is small for a standard cable used intermittently), and routing the draining water away so it doesn't freeze and build up at the end of the downspout.

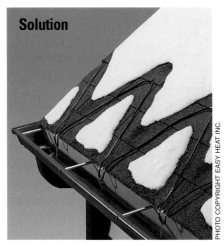

Solution

LEAKING ROOF

Our ceiling leaks under this section of roof whenever we have a severe rain and in the winter after heavy snowfalls. How do we stop it?

You're getting a double whammy from poor flashing and ice dams. The culprit is almost certainly the soffit that meets the roof, which is one of the toughest areas to waterproof. In your photo, you can still see signs of an ice dam. An ice dam occurs when snow melts and the water freezes when it hits the colder edges of your roof. Eventually, water pools behind the dam and works its way back up under the shingles and under the soffit until it finds an opening through your roof. The fact that you get leaks during severe rain also suggests a roof detailing problem.

Start with good flashing, since this should stop leaks from rainfall and might stop the leaks from ice dams as well. Begin by removing the shingles down to the wood sheathing and slip a strip of adhesive ice-and-water barrier (available where roofing products are sold) under the soffit/main roof joint. Depending on how the roofs join, you may have to cut a slot to work it in far enough. It should overlap another piece of ice-and-water barrier laid below, all the way down to the roof edge. This should cover the most leak-prone areas. Then reshingle, sliding metal step flashing behind the fascia board (the trim behind the gutter). The valley flashing, laid over the joint where the two roofs meet, should overlap the step flashing at least 2 in.

If leaks continue to occur from ice dams, consider installing roof edge heating cables. (Find them locally at hardware stores or home centers, or try the source given at left.) Improved attic insulation and ventilation are usually the best ways to prevent ice dams, but they might not be effective in this complicated roof situation.

6 Outdoor Structures & Landscaping

IN THIS CHAPTER

CONCRETE
GARDEN BENCH

*Make two simple forms, add three bags of concrete
and you'll have a bench in two weekends!*

by **David Radtke**

I n the mood to create something timeless and beautiful
for your garden? Build this fun three-piece concrete
bench a little at a time over the course of a week or so.
You can give it a unique personal design and then sit and
enjoy it for a lifetime.

All you have to do is build simple plywood forms, mix
and pour your own concrete to fill them, and then install
the bench in your favorite garden spot. You can build the
plywood and hardboard forms over the weekend, buy three
80-lb. bags of dry concrete mix, pour the forms after a few
days and wait for the magic. You can follow the
plan exactly as shown to learn the
process and then experiment with your
own shapes and designs.

The concrete forms for this bench are
not only cheap but also reusable. You'll spend
about $40 for form material and hardware. I
found I could make about five benches from a
single set of forms before they started to
deteriorate. And with concrete at $4 per
bag, this is one inexpensive project.

The bench details come from panels
built into the forms that appear as recesses
once the form is poured. You can leave the
recesses empty to create lines and shadow or fill them
with tile or stone to add color and texture. Note, however,
that you can raise the cost substantially if you buy fancy tile
or stone. I spent about $50 for the cut stone mortared into

the top recess, but you can achieve similar results using
bulk flat river stones, which are available from landscape
suppliers for a fraction of the cost. You can also use ceramic
tile, even broken tile, to create a unique personal design.

You can complete the project with ordinary carpentry
tools, including a circular saw and a jigsaw. But a table
saw would be helpful to cut the thin 1-in.-wide strips of
hardboard for the details in the form. Also, a wheelbarrow
is handy for mixing the concrete, but if you don't have one,
you can buy a tough plastic bin at a home center.

Get the right stuff

Our local home center sells 2 x 4-ft. panels of plywood and
hardboard next to the full-size sheet goods (plywood and
paneling). These small, easy-to-handle
sheets are all you need for this
project. Make sure to get standard
hardboard, not tempered, for this
project. Tempered hardboard has a very
hard, slick surface that won't make the tight
bends you'll need for the curved pieces on the
two leg forms.

Not all concrete mixes are
the same. For this project, use
only Quikrete or Sakrete 5,000-lb.
concrete. If you can't find it at
your home center or hardware store,
call (800) 282-5828 for a dealer near you.

Figure A: Seat Details

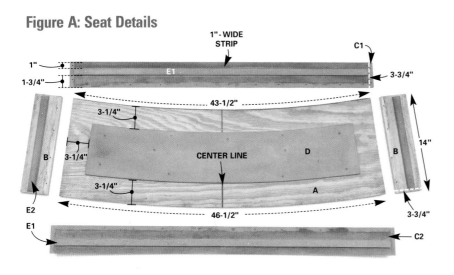

1"- WIDE STRIP · C1 · 1" · E1 · 3-3/4" · 1-3/4" · 43-1/2" · 3-1/4" · 3-1/4" · CENTER LINE · D · B · B · 14" · 3-1/4" · A · 3-1/4" · 46-1/2" · 3-3/4" · E2 · E1 · C2

Figure B: Leg Details

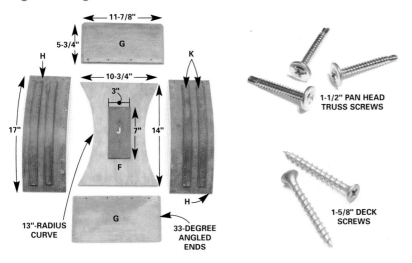

11-7/8" · 5-3/4" · G · H · K · 10-3/4" · 3" · J · 7" · 14" · 17" · F · H · G · 1-1/2" PAN HEAD TRUSS SCREWS · 13"-RADIUS CURVE · 33-DEGREE ANGLED ENDS · 1-5/8" DECK SCREWS

Ordinary twine works great for marking the curves

Find a large, wide-open space like a garage floor or a flat driveway to mark the curve onto the base of the seat form. Tape to your floor a large washer (**Photo 1**) with a length of twine tied to it. Draw a center line on the 2 x 4-ft. piece of 3/4-in. plywood as shown. Align the plywood so the taut twine falls right over the center line. Be sure the far edge of the plywood is 12 ft. 6 in. from the washer. Tie the pencil to the twine at this distance and scribe a curve along the whole length of plywood, keeping the twine taut. Next, scribe another arc

14 in. shorter than this onto the plywood. Now look at the dimensions on **Figure A**, above, and mark the outer sides of the plywood. Cut out the shape with your jigsaw and sand any irregularities along the curve with your belt sander.

Next, measure each end of the form base and cut the end pieces (B) from the other sheet of plywood. Predrill and screw these to the base (**Photo 2**). Next cut the 3-3/4-in.-wide sides from 1/4-in. hardboard, predrill them every 4 in. and screw them to the form base with pan head truss screws (see detail).

Scribe the inner 1/4-in. panel (**Photo 3**) to the curve of the seat,

OUTDOOR STRUCTURES & LANDSCAPING

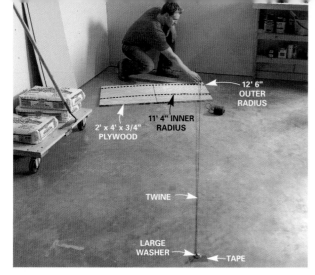

1 USING a pencil and twine, scribe the two concentric arcs onto a sheet of 2 x 4-ft. plywood to form the basic shape of the bench. The two arcs should be 14 in. apart.

2 SCREW 3/4-in. plywood ends (B) to the form base with 1-5/8-in. deck screws. Then cut strips of 1/4-in. standard hardboard, predrill pilot holes and screw them to the sides of the form base (A) and to the form ends (B). Use 1-1/2-in. truss screws.

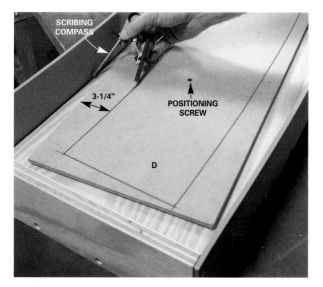

3 CUT a piece of 1/4-in. hardboard and screw it to the seat form with a pair of 3/4-in. screws. Then scribe the panel with a compass to mark an equal reveal on each side. Remove the panel, cut it to the line, then glue and screw it to the seat form base (A).

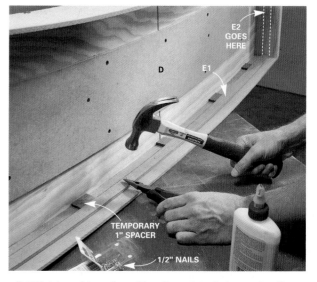

4 RIP 1-in.-wide strips of hardboard and glue and nail them to the middle of the form sides to form the edge recesses in the bench top. Use water-resistant glue.

then glue and screw it to the base of the form (this will form a recess in the top of the bench once you pour the concrete). If you plan to make a deeper recess, use 3/8-in. plywood instead. This may work out better if you plan to use thicker tile or stone for your inlay. Be aware, however, that any panel thicker than 3/8 in. will make it tougher to remove the form from the concrete.

To finish the seat form, rip strips from 1/4-in. hardboard

and then glue and nail them to the form sides with 1/2-in. wire nails, which are available at any hardware store (**Photo 4**).

Soak the hardboard for the leg forms in water overnight

Cut the pieces of 1/4-in. hardboard for the sides to the dimensions in the Cutting List. The lengths for the sides (H) are about 1 in. longer than needed, so it'll be easier to fasten them to the curved base bottom and the sides. You can trim them after assembly. Soaking makes them flexible enough to conform to the 13-in.-radius arc in the leg form.

Before you assemble the form, cut the base (F) and ends (G) to the dimensions in **Figure B**, p. 205. Predrill and screw the sides to the base using 1-5/8-in. deck screws.

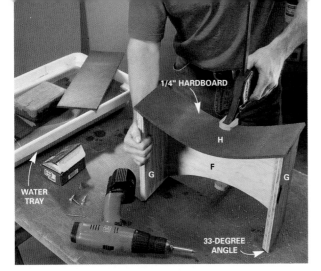

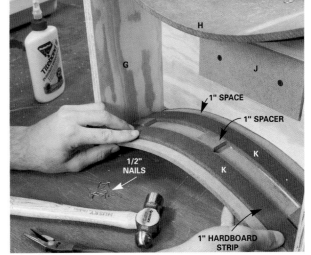

5 SOAK the leg form sides (H) and the strips (K) overnight. The next day, assemble a pair of leg forms. Clamp the center of the hardboard side and gently squeeze it to the curved base of the leg form. Then screw it into place with truss screws.

6 FIT 1-in.-wide hardboard strips to the inside of the leg form to make recesses in the leg fronts and backs. Let the curved side pieces dry for two hours for better glue adhesion before installing strips. Tack them in place with 1/2-in. nails. Let the form and strips dry overnight, then disassemble.

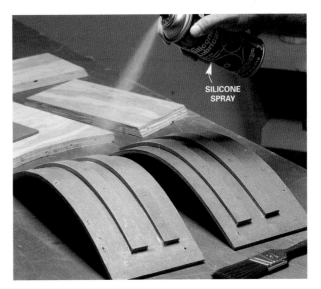

7 BRUSH ON two coats of polyurethane varnish or shellac to protect the insides of all the forms. It's best to take apart the form to get the entire surface.

8 SPRAY the entire inner surface of all the forms with a silicone spray lubricant. When the lubricant beads up, brush it into an even layer with a paintbrush.

You'll notice the angle cut on each end of G is about 33 degrees. You can cut this by setting your circular saw at a 33-degree bevel and then using a square as a guide against the foot of the saw to end-cut it square. Don't fuss about the 33-degree angle. If it's off by a couple of degrees either way, it'll still work out.

Grab the wet hardboard out of the soaking tank (a laundry tub works great) and set it onto the form (**Photo 5**). Gently squeeze the clamp onto the form until it bends into position. Then predrill and screw it every 1-1/2 in. along the curve. Work one screw at a time from the center out to keep the bottoms flush. Once you've fastened the long edge, screw the sides to the end pieces (G). Check the end pieces with a framing square to make sure they're square to the base (F). Complete the other side and then the second

leg form using the same method. Let the hardboard air-dry for about three hours before gluing and nailing the hardboard strips (K), as shown in **Photo 6**.

Remove the thin 1-in. hardboard strips (K) from the soaking tank. Cut them to length so they fit snugly into the corners against the ends (G). Next, glue the bottom and nail them into place as shown in **Photo 6**. Use the 1-in. spacers as shown to get them positioned properly. Let the strips and glue dry for several hours before the next step.

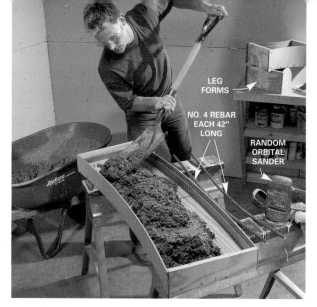

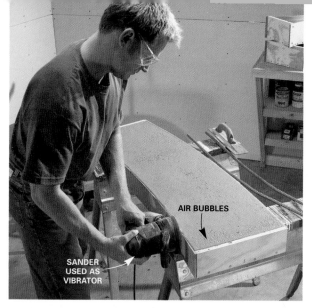

9 MIX the special concrete mix to the consistency of oatmeal. It should clump and settle a bit as you dump it into the form.

10 BOUNCE the forms a few times onto the tops of the sawhorses at each end to settle the concrete. Then hold a vibrating sander firmly along the entire perimeter of the forms and vibrate until you get air bubbles to appear (about two minutes).

11 POUND the rebar into the concrete as soon as you're finished vibrating it. Push it about 1-1/2 in. below the surface. You'll notice this fast-setting concrete getting stiff already.

12 FLOAT an even surface to the tops of the forms. Add a little concrete if necessary. Now wet the concrete left in the wheelbarrow and add the other bag, mix and pour the leg forms. Let it harden for two days.

Seal the forms before pouring concrete

When the forms are completely dry, label each piece and disassemble them. To help your forms release better later, ease the sharp inside edges with 100-grit sandpaper. Lay the pieces out on a workbench and brush two coats of waterborne polyurethane on the inside of all the forms. Let them dry for two hours.

Now you'll need to apply a lubricant to help release the forms from the hardened concrete. You can use silicone spray, vegetable oil or paste wax. We used silicone spray with good results. When you spray the silicone, it'll have a tendency to bead up on the polyurethane. To break the

surface tension of the liquid, brush it after spraying until it smooths out into a uniform coat. Let the surface dry to the touch and then screw the forms together. Next cut two lengths of rebar to 42 in. and prebend them to follow the curve of the form. Set them aside.

Mix the concrete to a stiff consistency

Set your forms onto sawhorses as shown in Photo 9. This special concrete sets up a bit faster than normal, so cancel all appointments and avoid distractions. Mix two bags of concrete to a firm but fluid consistency. Shovel the concrete into the large seat form to about two-thirds full, then

13 LAY the seat onto a pair of blocks, unscrew the sides and remove the forms piece by piece. The top is tricky to get off. To loosen it, gently pry it up, working your way around the form. Pull the top free and clean the forms for your next bench.

grab one end of the form and lift it a few inches and drop it onto the sawhorse. Do this several times on each end to settle the concrete and work it into the form. Now fill the form and then use a float to level the top. Next load your vibrating sander or random orbital sander with 100-grit sandpaper and place it firmly on each side for about 30 seconds each. The vibration from the sander will bring all the trapped air bubbles to the top. Now, grab your rebar lengths and insert them into the form as shown in **Photo 11**. Tap the rebar into the mix about 1-1/2 in. deep with a stiff-blade scraper. When both rebar pieces are submerged, smooth the top again even with the top edge of the forms (**Photo 12**) and let the mix harden.

You'll have a bit of concrete left in your wheelbarrow. Dump the next bag right in with it, add water and mix it again. Fill the leg forms to the top in the same way, vibrate them with your sander and level the tops. Let the concrete set for two days before you continue.

Remove the forms

The concrete seat top inside the form is heavy. Carefully lift the seat form and place it on your workbench upside down with some scraps of wood beneath it to elevate it above the worktop. Remove all the screws that hold the form pieces together. Remove the long hardboard sides first and then gently pry the ends away from the concrete.

The top piece of the seat form is the most challenging. Tap the stiff-blade scraper in between the top of the form and the concrete. Wiggle the blade back and forth, moving from corner to corner to coax the form free. Once the form is removed, use a concrete-sanding block to ease the edges (**Photo 15**).

To remove the forms on the leg pieces, start with the 3/4-in. plywood ends, then move to the flexible hardboard

14 POSITION the legs onto a solid patio or slab. Turn them in slightly to a pigeon-toed look and set the top onto the legs. Adjust the legs so the seat overhangs the legs about 6 in. on each side. Glue the legs to the top with landscape block adhesive.

15 EASE any sharp edges with an abrasive block, which is sold at tile stores and concrete suppliers. Work slowly and use a light touch.

sides and gently pry, being careful not to force the form from the concrete. You may need to slide a screwdriver into the grooves of the recesses to pry out the strips.

Finishing touches

You can now add tile or stone to your bench or leave it as is. To set up your bench, set the legs onto a level, stable base. The legs should be arranged about 6 in. in from the edge of the seat top and pigeon-toed slightly to follow the curve. Use landscape block adhesive to fasten the legs to the patio stones or other stable base. Then apply it to the tops of the legs to fasten the seat (**Photo 14**). Let it set up for a day before you use your bench.

SPRINKLER HEAD

RISER

RELOCATE A SPRINKLER HEAD

Could you show how to move a sprinkler head? I had to replace the one next to my driveway twice last year because it was run over.

First decide where you want the sprinkler head. You can move it up to 4 ft. with flex pipe (available at plumbing and irrigation supply stores) without affecting performance. Dig an 8- to 12-in.-deep trench from the current head location to the new location. Turn off the irrigation system at the controller. Unscrew the sprinkler head from the riser (**Photo 1**) and then unscrew the riser. Insert a flex pipe elbow into the existing combination elbow or riser tee. Tighten the elbow until it's hand-tight. Then attach a 3/8-in. flex pipe to the flex pipe elbow by sliding it over the nipple (the flex pipe has a smaller diameter than the water line pipe). The connection doesn't require clamps.

Fasten a flex pipe elbow to the other end of the pipe. Place the sprinkler head on the elbow, then turn it until it's hand-tight. Hold the sprinkler head in the location you want it. The top of the head should be at ground level. Backfill around the head with your free hand (**Photo 2**). Once the head is secure, fill in the trench and replace the sod.

NEW SPRINKLER HEAD LOCATION

SPRINKLER HEAD

FLEX PIPE

OLD SPRINKLER HEAD LOCATION

FLEX PIPE ELBOW

COMBINATION ELBOW

GAPS BETWEEN DECK BOARDS

You recommended leaving 1/8 in. between deck boards, but a contractor friend said to butt them tight. Who's right?

One of the great debates in deck building is how much space to leave between deck boards. Some builders say to butt them tightly together because they'll shrink within a few months and leave a nice 1/8-in. gap. Others say to gap the boards about 1/8 in. right off.

The answer, of course, depends on the moisture content of the boards you start with, because wood shrinks as it dries. If the boards are soaking wet (wet all the way through when you cut one), butt them together, edge to edge. If they're mostly dry (moisture around the center only), leave a 1/8-in. gap.

To illustrate the problem, we purchased 5/4-in. treated deck boards right off the rack at a local home center. They were heavy (one sign of high moisture content) and were wet all the way through when we cut them. We confirmed that they were wet with a moisture meter reading of 20 percent. We screwed the boards to a couple of joists, butting them tightly together (**photo above left**).

After two weeks of sitting inside, the boards had started to dry and shrink, opening 1/8-in. gaps. In just six weeks, the gaps had increased to about 1/4 in. (**photo**

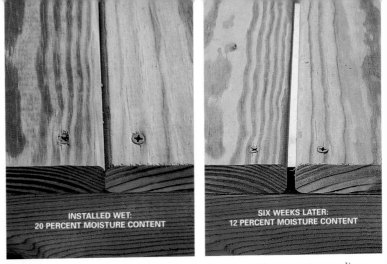

INSTALLED WET: 20 PERCENT MOISTURE CONTENT

SIX WEEKS LATER: 12 PERCENT MOISTURE CONTENT

above right). At that point, the moisture meter reading was about 12 percent (which is considered "air dry" in most climates). If we had gapped the boards 1/8 in. when we screwed them in place, the gap when dry would have been too wide and visually unacceptable.

Although the wood species and the way the wood is cut affect the amount of shrinkage a bit, the most important factor is moisture content. Since you aren't likely to have a moisture meter, be sure to crosscut several boards to see if they're wet all the way through. If so, butt them tightly. If the cross section is only a bit damp or wet near the center, gap the boards. Sometimes you can buy pressure-treated wood that's stamped "KDAT." This means "kiln dried after treatment," usually to 15 percent. You can gap these boards with reasonable assurance that they'll remain stable. Premium deck boards, like cedar, are often kiln dried as well, but ask when you buy or look for a kiln-dried stamp or label.

BURROWING CHIPMUNKS

I have a problem with chipmunks burrowing around the stoop at the front entryway of my home. How can I keep the little critters from digging there again?

You're experiencing a common problem that's now occurring in the city as well as in the suburbs and rural areas. Chipmunks typically start their tunnels next to something solid, such as front steps or sidewalks, and burrow under it for protection.

To keep the critters out, bury a strip of hardware cloth 2 ft. deep in the ground around the steps and along the sidewalk. Chipmunks won't be able to get through it and they won't dig down far enough to get under it. You

can buy 2-ft.-wide strips of hardware cloth at home centers, so you won't have to cut it.

If your chipmunk problem persists and they start to dig somewhere else on your property, simply catch them in live traps and relocate them away from residential areas.

FIRST AID FOR YOUR **LAWN**

Five remedies for your hurting turf

by **Lucie B. Amundsen**

Even the best lawns could use a little therapeutic attention now and again. To help you pull yours out of the rough patches, we've put together the best remedies for the most common turf maladies. We'll also tell you how to improve your lawn's natural defenses and reduce future maintenance chores.

USING a garden hoe, work up the shady area to remove any struggling grass. Plant ground cover or a shade garden.

PROBLEM: **SHADE**

■ **Symptoms:** Shaded grass will look thin and patchy. Some types of grass actually produce wider blades as the plant attempts to catch more rays. But they also produce fewer blades, resulting in a spindly appearance. The truth is, if your lawn gets less than six to eight hours of sun daily, you are unlikely to sustain lush grass.

■ **Cause:** Trees, buildings and bushes.

An Ounce of Prevention

Avoid the frustration of sun-starved grass by starting a shade garden or ground cover in any area that doesn't receive six to eight hours of good light.

■ **Remedy:** There are no good remedies. You can increase the sunlight as much as possible by trimming trees and shrubs. Also try starting areas in shade with sod instead of seed. The sod will adjust to the lower level of light. Although all seed varieties have their shade limitations, try overseeding your thin area with a shady grass mix.

Or throw in the towel, grab your trowel and plant a shade-tolerant ground cover. Many will thrive where your turf withered. Lamium (dead nettle) and ajuga (bugleweed) collaborate nicely in providing lovely blooms and an enthusiastic, but not invasive, carpet. This pair fares well, with a hearty tolerance spanning zones 3 to 8, and can be planted right up to your grass. They are fairly low growers and won't get more than a few nicks from a lawn mower.

Also, mulching between the ground cover plants will help retain moisture. This is especially wise if your new "shade garden" is on a slope; mulch will help prevent your fledging plants from washing out in a hard rain.

■ **Recovery time:** The plants and mulch will immediately boost the appearance of an area that was once thin grass. It'll take a couple of seasons for the ground cover to become established and blanket the area.

PROBLEM: DOG SPOTS ON GRASS

■ **Symptoms:** Dog spots are round patches about 4 to 8 in. in diameter with dead grass in the middle, encircled by dark green grass. They're most apparent in the early spring when dormant grass first begins to turn green again.

■ **Cause:** Dog urine contains high concentrations of acids, salts and nitrogen, which burn (dry out) the grass roots and kill them. As rain washes the area, the urine is diluted and the nitrogen spreads, causing the grass surrounding the spot to grow faster and turn greener.

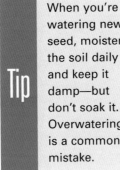

Tip When you're watering new seed, moisten the soil daily and keep it damp—but don't soak it. Overwatering is a common mistake.

■ **Remedy:** You have to replant your grass; it won't come back on its own. But first you have to dilute or remove the caustic urine from the soil (**Photo 1**). Thoroughly soak the area with lots of water. Let the hose run for at least three minutes. Then you can start the replanting process (**Photo 2**). Add a half inch of new soil to help absorb any remaining urine (**Photo 3**). Then you can spread new seed, as we show, or use a commercial yard patch mixture (available at most nurseries or home centers) or even sod. In any case, the secret of good germination is keeping the seed moist. And keep the area moist until the new grass is about 3 in. high.

■ **Recovery time:** Four to six weeks

An Ounce of Prevention

1. Soak your pet's favorite areas in your lawn to get the salts out of the root zone before they kill the grass.
2. Fertilize your lawn in the spring to boost the overall color and mask the darker green dog spots.
3. Train your pet to urinate in a designated area. Replace or repair the grass in this area annually or cover it with mulch.
4. Keep your pet well hydrated to make its urine less concentrated.
5. Become a cat person.

1 SOAK the patch until the grass is sopping wet to dilute the urine acids and salts and wash them deeper into the soil, beyond the grass roots.

2 SCRAPE up the dead grass with a hand rake and remove it. Rough up the area to loosen the soil 1/2 in. deep. Seeds germinate better in soft soil.

3 SPRINKLE on a 1/2-in.-thick layer of topsoil, then pepper it with grass seed. Cover with a pinch of new soil and press it to firm it up. Keep the area moist until the new grass is about 3 in. high.

PROBLEM: THATCH

■ **Symptoms:** If your grass feels soft and spongy when you walk on it, your lawn may have a thatch buildup. Thatch is a fibrous mat of dead stalks and roots that settles between the lawn's green leaves and the soil (**photo right**). When this mat becomes greater than 3/4 in. thick, it can cause your lawn to suffer from heat and drought. Affected lawns will rapidly wilt and turn blue-green, indicating they're hot and dry.

■ **Cause:** Cutting off too much at each mowing (letting the grass get too long) and cutting too low. Both will produce more dead grass tissue than microbes and earthworms can recycle. Thatch can develop in any soil but is most often associated with high clay content. Other causes are over-fertilization and frequent, light watering, which encourage a shallow root system.

■ **Remedy:** Slice open a section of your lawn (**Photo 1**). If your grass shows 3/4 in. or more of thatch, it's time to rent an aerator (about $70 per day). An aerator is a heavy machine that opens the soil by pulling up finger-size soil cores. The lawn will absorb more oxygen and water, which will encourage healthy microbe growth and give worms wiggle room.

Aerate in the spring or fall when the grass is growing but the weather is not too hot to stress the plants (**Photo 2**). If the machine isn't pulling plugs, your lawn may be too dry. To avoid this problem, water thoroughly the day before you aerate. You can also rake in topsoil (**Photo 3**) to increase the healthy microorganisms that aid thatch's natural decomposition. Topsoil is available at any garden center.

■ **Recovery time:** You can expect the thatch layer to decrease by about 1/4 in. per year, about the same rate at which it forms.

An Ounce of Prevention

1. **Mow often and cut no more than one-third of the grass height.**
2. **Water your lawn less often but for longer periods to prevent shallow root systems.**
3. **Reduce the amount of fertilizer you spread at any one time.**
4. **Reduce the use of pesticides. This will help keep the worm and microorganism populations healthy.**
5. **Aerate at least once every year if your lawn is prone to thatch.**

CAUTION: Call your local utility provider or 1-888-258-0808 to mark your underground utility lines before you aerate.

1 SLICE the turf grass with a shovel and pry it back. If the thatch depth measures more than 3/4 in., aerate at least 3 in. deep.

2 MAKE two or three passes with an aerator until you've made 3-in.-deep holes 2 in. apart throughout your yard.

3 SPREAD 1/4 in. of topsoil on the yard's most thatchy areas and then rake vigorously to fill the holes with loose soil.

PROBLEM: GRUBS

■ **Symptoms:** Grub-chewed turf has patchy areas that wilt and die. You can easily pull up the affected turf if you tug on it. Another indicator of grubs may be increased raccoon, bird or mole activity. They like to dig up and eat the grubs at night. While this may sound good, the moles will kill the grass as they forage for grubs.

■ **Cause:** Lawn grubs are the larval stage of moths and beetles. The grubs eat the roots of grass, setting them up for death by dehydration.

■ **Remedy:** Be vigilant. Are beetles swarming around your porch light? In the next month, keep an eye out for patches of grass that wilt or are blue-green on hot days. They may be larvae infested. Turn over some turf (**Photo 1**). If you count six to 10 grubs (white worm-like larvae with black heads) under a 1-ft.-square area of sod, consider using a grub insecticide (available at home centers and nurseries). Or talk to a professional ("Grass Service" in your yellow pages) about treating your yard. They will be familiar with the grub problems in your region and the most suitable treatment methods.

If you spot the grubs but your count is lower than six per square foot, baby your lawn to strengthen its natural defenses. Mow on higher blade settings and water thoroughly but infrequently to encourage the grass to grow new, deep roots. Do not cut off more than one-third of the grass height at each mowing, to avoid stressing the plant.

Tip
A grub problem is often indicated by increased mole, bird and raccoon activity. They dig up and feed on grubs at night. This may sound good, but moles kill your grass along with the grubs.

Renting a lawn aerator

If your goal is to have one of the nicest lawns on the block, you can go a long way toward achieving it with annual aeration.

When a lawn lacks sufficient air (a "compacted" condition), it grows slowly and becomes vulnerable to disease, insects and heat damage. The soil will become impermeable and shed water instead of absorbing it.

Gas-powered aerators are available at most tool rental stores. They're slow-moving but powerful machines, so ask the clerk for handling directions. An aerator weighs about 200 lbs., so be prepared for some heavy lifting or ask your rental store for a ramp to get it into a truck bed or van.

Cool-season grasses should be aerated in the late summer or early fall. Spring is best for warm-season types. (If you're not sure what type you have, take a sample to an expert at a local garden center.)

Resist the temptation to remove the thatch with a rented power rake. Power raking is less effective than aerating because it typically removes less than 15 percent of thatch and may damage the healthy grass as well.

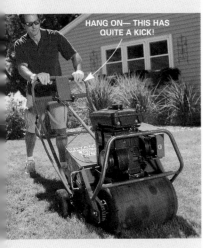

HANG ON— THIS HAS QUITE A KICK!

An Ounce of Prevention

Inspect your turf periodically by pulling on patches that look unhealthy, or have a professional inspect your lawn if you suspect a problem.

GRUBS

1 PIERCE lawn with a shovel in a U-shape. Peel back the lawn (as though rolling up a rug) and count the white grubs in a 1-sq.-ft. area.

2 TREAT your lawn with an insecticide if the count is six to 10 grubs in a square foot. Follow the manufacturer's directions carefully. Or consult with a yard service.

PROBLEM: FAIRY RING

■ **Symptoms:** Fairy rings are circles approximately 3 to 8 ft. wide that consist of a dark green and fast-growing area of grass surrounding an inner area of partially dead or thin grass. Some rings also produce mushrooms.

■ **Cause:** Fairy rings are caused by fungi that live in the soil. As the fungi feed on organic matter, they release nitrogen, causing the grass to turn dark green. As the colony grows, it disturbs the flow of needed water to the turf roots, creating thin or dead spots. Fairy rings often begin with the decomposition of organic matter, such as an old tree stump buried under the lawn.

■ **Remedy:** By bringing up the color in the rest of your lawn with a nitrogen fertilizer, you can mask much of the overgreening of the fairy ring (**Photo 1**). Hand-aerating the ring will break up the fungus and allow the flow of water and other nutrients to the grass roots (**Photo 2**).

■ **Recovery time:** Generally fairy rings can be masked with the application of fertilizer, with results in 10 to 14 days. The grass within the ring will thicken up with aeration in about two to three weeks. 🏠

Consultants • DR. HENRY WILKINSON, TURF PATHOLOGIST; PROF. ROBERT MUGAAS and BETH JARVIS, UNIVERSITY OF MINNESOTA EXTENSION

An Ounce of Prevention

Aeration will help with fairy rings, but maintaining a healthy lawn with a balanced fertilization program is essential. Apply three doses:
1. Apply 1/2 lb. per 1,000 sq. ft. in late April or early May to give the overwintering grass roots a bit of a boost.
2. Add no more than 1/2 lb. per 1,000 sq. ft. at the end of June or in early July when temperatures are not at their peak. Stimulating growth during a heat wave will stress the plants.
3. Spread 1 lb. per 1,000 sq. ft. at the end of October. The best root growth takes place when the soil temps are between 58 and 65 degrees F. The roots store energy over the winter, making the entire lawn healthier the following spring.

DO NOT FERTILIZE THE RING ITSELF

1 SPREAD 1/2 lb. of nitrogen fertilizer per 1,000 sq. ft. to green up your lawn, but skip the fairy ring zone. This masks the lush green of the fairy ring by blending it into the rest of your yard.

CORE PLUGS

2 BREAK UP the fungi with a hand aerator ($20 at a home center or garden store). Punch holes every 2 to 4 in. throughout the ring and 2 ft. beyond.

DECAYING WOOD

3 GO "treasure" hunting if you see no improvement in three weeks. Dig out rotting stumps, roots, construction debris or other organic materials under your lawn.

SharpenYourSkills

SHARPEN A MOWER BLADE

One of the best ways to encourage a greener, fuller and healthier lawn is to sharpen your lawn mower blade. A dull blade rips and pulls the grass blades, leaving ragged tears that both weaken the plant and promote fungal growth and other grass diseases. A sharp blade, on the other hand, cuts cleanly, allowing the plant to heal and recover quickly. Sharp blades also let you complete your lawn-cutting chore faster and with less stress on the mower.

Sharpening is a simple task, even for a novice. It'll take a few sharpenings to master the technique. After that, the chore will take less than 10 minutes. Plan to do it twice every mowing season. We show here the steps that will work for just about any walk-behind mower. Riding mowers require different blade removal techniques, which we won't show here.

Mark your new blade

SPRAY PAINT

Mark your blade with spray paint before you remove it so you know which way to reinstall it. Mower repair pros say that the biggest mistake homeowners make is installing a blade upside down after sharpening it. The blade won't cut—and they'll go nuts trying to figure out why!

1 PULL the spark plug wire from the spark plug to prevent the motor from accidentally starting. Tape or tie it back so it doesn't flop back into contact with the plug.

Play it safe when removing the blade

We recommend always removing the spark plug wire before you touch the blade (Photo 1). The blade and shaft are directly connected to the motor, and in some cases turning the blade by hand could cause the motor to fire.

Then look for the carburetor and air filter. The carburetor is usually easy to recognize because it has throttle cables running to it. If you keep this side up when you tip your mower over to get at the blade (Photo 2), you won't get a smoke cloud from leaking oil the next time you start it. Some mowers have gas caps with air holes that could leak a little gas onto your garage floor, so work outside or keep a rag handy to clean up drips. Once the blade is off, set the mower back onto all four wheels until you're ready to reinstall your blade.

OUTDOOR STRUCTURES & LANDSCAPING

Sharpen Your Skills

AIR FILTER

2 TURN the mower onto its side with the air filter and carburetor side up. This keeps oil and gas from dripping into the air filter.

BLADE WEDGED

3 WEDGE a short 2x4 between the blade and the deck to clamp the blade. Loosen the bolt (or nut) with a long-handled wrench. Turn counterclockwise. Remove the bolt and blade.

You'll usually find a single bolt or nut holding the blade on. It's usually very tight and you'll need to clamp the blade to loosen it. The 2x4 method we show (**Photo 3**) is simple, quick and safe. Don't use your foot! A good tool to keep handy to loosen the bolt is a 10-in. breaker bar with a socket to match the bolt. It'll give you plenty of leverage to loosen extremely tight bolts, and you can keep your knuckles well away from the blade when bearing down. Use a squirt of penetrating oil on really rusted, stuck bolts. Wait 10 minutes to give it time to work.

Sharpen it with a file

Once you remove the blade, examine it to determine whether to sharpen it or replace it. (See "Do You Need a New Blade?" at right.) We recommend that you sharpen it with a hand file (**Photo 4**). Mower blades are made from fairly soft steel. You can sharpen most with fewer than 50 strokes of a clean, sharp "mill bastard" file that's at least 10 in. long. Grinders also work, and much more quickly. (Pros use them.) But they're more difficult to control and you might overheat and ruin the blade.

Tip Keep a second blade on hand. The store will probably be closed when you need it!

Always sharpen from the top side of the cutting edge; this will give you the longest-lasting edge on the blade. The file cuts in one direction only, on the push stroke; you'll feel it bite into the steel on the blade. If you don't feel that cutting action, your file is probably dull or you're not pressing down hard enough. Don't try to make your

Do you need a new blade?

Examine your blade when you remove it and look for the problems shown. If you're unsure of the condition of the blade, take it to a hardware store or home center and compare it with a new one.

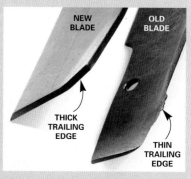

NEW BLADE | OLD BLADE
THICK TRAILING EDGE | THIN TRAILING EDGE

Thin trailing edge
The trailing edge, or fin, is the edge opposite the cutting edge. This fin is often slanted upward, which creates an updraft to lift the grass and grass clippings. Dust and sand will wear this fin down. When it's thin, replace the blade.

NEW BLADE

Bent
Set your old blade on your workbench and check for bends. If you're unsure, compare it with a new blade.

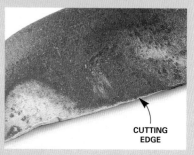

CUTTING EDGE

Dents in cutting edge
Replace blades that have deep dents that you can't file out and erosion from wear and sharpening. Also replace any blade that has cracked.

218

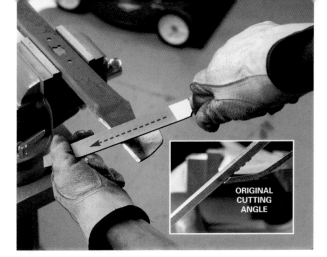

4 CLAMP the blade in a vise and sharpen the cutting edge with a mill bastard file, held at the same cutting angle as before. File until the blade is "butter knife" sharp.

ORIGINAL CUTTING ANGLE

5 HANG the blade on a nail to check the balance. If one side dips, file a bit more off that side until the blade remains horizontal.

NAIL

blade razor sharp; it'll dull more quickly. "Butter knife" sharp will do.

Sharpening mulching blades is sometimes more difficult. (See "Buying a New Blade," below right.) Mulching blades may have longer or curved cutting edges, and you may need several types of files to sharpen them. In some cases, you may have to resort to a 4-1/2-in. angle grinder. If your blade is too difficult to sharpen, take it to a hardware store or a blade sharpening service. You can have it sharpened for about $6.

Balance it before reinstalling

Before you reinstall the blade, be sure to balance it. An unbalanced blade will cause vibration and possibly ruin the blade shaft or bearings. To check the balance, simply drive a nail into a stud and set the blade onto it like an airplane propeller (Photo 5). If one side falls, it's heavier, and you have to file more metal off it. Keep filing until the blade stays level.

Reinstall the blade and hand-tighten the bolt. Insert the 2x4 in the reverse direction so you can bear down on the breaker bar to tighten the bolt. It's difficult to overtighten the bolt. Mower sharpening pros say that the second most common mistake they see is undertightening the bolt. A loose blade throws off the engine timing and sometimes makes the mower hard to start.

No excuses!
To get in the habit of keeping your blade sharp, dedicate a set of tools for sharpening only. Hang them nearby so they're ready to go. And keep a second, sharp blade handy too. You can slip it on and sharpen the dull one later.

BREAKER BAR

6 REINSTALL the blade and screw in the bolt. Then wedge the 2x4 back in and tighten the bolt firmly with your socket and breaker bar.

Buying a new blade

Always replace your blade with an exact replacement blade, or the blade recommended in your owner's manual. Resist the temptation to convert your regular straight-blade mower to a fancier mulching mower by simply changing the blade. Your mower probably won't work any differently than before, and it may not work as well. The mower deck on a straight-blade mower is shallow and has a side discharge to eject the grass clippings quickly. A mulching mower has a deeper deck without a side discharge; the grass is chopped three or four times before it drops to the ground. The mower design is as important as the blade.

REGULAR BLADE

MULCHING BLADE

GreatGoofs®

Blower-bag bungle

I was house-sitting for friends who have several huge trees in their yard, and I decided to take on the leaf cleanup. My dad's new leaf blower/vacuum seemed like just the right tool to suck up the leaves.

Leaves had collected on a porch off the kitchen, so I looked for an outlet, found one just inside the doorway and started vacuuming. The blower/vac sucked up the pile of leaves instantly. Then I caught something out of the corner of my eye: Mulched leaves were flying through the kitchen like confetti. I had forgotten to zip up the bag before starting the machine. I could only clean up the mess, laugh and swear never to tell anyone.

Lattice lesson

After finishing my porch deck, I decided it needed a skirt to hide the ugly footings. After cutting a couple of 4 x 8-ft. lattice sheets to size, I crawled underneath the deck to nail them up. Relieved that the job was nearly done, I started to wiggle out through the last open portion—only to realize it was too small. I had jailed myself in!

Fortunately I was able to pull free a good-size section and make my hasty escape before the neighbors could catch the show.

Bottom's up

The word "mechanical" and my father are not synonymous, but he decided to sharpen the blade on our rotary lawn mower after Mom told him it wasn't cutting well. He removed the blade and sharpened it and then put it back onto the mower. When Mom started the mower and began to cut the lawn, she noticed it cut worse than ever. Dad couldn't believe it. He then shut off the mower and looked underneath. The back edge of the blade opposite the cutting edge was now shiny. He'd obviously installed the blade upside down. His "non-mechanical" reputation is still intact!

Fire water

My 84-year-old mother decided to clear brush behind her house and burn it. She built a good, hot fire and was watching with satisfaction when a fountain of water sprang up in the middle of the flames. She thought she was seeing a miracle, a wonder of wonders—water and fire living together!

Then she remembered the plastic water pipe running right under that spot to the garden spigot.

No wonder.

Goofy grass

I had to replace a worn 4 x 6-ft. section of my lawn with new sod. I was advised to completely kill off any grass before rolling out the new turf.

Wanting to do a good job, I purchased the best lawn killer I could find and meticulously sprayed out a perfect square.

A few days later, the area started to turn brown as expected. I also noticed that a few spots outside the square were starting to die out too. I was irritated that my sprayer had leaked on my otherwise perfect lawn.

As the grass killer proceeded to do its job, the mystery spots began to take shape—they were the perfect imprints of my shoes! Evidently I had walked through the sprayed area while heading back to my garage.

Warm birdbath?

We'd always used a well to water our gardens and clean out the birdbaths. However, I was having a pump problem and figured the time had come to connect my outside water to the city system.

I hooked up a valve, soldered some basement pipes and went outside to check my work. The water came out hot at first—because I had just sweated the pipes, I told myself. But to my surprise, the water stayed hot and then got even hotter.

Downstairs, I followed the pipe all the way back to our water heater. I had to spend the rest of my day redoing plumbing—or only the birds would have gotten a hot bath at our house.

GRAB-AND-GO
GARDEN TOOL CABINET

Give your garden tools their own home so they're easy to find

by **David Radtke**

Imagine this: You drive home with a carload of new plants and flowers. You open your new outdoor garden tool cabinet and grab your shovel, bulb planter, trimmer or whatever you need—and it's all there in plain view! This scenario doesn't have to be a dream. You can build our cabinet in one weekend and paint and organize it the next.

This cabinet is compact, but it can store all of your garden hand tools and still have room for boots, fertilizers and accessories. Most gardeners set aside a tiny spot in their garage for their tools, which often end up tangled in a corner. Now your garden tools can have a home of their own, outside the garage. The design is flexible, so you can customize the interior to suit your needs and add a lock if you wish.

In this article, we'll show you how to assemble the cabinet in your garage and then wheel it out and mount it on your garage wall. And you don't have to be a crackerjack carpenter or own special tools to build it.

Besides being good looking, this project is designed to last. The shingled roof will keep the rain out. And if moisture does get in, the slatted bottom and 4-in.-diameter vents near the top allow enough air circulation to dry everything out. We mounted this storage cabinet on the outside of a garage, but you can easily mount it to the back of your house or to a shed.

The 4-ft. by nearly 8-ft. cabinet is made from exterior plywood with pine trim. All the materials are available at home centers and lumberyards. You can find a huge variety of tool mounting clips and retainers at hardware stores for hanging rakes, shovels, clippers and everything else. Just let your imagination solve the need. Figure on spending about $250 on the materials, not including hardware or paint. So what are you waiting for? Get the materials, read the photo sequence, examine the detailed drawings and text instructions, and get started.

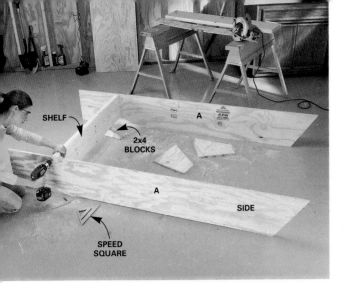

1 CUT the plywood sides and 2x10 shelf, prop up the shelf with 2x4 blocks and fasten the sides into the shelf with 2-in. deck screws.

2 TURN the assembly over and screw the back to the sides and center shelf. Use a level or straightedge to mark the shelf location on the back side of the plywood.

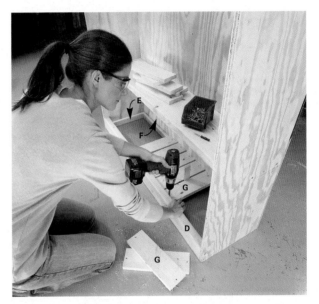

3 CUT the subrails (D) and the roof supports (H), then screw them into place. Use 2-in. screws for the subrails and 3-in. screws for the roof supports.

4 GLUE AND NAIL the 1x2 cleats (E and F) to the sides, back and subrail (D) and then screw the 1x4 floor slats (G) to the cleats. Start with the center slat and leave 7/16-in. gaps.

Assemble the main box

Exterior-grade plywood is the basic building material for this project. Unfortunately, you'll never find absolutely flat pieces of plywood at a home center or lumberyard, but the flatter you can find them, the better this project will turn out. Choose a BC grade of plywood. This will ensure you have one good side "B" that'll look good on the outside, and the "C" side can go inside.

Once you get the plywood home, keep it out of the sun or your flat panel will turn into a tortilla chip in no time. It's best to cut the pieces in the shade or in your garage. A long straightedge cutting guide for your circular saw will help you get nice straight cuts if you don't have a full-size table saw. Look at the Cutting List on p. 225 and cut all the parts to size except the door stiles, rails and trim

pieces, which are best cut to fit once you've constructed the main plywood box.

Choose the flattest sheet of 3/4-in. plywood for the door cores. As you lay out all the pieces, choose the best-looking side of the plywood for the painted parts. The sides of the cabinet form a 30-degree slope for the roof. Use a Speed square (see **Photo 1**) to mark the angled roof supports (H) and ends of the trim pieces that follow the roofline. It's easier to cut accurate slopes on the larger side pieces (A) by first measuring each side, marking a diagonal line from point to point and then cutting along the mark. Assemble the main box of the cabinet as shown in **Figure A** and **Photos 1 – 5**. Drill pilot holes for all screws with a No. 8 combination countersink and pilot bit. Use 2-in. galvanized deck screws to fasten the sides to the

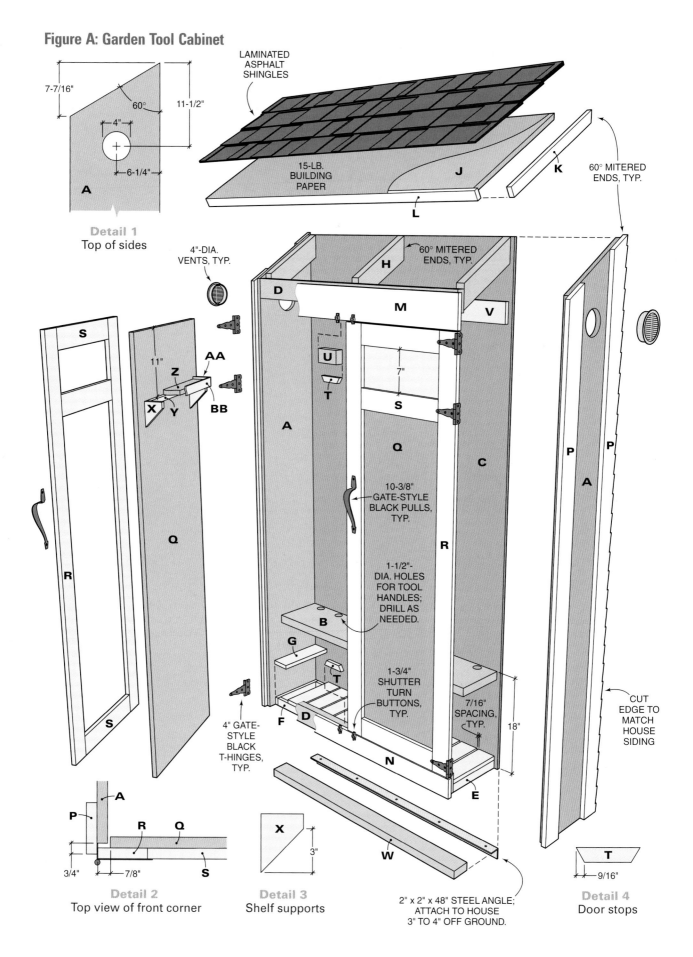

Figure A: Garden Tool Cabinet

7-7/16"
60°
11-1/2"
4"
6-1/4"
A

Detail 1
Top of sides

LAMINATED
ASPHALT
SHINGLES

15-LB.
BUILDING
PAPER

J

K

L

60° MITERED
ENDS, TYP.

4"-DIA.
VENTS, TYP.

60° MITERED
ENDS, TYP.

D

H

M

V

S

11"

Z

AA

X **Y**

BB

U

T

7"

S

A

Q

C

10-3/8"
GATE-STYLE
BLACK PULLS,
TYP.

R

S

Q

R

B

1-1/2"-
DIA. HOLES
FOR TOOL
HANDLES;
DRILL AS
NEEDED.

G

T

1-3/4"
SHUTTER
TURN
BUTTONS,
TYP.

F **D**

N

7/16"
SPACING,
TYP.

18"

E

CUT
EDGE TO
MATCH
HOUSE
SIDING

P **P**

A

4" GATE-
STYLE
BLACK
T-HINGES,
TYP.

W

2" x 2" x 48" STEEL ANGLE;
ATTACH TO HOUSE
3" TO 4" OFF GROUND.

A
P
R **Q**
3/4" 7/8" **S**

Detail 2
Top view of front corner

X
3"

Detail 3
Shelf supports

T
9/16"

Detail 4
Door stops

224

5 MOUNT the 1x2 roof trim to the 3/4-in. plywood roof, then center it and mark the position. Then temporarily screw it to the roof supports with a pair of 2-in. screws on each side.

6 GLUE AND SCREW the 1x4 side trim to the plywood sides, keeping the trim pieces 3/4 in. proud at the front. Cut the 4-in.-diameter side vents.

shelf and 1-5/8-in. screws to fasten the back to the sides. **Note:** Cut a piece of 1/4-in. hardware cloth to fit under the floor slats of the cabinet. This wire mesh will keep furry critters from making your tool cabinet into a cozy winter home.

Cut the roof panel (J) and trim pieces (K and L), then glue and nail the trim to the front and side edges of the roof panel. Center the panel (**Photo 5**) and temporarily

screw it to the roof supports so you can install the side trim (P) and the upper rail (M). **Note:** You'll need to remove the roof and the doors after assembly to make the project light enough to move to your site.

Add trim and assemble the doors

Make sure to extend the front edge of each side. Set the

MATERIALS LIST

ITEM	QTY.
3/4" x 4' x 8' BC plywood	2
1/2" x 4' x 8' BC plywood	1
2x10 x 4' pine	1
2x4 x 8' pine	2
1x6 x 8' pine	1
1x4 x 8' pine	12
1x2 x 8' pine	3
2x4 x 8' treated wood	1
12" x 48" hardware cloth (1/4" grid)	1
Bundle of asphalt shingles	1
3' x 5' strip of 15-lb. building paper	1
1-5/8" galv. screws	2 lbs.
2" galv. screws	2 lbs.
3" galv. screws	1 lbs.
4" T-hinges	6
Shutter turn buttons	4
4" round vents	2
1-1/4" finish nails	1 lb.
1/4" x 3" galv. lag screws and washers	9
2" x 2" steel angle	1
7/8" shingle nails	1 lb.

CUTTING LIST

KEY	QTY.	SIZE & DESCRIPTION
A	2	3/4" x 12-7/8" x 90" plywood sides
B	1	1-1/2" x 9-1/4" x 46-1/2" pine shelf
C	1	1/2" x 48" x 90" plywood back
D	2	1-1/2" x 3-1/2" x 46-1/2" pine subrails
E	2	3/4" x 1-1/2" x 11-3/8" pine bottom cleats
F	2	3/4" x 1-1/2" x 45" pine bottom cleats
G	12	3/4" x 3-1/2" x 11-3/8" pine bottom slat
H	3	1-1/2" x 3-1/2" x 15-1/8" pine roof supports
J	1	3/4" x 21-7/8" x 60" plywood roof
K	2	3/4" x 1-1/2" x 21-7/8" pine roof trim
L	1	3/4" x 1-1/2" x 61-1/2" pine roof trim
M	1	3/4" x 5-1/2" x 48" pine upper rail
N	1	3/4" x 3-1/2" x 48" pine lower rail

KEY	QTY.	SIZE & DESCRIPTION
P	4	3/4" x 3-1/2" x 91" pine side trim
Q	2	3/4" x 23" x 72-3/4" plywood doors
R	4	3/4" x 3-1/2" x 72-3/4" pine door stile
S	6	3/4" x 3-1/2" x 16-7/8" pine door rail trim
T	2	3/4" x 1" x 4-1/2" pine door stop
U	1	1-1/2" x 2-7/16" x 4-1/2" pine door stop support
V	1	3/4" x 3-1/2" x 46-1/2" pine hang rail
W	1	1-1/2" x 3-1/2" x 48" treated mounting board
X	1	3/4" x 3" x 4" pine shelf supports
Y	1	3/4" x 3/4" x 16-1/2" pine shelf-mounting cleat
Z	1	3/4" x 3" x 20" pine shelf
AA	2	1/4" x 1-1/2" x 3" pine shelf edging
BB	1	1/4" x 1-1/2" x 20-1/2" pine shelf edging

OUTDOOR STRUCTURES & LANDSCAPING

7 COUNTERSINK the holes in the inside of the hinge flaps to accept the tapered heads of the mounting screws.

8 POSITION the flaps of the hinges against the plywood sides at the centers of the door rail locations. Drill pilot holes and drive the screws into the side trim to secure the hinges.

trim (P) 3/4 in. beyond the front edge of the plywood side (**Photo 6**). Next cut and nail the front upper rail (M) and the lower rail (N) to the subrails. Both ends should butt tightly to the side trim.

Even though the doors are made mainly from plywood, the rail and stile trim boards glued and screwed to the front side give the doors a handsome frame-and-panel look. Be sure to lay the doors out on a flat surface and then glue and nail the rails (long vertical pieces) and stiles (short horizontal pieces) to the plywood surface. The stile on each hinge side must hang 3/4 in. past the plywood (see **Photo 10 inset**).

You'll need to alter the factory T-hinge for the inset design of the doors. The hinge flap is screwed to the side trim (P) as shown in **Photo 8**. If you were to use the factory-supplied pan head screws, the door would bind on the screw heads. To solve this problem, taper the edges of the existing holes with a countersink bit. Remove just enough steel (**Photo 7**) so the head of the tapered No. 8 x 3/4-in. screw fits flush with the hinge flap surface.

Cut the small doorstops with a handsaw and then glue and nail them to the edges of the subrails. With the doorstops in place, set the doors into the opening. Make sure you leave a 1/8-in. gap at the top and bottom and a 3/16-in. gap between the doors. You may need to plane or belt-sand the door edges to get a good fit. **Note:** Because the flaps of the hinge that fasten to the side trim are about 7/8 in. wide instead of 3/4 in., your doors will sit about 1/8 in. proud of the side trim.

Mount the cabinet to the wall

Fasten a 4-ft. 2x4 to the top flange of a 4-ft.-long piece of steel angle (**Figure A**). At a hardware store, you can usually find steel angle that measures 1-1/2 in. x 1-1/2 in. with

holes drilled every 3 in., but any steel angle that's 1/8 in. thick or larger will do.

Locate the exact position of your cabinet on the wall at least 3 in. above grade and then fasten the angle to the wall with 1/4-in. galvanized lag screws. It must be level. You may need to cut a course or two of siding to get the angle to lie flat. Our garage slab was several inches off the ground, so I drilled holes into the side of the slab, installed lag shields and fastened the angle. If your slab is too close to the ground, you can fasten the angle farther up into the wood studs of the garage. The weight of your cabinet rests entirely on this wall cleat. It's not necessary to fasten the bottom of the cabinet to it.

<aside>

Editor's Note

If you have vinyl, aluminum or steel siding, here's how to prevent the siding from deforming as you tighten the cabinet to the wall. Instead of tightening the lag screws one at a time, gently tighten them alternately to even out the pressure as you go.

— David

</aside>

Measure the locations of the wall studs and transfer these to the cabinet back. Locate three 1/4-in.-diameter pilot holes in the hang rail (V) near the top of the cabinet and another three holes 4 in. up from the bottom at the stud locations.

Now, strap your cabinet to a furniture dolly (with the doors and roof removed to reduce the weight) and wheel it over to the wall cleat. Set the bottom of the cabinet onto the cleat, center it and temporarily brace it against the wall. Drill 5/32-in.-diameter pilot holes into the wall studs using the existing pilot holes as a guide. Drive the 3-in. lag screws (including washers) and snug the cabinet to the wall.

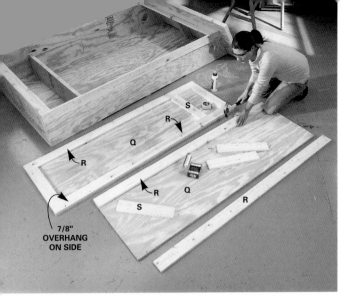

7/8"
OVERHANG
ON SIDE

9 GLUE AND NAIL the door rail and stile trim to the 3/4-in. plywood core. Overhang the stile on the hinge side of each door 7/8 in. See Figure A for the exact placement.

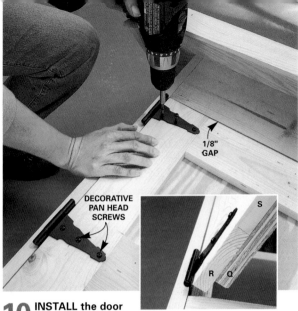

1/8"
GAP

DECORATIVE
PAN HEAD
SCREWS

10 INSTALL the door stops (Figure A), then set each door into its opening. Use the decorative pan head screws provided by the manufacturer for the long decorative flap on the door surface.

2x4 x 8'
BRACE

2x4 x 4'
MOUNTING
BOARD

2" x 2" STEEL
ANGLE

11 FASTEN a steel angle to the foundation with a 2x4 attached to its top (Figure A). Lift the cabinet into place and stabilize it with a 8-ft. 2x4 brace against the ground, forcing the cabinet back against the wall.

2x4
BRACE

NOTCHES
FOR SIDING

P

P

12 SCRIBE the 1x4 side trim to fit the siding. Cut the notches with a jigsaw. Nail it to the cabinet side. Screw on the roof panel and shingle it.

Finishing touches

Lay the side trim (P) against the siding. You may need to trim it with your jigsaw to conform (**Photo 12**). Screw the roof panel to the cabinet. Staple a layer of 15-lb. building paper to the roof panel and shingle the panel using 7/8-in. roofing nails. Avoid driving shingle nails through the over-hangs where the points might show. When you get to the last course, trim the shingles to fit and run a bead of matching caulk at the siding to seal the edge.

Rehang the doors and then mount the door handles and the catches at the top and bottom of the door. Wait to add your vents until you've finished painting. We spray-painted the vents to match the color of the sides.

Take a trip to the hardware store and shop for a variety of fasteners, from angle screws to rake and broom holders. Once you finish organizing the cabinet, prime it and then paint it to match your building. 🏠

OUTDOOR STRUCTURES & LANDSCAPING

HandyHints®

FLIP-UP DOWNSPOUT

Pulling off downspout extensions and jamming them back on is a nuisance when you're mowing. But you can convert all your extensions to flip-up versions in about an hour with $4 worth of hardware. Make a 1/2-in.-deep cut across the extension about 3 in. from the end with a hacksaw. Then use metal snips to finish cutting out a notch. Fasten the extension to the downspout with sheet metal screws or 1/8-in. aluminum rivets. For smooth operation, place plastic fender washers between the two parts. Make sure the extension hangs about 1/2 in. below the downspout.

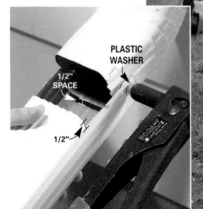

PLASTIC WASHER

1/2" SPACE

1/2"

NONSTICK MOWER DECK

If the underside of your lawn mower develops a thick crust of grass clippings, scrub it clean and then give it a coat of spray lubricant. Products that contain silicone or Teflon work best and cost about $5 at home centers and hardware stores.

LOAD SUPPORT

Next time you head to the home center to pick up long, floppy materials like trim, plastic pipe or vinyl siding, take your extension ladder. It provides a stiff support for your flimsy load. Include some heavy weights to hold down the end of your cargo and plenty of elastic cords to strap your load to the ladder. Also tie down the ladder so it doesn't slide from side to side.

NO-TRIM WALL BORDER

If you're building a fence, a retaining wall or a planter, set a course of protruding stones in the soil beneath it. That way, your mower can cut all the grass—no trimming by hand needed. The stones should protrude about 4 in. from the wall and stand at least an inch above the soil so grass doesn't creep over them. You'll still have to pull out grass from between the stones occasionally.

TARP TRAILER

With a big plastic tarp, you can easily drag leaves, branches or mulch around your yard to wherever you need it. A 9 x 12-ft. tarp costs about $8 at home centers and hardware stores.

HandyHints®

GARDEN TOOL HIDEAWAY

A mailbox near your garden provides a convenient home for tools. A small mailbox like this one costs less than $10 at hardware stores and home centers. King-size models cost about $25.

SOAKER BUCKET

When it comes to watering, slower is better because water soaks in rather than runs off the soil. Slow watering usually means running your garden hose at a trickle or using a soaker hose. Here's a way to soak the soil without dragging hoses around: Drill four 1/8-in. holes in the bottom of a bucket and set it next to thirsty plants.

RAPID INFLATION

On many shop vacuums, you can plug the hose into the exhaust port. And that lets you turn your vacuum into a power inflator for toys and air mattresses. A small transmission funnel ($5 at hardware and auto parts stores) makes a perfect nozzle.

FUNNEL

DUCT TAPE

WordlessWorkshop™

by **Roy Doty**

DECK RAILING PLANTER

OUTDOOR STRUCTURES & LANDSCAPING

STONE WALLS

New modular block systems stack up so easily that you can build a handsome, freestanding wall in a weekend

by **Travis Larson**

Building a low stone wall is a simple project that will have a big impact on the front of your house. It's a welcoming portal drawing guests to your front door, and it can complement other yard features like patios, walks, flower beds and arbors as well. But natural stone walls are expensive, and the stones' irregular shapes and sizes make them tricky to lay up. In the last few years, new, natural-looking concrete modular blocks have become available at landscaping centers. These modular wall blocks offer significant cost savings and simple installation techniques.

In this article, we'll show you how to assemble one of these systems from start to finish. We'll include the critical base setting details that ensure stability and longevity. And we'll also show you how to cap a wall with handsome natural stone.

You won't need any expensive tools for this project, just standard digging tools, a sturdy wheelbarrow, a 4-ft. level for establishing a level footing, and a 2-ft. level for setting the blocks. It's also handy to have a 3-lb. hand maul or sledgehammer for fine-tuning block positions and a hand tamper to compact the gravel base (**Photo 3**). If you have overlying sod, it's worth renting a sod cutter ($25 a day). To trim the natural stone top cap to fit, buy a diamond circular saw blade ($40).

Choose a compactable footing material

Measure the desired length of your wall and take that figure to the landscape supplier. The staff will help you calculate how many blocks you need for the style you select.

Order the gravel footing material at the same time so you can have it delivered with the wall blocks. Your choice will depend on what's offered at the landscape center. The key is to select a granular material that's easy to shovel and level and that will compact when you tamp it. We used "Class II" (as in "2") fill, a coarsely ground limestone combined with finer granules. It's a great footing because it packs and drains well and is easy to level. With moisture and compaction, it forms a semi-solid footing. If Class II isn't available in your area, you can use any type of 1/2- to 3/4-in. crushed gravel. But avoid rounded stone; it won't compact. The landscape center staff will advise you on the best available material.

Figure the footing volume by multiplying 1.6 ft. (trench width) by .66 ft. (8 in.; the depth) by the length of the trench. That'll give you the volume in cubic feet. Divide that by 27 to get the quantity, in cubic yards, that you'll need to order.

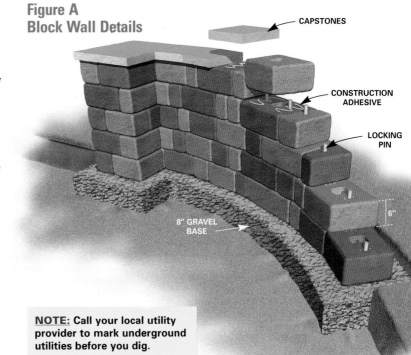

Figure A
Block Wall Details

CAPSTONES

CONSTRUCTION ADHESIVE

LOCKING PIN

8" GRAVEL BASE

6"

NOTE: Call your local utility provider to mark underground utilities before you dig.

Lay out the footings and dig the trench

Straight walls are easy to lay out; just use marking paint to outline a trench 6 in. wider than the width of the blocks. But if you're planning on a curved wall like ours, first lay a row of blocks on the ground and adjust the pieces until you get the even, gradual curve that you want. Then use marking paint to mark the trench outline 6 in. on both sides of the blocks (**Photo 1**). Remove the overlying sod and dig the trench to a depth that'll allow for 8 in. of gravel plus one-third the thickness of the first row of block. Our blocks were 6 in. high, so we dug down 10 in. Setting the first row of blocks slightly below the ground looks best and locks the wall into place. As you dig, check the bottom of the trench with a 4-ft. level to keep a reasonably consistent, level grade. The gravel will take care of minor variations. If your yard has a slope, begin your trench at the low end. (For steeper slopes, see box below.)

Ideally, this depth will get you through the topsoil and into solid subsoil (clay, sand or a mixture). Topsoil can settle and cause the wall to sag or lean over time. So if

Building on slopes

If your yard slopes less than about 6 in. or so over the length of the wall, dig your footing down to the proper depth at the lowest part of the wall and level the whole trench bottom from that point. At the high end of the slope, the first row of the stones will be nearly buried. But if your yard slopes more, you'll have to "step" the footings. The manufacturer's instructions will help with the details.

COLUMN BASE

MARKING PAINT

1 LAY OUT the stone on the ground to best shape the curved wall. Then mark the footprint of the wall 6 in. on both sides of the stones with marking paint.

2 DIG a trench 10 in. deep, keeping the bottom roughly level. Fine-tune the trench depth using a level and board so the blocks in each wall line up.

3 DUMP IN 4 in. of crushed limestone, pack it, then pack in an additional 4 in. Flatten the surface and level it both ways.

4 LEVEL each successive stone with the previous one. Tamp high stones lower with light taps from a sledge. Sprinkle more fill beneath low blocks.

5 DRY-FIT the entire next row using locking pins. Then remove each block, apply two beads of adhesive under each and set it.

6 STARTING at one end, fit the capstones by butting them together. Lay a straightedge across the joint and mark cutting lines on both stones.

digging a few extra inches gets you down to subsoil, it's worth the trouble. Pack any disturbed soil at the bottom of the trench with a hand tamper before you pour in the footing material.

It looks best to match the horizontal joint lines with the lines on nearby walls. Our two walls flank a sidewalk, so we leveled across from the lowest block on the first wall to position the second wall (**Photo 2**). Add the block and footing thicknesses to establish the bottom of the trench. Use the same technique later when you're packing in the footing material so the first row of blocks will line up with the other wall.

A level, compacted base will keep the wall true

If you're using crushed gravel as your footing, just pour it in, level it, pack it and start the wall. But if the footing material contains clay or is crushed limestone like ours, add the footing in two 4-in.-deep "lifts" (layers). Roughly rake the first lift flat and then mist it with a garden sprayer

and compact it with the hand tamper. Dampening the footing makes the material compact easier and better. Overlap each tamper footprint, working your way from one end of the trench to the other. For extra insurance against settling, tamp it twice.

Use more care when you're leveling the second layer. Rake it flat and use a level to fine-tune the grade before tamping. Use a shorter level to make sure the footing is level across the width as well so the wall won't lean. Strive for a grade that varies no more than 1/8 in.

Lay the block

The first row of blocks is critical to your wall's appearance. It defines all of the overlying rows. Small variations will create gaps and cause the wall to lean, so take your time. Start your wall at ends that abut other walls or sidewalks. Alternate block sizes for variety. Be patient and level each block perfectly both ways before you set the next one (**Photo 4**). Light taps from a sledgehammer will nest blocks into the footing slightly to help with the leveling. Be

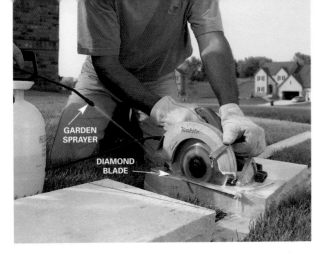

GARDEN SPRAYER

DIAMOND BLADE

7 CUT the miters with a diamond saw blade and set the capstones with beads of adhesive.

Choosing modular block

Realistic cast wall materials rival natural stone in looks, but not, fortunately, in cost (or in tricky fitting techniques!). In fact, a modular block wall costs less than half as much as a natural stone wall. Manufacturers mimic the natural appearance of stone by varying the sizes, colors and textures of each block. You mix up the blocks while assembling the wall to better mimic the random sizes of natural stone.

Most systems offer blocks that are finished on all four sides. You'll need them for corners, especially if you build columns at the wall ends. Be sure to include capstone for the top of your wall. Most manufacturers offer thinner cast versions of the blocks for this. Instead, we decided to use natural Indiana limestone and cut it to fit to add to the natural appearance of the wall (**Photo 7**). However, because each 16-in. x 2-ft. stone costs $40, the cost of a natural top cap can rival the cost of the block wall itself!

careful—pound too hard and you could crack the block. If a block is too high to level by tapping, remove the block and scrape away some of the gravel. If a block is too low, sprinkle in more footing material, retamp it and try again.

The next rows go on fast. In fact, building the rest of the wall will usually take less time than setting the base course. With each row, dry-lay the blocks with pins (no adhesive), choosing widths so the blocks straddle (offset) the seams below. This takes a bit of picking and choosing and switching sizes. You also want to get a good random mix of colors. The instructions will tell you how many pins are needed and where they should be placed. There may be concrete "crumbs" plugging some of the holes. Just scrape those away with a screwdriver.

When you're satisfied with the look, remove the blocks one at a time, add a few beads of adhesive and set the block back into place. Keep the adhesive away from the edges, where it could ooze out and be visible. Use tubes of polyurethane adhesive for dry blocks (or the adhesive recommended by the manufacturer). If blocks are damp, use a liquid polyurethane glue like Gorilla Glue or Elmer's Ultimate Glue, which stick and cure on damp surfaces.

Add the top capstones

Simply follow the manufacturer's directions if you're capping the wall with modular units. Usually that's just a matter of fitting and gluing down the cap blocks without pins. But fitting natural stones calls for cutting as well, especially on a curved wall. The trick for nice tight joints is to set the stones into place and scribe the cutting lines (**Photo 7**).

Start by laying the first stone into place, scribing and cutting an angle on the end if it's needed where the wall abuts an existing wall or column.

Cutting stone is easier than it sounds. A diamond blade in a circular saw does the trick. Just follow the line with the blade, just as if you were cutting wood. The stone we used was soft enough to cut in one pass with the blade all the way down. But harder stones may need several passes: a shallow cut first and then deeper cuts. It works great to rest the stone right on the grass while you cut. It's a dusty, noisy process, so wear a dust mask, safety glasses and hearing protection. Reduce dust by having a helper aim a thin stream of water from a garden sprayer into the part of the blade that generates the most dust (**Photo 7**).

Center the second capstone on the wall and butt it against the first. Center a straightedge over the joint and draw cutting lines on each stone. Adjust the lines if necessary to minimize stone waste. After cutting, set the stones into place and add the next stone, draw lines, cut and so on. You can cheat the stones around a bit to close up small gaps, but not too much. Otherwise variations in the overhangs will start to be obvious. 🏠

Gallery of Ideas

STONE FOUNTAIN

If you're looking for an eye-catching feature for your patio, deck or even front entry, this natural-looking artesian fountain will do the trick. Water from a pump gurgles up and through a 1-in. hole drilled through a large rock, into a gravel-filled reservoir and is then recirculated. You can use your own creative eye and inspiration for installing the stones and plants, and selecting the shape.

Project Facts
Cost: $200-$1,000
Skill level: Beginner to intermediate
Time: 1-2 days

FROM MARCH, 2006, p. 28

SCREEN PORCH

FROM MAY, 2006, p. 42

If you want to beat the bugs and spend more time outside this summer, this project is for you. This screen porch is a big improvement to your backyard—but it's also a big project. You'll need to modify your house to accommodate the new structure and building it involves tasks ranging from pouring concrete footings to shingling the roof. But the design has been simplified by using standard dimensional lumber, without heavy beams or complex joints. The project can be built for less by substituting treated material for the cedar decking and tongue-and-groove pine for the cedar on the ceiling.

Project Facts
Cost: Around $6,500
Skill level: Advanced
Time: A summer's-worth of weekends

COMPACT STORAGE SHED

If you need a place to store all your garden tools and supplies, but have limited yard space, this small shed is a perfect storage solution. With its 6 x 6-ft. footprint and classic Georgian styling, it fits into tight spots and adds charm to any backyard. The "front room" (53 x 65 in.)

provides plenty of space for shelves and even a small potting bench, while the double door on the back of the shed creates a spacious easy-access tool locker.

FROM JUNE, 2006, p. 35

Project Facts

Cost: About $1,300
Skill level: Inter-
    mediate
Time: 4-6 days

ENTRY ARBOR AND TRELLIS

FROM JULY/AUGUST, 2006, p. 56

You don't have to hire an architect to redesign your front entry to make it attractive and inviting. Sometimes a simple, inexpensive arbor or trellis will do the trick. The trellis helps break up the expansive wall of siding, while the arbors flanking each side of the sidewalk help frame the front door and entry area. The only power tools you need are a circular saw and screw gun. You cut and assemble everything in place, so it's easy to measure and cut the pieces to fit as you go.

Project Facts

Cost: Arbor, around $100; arbor with trellis, around $200
Skill level: Beginner to intermediate
Time: 1-2 days

OUTDOOR STRUCTURES & LANDSCAPING

To order photocopies of complete articles for the projects shown here, call (715) 246-4521, email familyhandyman@nrmsinc.com or write to: Copies, The Family Handyman, P.O. Box 83695, Stillwater, MN 55083-0695. Many public libraries also carry back issues of _The Family Handyman_ magazine.

CLASSIC
GARDEN ARBOR

Build this sturdy garden structure for half the cost of a store-bought model

by **Kurt Lawton**

This simple, elegant arbor is tall and wide enough to span a path in your backyard or make an attractive garden entry. It's strong and durable too. We used 4x4s for the corner posts and 2-by lumber for all crosspieces and the overhead structure. And we built the entire project out of cedar, for its natural rot resistance. For the gardener, we added plenty of lattice, so it can support climbing vines and other plants.

In this article, we'll walk you through the simple techniques for building this arbor, including one tricky part, cutting pockets in the posts for the crosspieces. For a touch of style, we made the cross-pieces look as if they extend right through the posts, as if we had cut fancy mortise-and-tenon joints. However, the pockets only extend 3/4 in. deep and the "stubs" on the outside are only 3 in. long. You can cut these pockets quite easily with a special Forstner bit and sharp chisel (**Photos 3 and 4**). In fact, you can complete all the joint work as well as most of the assembly in your shop or garage. Then it'll only take you about half a day to assemble the project in your yard. All together, give yourself a full weekend to build it.

Other than a little experience with basic carpentry tools, you don't need any special skills to build this arbor. A table saw comes in handy for ripping the 2x3s from 2x6 lumber. Otherwise, a circular saw will do. In addition, a pneumatic finish nailer will speed up lattice assembly, and a drill guide that turns your hand drill into a simple drill press ($30; see photos, p. 240) will speed up pocket cutting. We recommend that you buy a 1-1/2-in. Forstner bit ($19) to cut splinter-free holes for the crosspiece pockets and a 1/4-in. drill bit that's 12 in. long to bore completely through the posts and lintels (**Photo 11**).

The cedar and other materials for this project cost about $200. You could cut that cost to about $100 if you use pressure-treated wood, which would look just fine if painted or stained.

Figure A
Arbor Details

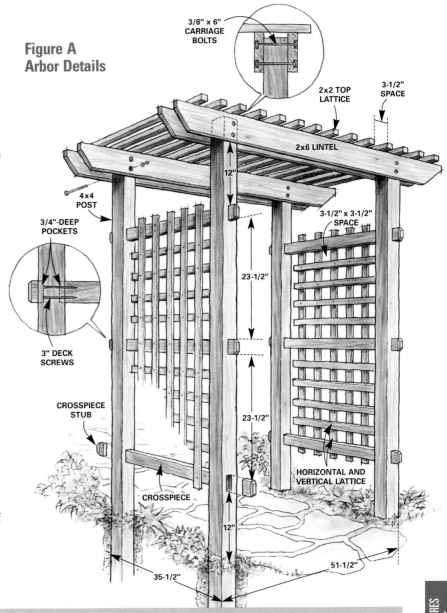

SHOPPING LIST

ITEM	QTY.
4x4 x 10' cedar	4
2x6 x 8' cedar	5
1x2 x 8' cedar	12
1x4 x 8' pine (temporary braces)	2
2x2 x 8' cedar	7
Wolfcraft Model No. 4525 Drill Guide/multi-angled* ($30)	1
1-1/2" Forstner drill bit ($19)	
1/4" x 12" drill bit ($8.50)	1
3/8" and 1" spade bits	1 ea.
3/8" x 6" carriage bolts (flat washers, nuts)	8
3" deck screws	24
No. 10 galvanized casing nails	1 lb.
Tube of construction adhesive	1

CUTTING LIST

SIZE & DESCRIPTION	PCS.
3-1/2" x 3-1/2" x 9' cedar posts	4
1-1/2" x 2-1/2" x 30" cedar crosspieces	6
1-1/2" x 5-1/2" x 73-1/2" cedar lintels	4
3/4" x 1-1/2" x 59-1/4" cedar vertical lattice	10
3/4" x 1-1/2" x 25-1/2" cedar horizontal lattice	16
1-1/2" x 1-1/2" x 42-1/2" cedar top lattice	14
1-1/2" x 2-1/2" x 3" crosspiece stubs	12

*Wolfcraft Model No. 4525 Drill Guide/ multi-angled: (630) 458-4000, www.wolfcraft.com

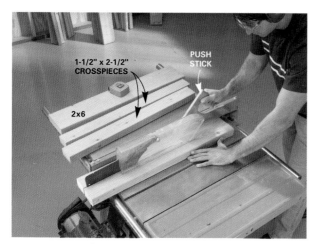

1 RIP 2x6s in half for the crosspieces. Then trim off the rounded edges to reach the 2-1/2-in.-width dimension. Cut them to length.

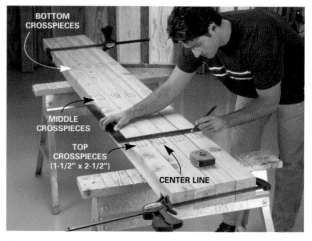

2 CUT the 4x4 posts to length, clamp them side by side and mark the exact crosspiece pocket positions with a pencil. Flip all posts over to the opposite side and repeat for the stubs.

3 CENTER a 1-1/2-in. Forstner bit and drill overlapping holes 3/4 in. deep at each crosspiece location. The drill guide keeps the drill perpendicular.

4 SQUARE and clean out each pocket with a hammer and sharp wood chisel until a crosspiece fits snugly.

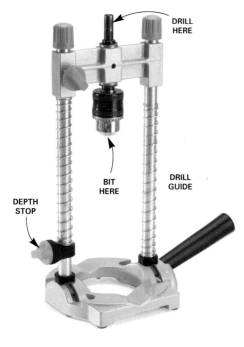

Build the side panels on a flat area

The first step is to cut out and assemble two sets of posts and side panels (**Figure A**). Work on a flat surface. Begin by cutting the lintels and crosspieces from 2x6 lumber (**Photo 1**). Then rip the crosspiece 2x6s in half and trim off the factory side to bring the width down to 2-1/2 in. This eliminates the rounded edge and leaves all four corners crisp and square.

Next, mark the crosspiece locations (**Photo 2**). Be sure to mark a center line at each position; you'll use it as a starting point for the center point of the drill bit. Draw the crosspiece position accurately to ensure a tight fit when you chisel out the corners and sides (**Photo 4**).

Then drill the recesses (**Photo 3**). Bits that cut wide holes can be difficult to control. The Forstner bit is the easiest to handle. It also cuts the cleanest and leaves a flat hole bottom. If you use other types of bits, test them on a scrap of cedar to make sure they cut accurately and cleanly. The drill guide we're using helps steady the drill and has a stop

1-1/2"
FORSTNER BIT

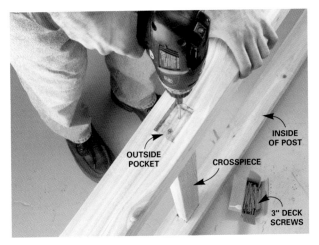

5 SLIP the crosspieces into the pockets between two 4x4 posts and fasten them with 3-in. deck screws driven through the outside pockets.

Labels: OUTSIDE POCKET, INSIDE OF POST, CROSSPIECE, 3" DECK SCREWS

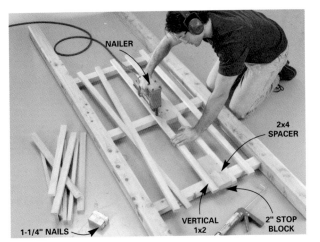

6 SQUARE the frame, then attach the vertical 1x2 lattice to the outside of the crosspieces with a pair of finish nails. Use a 2x4 with a 2-in. stop block to space them evenly.

Labels: NAILER, 2x4 SPACER, VERTICAL 1x2, 2" STOP BLOCK, 1-1/4" NAILS

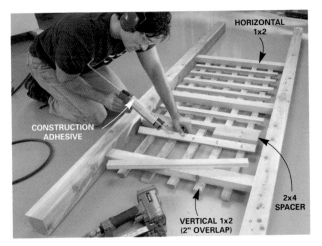

7 FLIP the frame assemblies over and glue and nail the horizontal 1x2 lattice to the inside of the vertical 1x2s.

Labels: HORIZONTAL 1x2, CONSTRUCTION ADHESIVE, VERTICAL 1x2 (2" OVERLAP), 2x4 SPACER

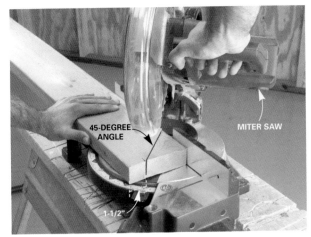

8 CUT the four 2x6 lintels to length, then cut the 45-degree decorative angles on both ends of each lintel. Start the cut 1-1/2 in. from one edge.

Labels: 45-DEGREE ANGLE, MITER SAW, 1-1/2"

to ensure a consistent depth. If you don't have a stop, drill gradually and measure often until you're deep enough.

Use a sharp chisel to cut the edges of the hole cleanly (Photo 4). Trim it slightly on the small side, test it with a crosspiece, then shave it larger as needed.

Now, lay the posts on a flat surface and insert the crosspieces. You'll probably have to stand the assembly on edge and knock them together until the inside measurement from post to post is 28-1/2 in. Check the assembly for square and screw it together (Photo 5).

Assemble the lattice in two stages—first the vertical 1x2s and then the horizontal 1x2s (Photos 6 and 7). Space them 3-1/2 in. apart using two 2x4 scrap pieces as spacers. And since the 1x2s will overhang the top and bottom crosspieces by 2 in., screw a 2-in. piece of 2x4 onto

Labels: 2x4 LATTICE SPACER, STOP BLOCK, 2"

the bottom of one of the spacers to quickly align them (Photo 7). Keep in mind that the vertical lattice goes toward the outside of the panel and the horizontal lattice toward the inside. The nailed joint between the two lattice members is the weakest; strengthen it with a dab of construction adhesive (Photo 7).

The final task in the shop is to precut the pieces for the top of the arbor—the 2x6 lintels as well as the top 2x2 lintel cross lattice (Photo 8).

Set the panels and add the top

Lay out the arbor dimensions (35-1/2 x 51-1/2 in.) on the site and dig 8-in.-diameter round holes 2 ft. deep. With a helper, carry the panels out and drop them in the holes. To level and plumb them:
1. Clamp a leg support to each post at ground level so you can lift or lower a post to level the

9 DIG holes 2 ft. deep and erect one side panel. Level the panel with leg supports and clamps and plumb it with angle braces.

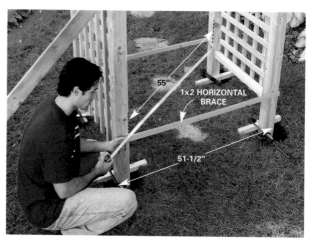

10 ERECT the second panel, level it and plumb it by connecting it to the first panel with 1x2 horizontal braces. Measure diagonally to check for square.

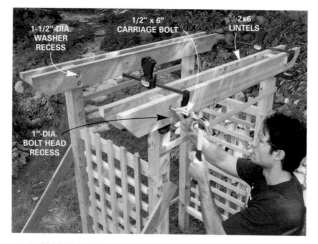

11 MARK the lintel positions and clamp them to the posts. Drill 3/8-in. holes and bolt the lintels to the posts. (See text for details.) Push the crosspiece stubs into their pockets and toenail them with 10d galvanized nails.

12 CUT the top lattice 2x2s to length and attach them to the top of the 2x6 lintels with 10d galvanized nails. Use a 2x4 spacer to evenly position each 2x2.

panel. Set the bottom crosspiece about 12 in. from the ground (**Photo 9**).

2. Screw 1x4 braces to the posts to keep them perfectly plumb (vertical).

3. Attach four 1x2 horizontal braces to the top and bottom of both panels to hold the second panel plumb and evenly spaced from the first panel (**Photo 10**). Level across from one panel to the other to make sure they're at the same height.

4. Measure diagonals and shift the panels until they're equal (**Photo 10**).

Fix the post positions by filling the holes with soil. Tamp the soil firmly as you fill.

Drilling the lintels and posts to make the bolt heads less visible can be tricky. Follow these steps:

■ Position and clamp the lintels to the posts (**Photo 11**).

■ Locate and drill 1-in. holes 1/2 in. deep for the carriage bolt head.

■ Drill through the center of the 1-in. hole and on through the 2x6 lintels and the 4x4 with a 12-in.-long 1/4-in. bit.

■ Drill a 1/2-in.-deep recess in from the other end with a 1-in. bit for the washer and nut.

■ Drill in from both sides with a 3/8-in. spade bit.

Now tap the 3/8-in. bolts into place and tighten the washers and nuts with a socket wrench.

Next, cut the crosspiece stubs, add construction adhesive and insert them into the outer pockets in the 4x4s. After nailing them, bevel their edges slightly with a router and 45-degree chamfer bit.

Finish by nailing on the top lattice (**Photo 12**) and applying an oil-based stain for a more attractive appearance and greater longevity. 🏠

7 Auto & Garage

IN THIS CHAPTER

GARAGE
MEGA-SHELF

The average garage has more than 150 sq. ft. of unused storage space.
We'll show you where to find it.

by **Travis Larson**

The average two-car garage has the upper regions of three 24-ft.-long walls ready and available for big-time storage. Add a continuous 2-ft.-deep shelf on all three walls and you're talking about a huge, accessible storage platform without taking up any floor space whatsoever. This project will work on just about any garage on the planet, although you may have to customize it a bit for your garage. (More on adapting it later.) We show this project in a garage with finished walls, but the assembly techniques will also work on garages with open studs.

While these shelves aren't sturdy enough to store your anvil collection, they're plenty strong enough for off-season clothes, sporting goods and camping gear. In short, just about anything you'd want to hoist up onto an 8-ft.-high

shelf and out of the way. In general, keep the weight under about 30 lbs. per linear foot.

The 23-in.-high apron under the shelf is a great place to drive nails and hooks for hanging garden tools, cords and hoses—all that other stuff that clutters up the garage. Add a closet rod between a couple of braces and you have a convenient place to hang jackets, raincoats or other clothes.

Cutting and installing the parts for an entire garage will only take you a weekend. As for skills, it's a project any weekend warrior can tackle. If you can handle a circular saw, a screw gun and basic hand tools, you'll have no problems. For the cleanest look, use a miter saw to cut the trim. And to speed up the job, use an air compressor and brad nailer for most of the nailing.

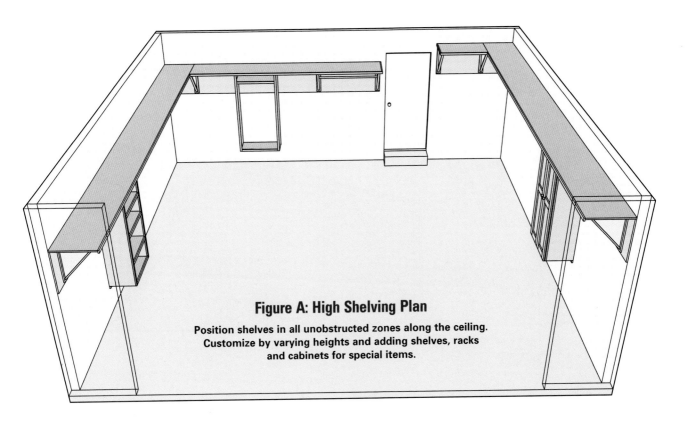

Figure A: High Shelving Plan

Position shelves in all unobstructed zones along the ceiling.
Customize by varying heights and adding shelves, racks
and cabinets for special items.

Choosing the materials

Our shelving system, made from oak plywood and solid oak trim, costs about $55 per 8 ft. of length. If you choose 3/4-in. CDX (construction grade) plywood and pine trim, you'll whittle down the cost to about $40 per 8-ft. section. We prefinished everything with two coats of polyurethane. If you choose to finish your shelves, roll the finish on the full sheets of plywood and brush the finish on all of the trim boards before cutting. That'll take scads less time than finishing it later.

Measure the overall length of shelving you intend to build and then use the dimensions in **Figure B** to help calculate the materials you need.

Planning your shelves

There are no magic heights or widths for your shelves; you'll want to customize them for your garage and needs. The best strategy is to build a 3-ft.-long mockup of our shelf and hold it against the walls in various positions to test the fit. It just takes a little effort and may help prevent headaches later. Then you can decide what height and size the shelves need to be in order to clear obstacles.

Some rules of thumb for sizing and positioning:

- Choose shelf heights that'll allow for enough space between the ceiling and the shelf for the tall items you plan to store.
- Make sure that shelves and braces will clear obstructions like garage doors, garage door tracks and service doors.
- In foot traffic areas (near car doors, for example), keep braces above head level and back from doorways, so you don't bump into them.
- If you have an SUV or a pickup truck, make sure the braces won't obstruct the doors.
- If you need to build narrower shelves, just shrink the plywood braces and shelves by the same amount.

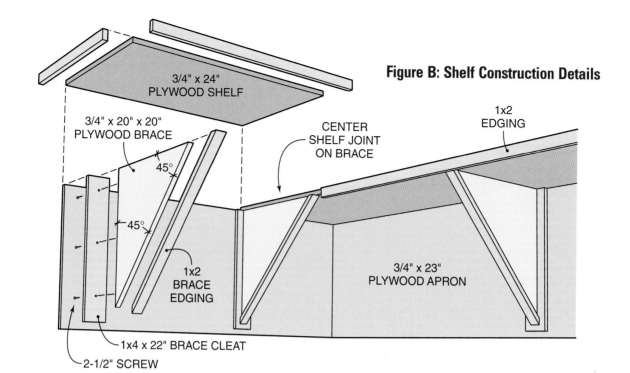

Figure B: Shelf Construction Details

3/4" x 24"
PLYWOOD SHELF

3/4" x 20" x 20"
PLYWOOD BRACE

45°

45°

1x2
BRACE
EDGING

1x4 x 22" BRACE CLEAT

2-1/2" SCREW

CENTER
SHELF JOINT
ON BRACE

1x2
EDGING

3/4" x 23"
PLYWOOD APRON

FACTORY
EDGE

1 RIP 24-in.-wide shelves and 23-in.-wide aprons from each 3/4-in. sheet of plywood. Use a factory edge as a straightedge guide.

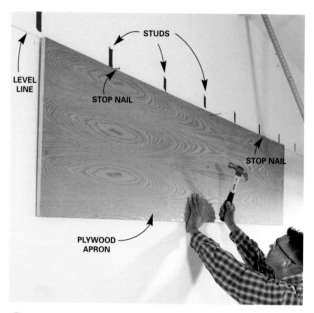

STUDS

LEVEL
LINE

STOP NAIL

STOP NAIL

PLYWOOD
APRON

2 SNAP a chalk line to mark the top of the apron and then mark the stud locations. Hold the plywood apron even with the line and nail them with 16d finish nails, four to each stud.

Lay out the walls and mount the aprons

Rip each sheet into one 23-in.-wide apron and one 24-in.-wide shelf. Use the factory edge of a "freehand" cut shelf as a saw guide for straight cuts on the other shelves and aprons (**Photo 1**).

Snap a line on the wall to mark the top of the apron and then mark all of the studs with masking tape. Take your time with this step; it's important that the apron nails anchor into solid framing, since they support the entire weight of the shelf. To be sure, poke nails through the dry-

wall (just below the line, where holes will be hidden) to find the centers of studs. Start the first apron somewhere in the middle of the wall, making sure that both ends fall on the centers of the studs. Then work toward the corners where the freehand crosscut ends will be hidden. If you're working alone, partially drive a couple of "stop" nails at the chalk line to help align the apron (**Photo 2**). That'll eliminate any guesswork. Prestart a couple of nails at stud locations before hoisting the apron into place so you can tack it to the wall while supporting it with one hand.

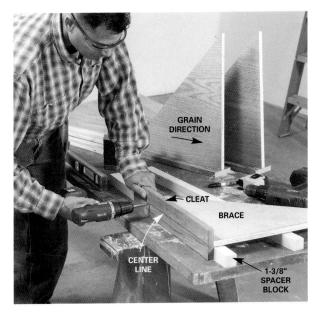

3 RIP 20-in.-wide lengths of plywood and cut them into 20-in. squares. Draw a diagonal line and cut the triangular braces. Use a sharp blade to minimize splintering.

4 REST the braces on 1-3/8-in.-thick spacer blocks, then mark the center of each 1x4 cleat. Predrill 1/8-in. holes and screw them together with three 2-1/2-in. screws.

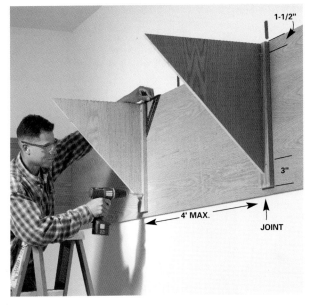

5 FASTEN each brace to the apron, flush with the top, with four 1-5/8-in. screws. Space the braces at the ends and middle of each full sheet.

6 NAIL the shelves to the apron and to the braces with 2-in. nails spaced every 8 in. Make sure joints meet at the center of the 3/4-in. braces.

Cut and mount the braces

Cut the triangular braces from 20-in. squares (**Photo 3**). You can cut the diagonal freehand because the trim will hide minor cutting flaws. Use two 1-3/8-in.-wide spacers to center and support the brace while you're screwing the 1x4 brace cleat to the back side (**Photo 4**). Drill 1/8-in. pilot holes into both pieces and countersink holes in the cleats to prevent splitting. Use three 2-1/2-in. screws, one about 2 in. in from each end and one more centered. For the best appearance, run the wood grain the same direction on each brace.

Drill four pilot holes in the cleats, two 1-1/2 in. from the top and two more 3 in. up from the bottom. Then screw each brace assembly to the apron (**Photo 5**). Use finish washers under the screws for a polished look. Position them directly over each apron seam and then place one more in the center so no shelf span is more than 4 ft. Make sure they're flush and square with the top of the apron. When shelving turns a corner, center a brace exactly 24 in. from one wall (**Figure B**). This brace will support the front edge of the shelf on the adjoining wall as well as a shelf end.

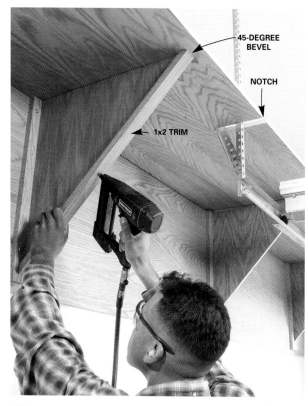

7 CUT the 1x2 brace trim pieces to fit with opposite 45-degree bevels at each end. Glue and nail them to the braces with 2-in. brads.

8 CUT the 1x2 edge trim to length, and glue and nail it to the front edge of the shelf with 2-in. brads.

Nail on the shelves and add the trim

Lay the shelves in place so joints fall over the braces and nail them to the braces and the apron with 2-in. brads spaced every 8 in. As with the apron, start somewhere in the center of each wall so you'll have factory edges abutting each other at joints and the saw cuts will be hidden at the ends. Angle the nails slightly at joints so they hit the center of the braces.

Add trim to the raw plywood edges for a nice finished look. Trim also strengthens the assembly and stiffens the shelves. Cut the brace trim to fit with opposing 45-degree bevels at each end. Then glue and nail them to each brace with 2-in. brads (**Photo 7**).

Starting at one end of each wall and working toward the other, cut the shelf edging to fit (**Photo 8**). Overlap plywood joints by at least 2 ft. for better support. The plywood will be a little wavy, but it'll straighten out as you nail on the trim.

Editor's Note: Custom cabinets

You can easily customize this shelving to fit special items like golf clubs, hanging clothes or anything else that's best stored in a cabinet or on open shelving. Just assemble a cabinet box like the one we show here so that the sides fall over the wall studs. Go as narrow as 16 in. or as wide as 4 ft., but make sure you can attach the cleats directly to wall studs. Attach those cleats to the back of the cabinet with 2-in. screws placed every foot just as you did with the braces, and then screw the assembly to the wall. The cabinet sides replace the 45-degree braces and supports the shelf. A simple unit like this one takes no more moxie than the shelves required. If you're interested in drawers or fancier cabinetry work, you're only limited by your cabinetmaking skills.
— Travis

HandyHints®

NO-SPILL FLUID JUGS

To avoid getting more windshield washer fluid on the tank than in it, store washer fluid in an empty laundry detergent bottle with a built-in funnel. Not only will you get a cleaner pour, but the detergent bottle is much sturdier than the flimsy one the fluid comes in, and it won't leak in your trunk.

DOUBLE-DUTY SHELF BRACKETS

Shelf brackets designed to support clothes hanger rods aren't just for closets. The rod-holding hook on these brackets comes in handy in the garage and workshop too. You can bend the hook to suit long tools or cords. Closet brackets cost about $3 each at home centers and hardware stores.

TRUNK BUMPERS

Keep a couple of sections of 3/4-in. pipe insulation in your trunk to protect both the car's paint and your oversized cargo. A package of pipe insulation costs about $4 at home centers and hardware stores.

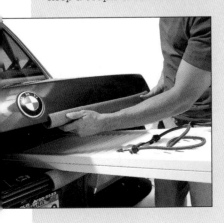

QUICK REFERENCE GUIDE

Keep a straightforward "how-to" reference guide attached to any tool that requires a series of steps to operate safely. Write concise instructions on an index card. Strengthen the paper by laminating it with packing tape. Finish by punching a hole and cable-tying the guide to the device.

AutoCare

JUMP YOUR CAR SAFELY

Carrying a set of jumper cables can help you help a fellow motorist—or the other way around. Jump-starting a vehicle is usually pretty simple, but it's serious business and you have to do it right to do it safely. Every year people are seriously injured while attempting to help another driver with a "jump." Clip this article and put it in your glove box. Then, before you even connect the cables, go through these steps:

- Make sure both batteries are the same voltage (most batteries are 12 volts) and the same polarity (both have a negative ground). You can check this information in your owner's manual in your glove box.
- Pull your cars close enough to each other to connect the cables, but never let the vehicles touch. This could cause a short.
- Shut off the ignition switch, lights and accessories in both cars. Be sure the vehicles are in park or neutral and that the parking brake is set. Wear safety glasses.
- Don't smoke. Sparks near a battery can cause an explosion.
- If the weak battery is frozen, don't try to jump it! It could explode. You can tell if it's frozen by looking through the inspection cap to see if the water is frozen. One or more sides of the battery case will bulge if it's frozen.
- Make sure you can identify the positive and negative terminals of both batteries.

Also be sure you'll have enough room to clamp to the cable terminals. The positive terminal is most likely connected to the car's starting/charging system with a red cable that has a plus sign. The negative is connected to the body/frame of the vehicle and usually has a minus sign.

WEAK BATTERY

GOOD
BATTERY

1 Clamp the positive (red or yellow) cable to the positive terminal of the weak battery. Make sure the other end doesn't touch any part of the car's engine or body or you could get a dangerous spark.

2 Clamp the other end of the positive cable to the positive terminal of the good battery.

3 Clamp the negative cable (black) to the negative terminal of the good battery.

4 Clamp the other end of the negative cable to a clean metal part of the engine (like a bolt head or bracket) in the car with the weak battery. Keep the clamp away from the battery, any moving parts and the fuel system. **Caution:** Don't attach the negative cable to the negative terminal of the weak battery! This common mistake could ignite hydrogen gas directly over the battery. Battery explosions can cause serious injury. Even if you've gotten away with it before, use a metallic engine part instead.

Now start the car with the good battery, let it charge the weak battery for 15 seconds, then try to start the car with the weak battery. If it doesn't start, shut off both ignitions, make sure the cable clamps are making good contact and then try it again. When the car with the weak battery starts, wait (about 15 seconds or so) to make sure it doesn't stall.

Disconnect the cables in the reverse order: First remove the negative cable from the car you jumped, then the negative cable from the car with the good battery. Then remove the positive cable from the car with the good battery (don't touch a grounded part of either car with the clamp of the positive cable). Finally, remove the positive cable from the car with the weak battery. Remember, both engines will be running (with any luck!), so work carefully as you remove cables to avoid belts, fans and other moving parts.

> **Tip**
>
> If you live in a very cold climate, buy the thickest-gauge cables you can find (the lower the number, the thicker the cable).

AUTO &
GARAGE

INSPECT YOUR **TIRES!**

Regular maintenance can keep you safe and save you money

Most drivers don't give their tires a second thought until they make strange noises or worse yet, go flat and leave them stranded. In this article, we'll show you how to check your tires' air pressure, we'll explain tire rotation, and we'll show you the telltale signs of tire wear and what to do about it. You'll drive more safely, improve your gas mileage and extend the life of your tires.

Maintain tire pressure

Check your tire pressure regularly and give your tires a quick inspection every time you fill up with gas (**photo above**). Pressure is measured in pounds per square inch (psi) with a tire

pressure gauge. You can buy one at any auto parts store. We found that the $10-and-up dial and digital gauges performed better in the long run than the less-expensive pencil-style gauges. Tires typically lose pressure slowly (usually about 1 psi per month). If you neglect them, they can get dangerously low, build up excessive heat, wear unevenly and deteriorate faster— all of which spell bad handling and reduced mileage.

To get an accurate reading, check the tire pressure when the tires are "cold." Obviously

DIGITAL GAUGES

DIAL GAUGE

PENCIL GAUGE

NOTE: For the proper inflation pressure for your vehicle tires, look for an inflation chart on the driver's-side door post or in your manual. Front and rear pressures may differ.

"cold" can mean completely different things in a northern Minnesota winter and an Arizona summer. For tire pressure, however, it simply means the air temperature inside the tires is the same as the air temperature outside the tires. The temperature usually takes about three hours to equalize after your tires are hot from driving. For the proper inflation pressure, look in your owner's manual or look for a sticker on the driver's-side door post. **Note:** Extremely low temperatures (below 0 degrees F) may cause the inflation valve to stick, and all the air will leak from the tire. So if it's really cold, drive the car a few miles to warm the tires first. The reading may be a bit higher, but at least you won't be stranded.

Rotate regularly

Many auto owners I've talked with know they should rotate their tires but don't do it. When you rotate tires from one wheel to the next, you distribute the wear more evenly over all four tires, giving them a longer life. This service is usually provided free by the tire dealer or you can get it as part of a maintenance contract for just a few dollars. Or take a half hour and do it yourself. Manufacturers differ on the rotation pattern and the process can differ depending on whether you have a rear-wheel-, front-wheel- or four-wheel-drive auto, so check your owner's manual. Most vehicles should have their tires rotated every 4,000 to 8,000 miles, or about every other oil change.

Watch for uneven wear

Check the condition of your tire treads every month or so and watch for the telltale signs of uneven wear (see **Figure B**).

Figure A: Suggested Tire Rotation

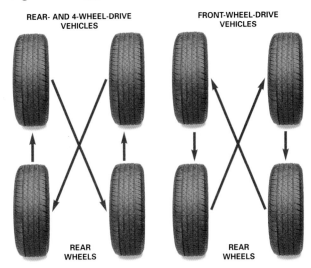

REAR- AND 4-WHEEL-DRIVE VEHICLES

FRONT-WHEEL-DRIVE VEHICLES

REAR WHEELS

REAR WHEELS

NOTE: If your vehicle has directional wheels or tires, rotate them front to back on the same side of the vehicle. Check with your dealer or tire manufacturer if you're unsure.

Stick a penny upside down into the tire tread. If you can see the top of Lincoln's hair, the tread is worn down too far and your tires should be replaced.

Figure B: Reading Tread Wear Patterns

If your tires show wear on the center of the tread only, you have overinflated tires. Check the tread depth and replace the tires if necessary or fill them to the proper pressure.

If your tires show wear on the outer edges of the tread, you're probably driving on underinflated tires. Check the tread wear and replace the tires if necessary or fill them to the proper pressure.

If your tires are worn on either the inside or outside of the tread, you'll need to have your vehicle's alignment checked.

WEAR ON CENTER

Overinflated

WEAR ON OUTER EDGES

Underinflated

WORN ON ONE SIDE

Bad Alignment

AUTO & GARAGE

TIME FOR A **FILTER CHANGE?**

Evaluate your own air filter and PCV valve

You take your car in for an oil change. The work is almost done when the technician comes out to talk to you. He's holding your air filter and PCV valve and recommending that you replace both because they "look dirty." Without missing a beat, he explains how critical the air filter is to the efficient operation of your car. He tells you that a clogged air filter, or one that's nearly clogged, can easily cost you 10 percent in gas mileage. With gas prices going through the roof, he adds, replacement will probably save you more than the cost of the filter. Plus, a dirty PCV valve, well, that's never a good thing. Then he waits for your decision. It's tough to make up your mind about a $25 air filter and an $11.95 PC-whatchamacallit valve when you don't know what to look for.

It's not difficult to check the air filter and PCV valve yourself. Here's what you need to know:

AIR FILTER CHECK

First, ignore the dirt on the leading edge of the air filter pleats. All air filters accumulate dirt on the leading edges in as little as a few thousand miles. Yet most last for about 12,000 miles. You want to know how much dirt has penetrated deep into the pleats. To test the true condition of your filter, hold a shop light behind it. See how much light passes through the inner pleats and compare yours with the three sample photos below. The filter shown on the left is totally clogged and cost the owner a fortune in wasted gas. The filter in the middle shows a clogged area, but the rest of the filter has decent light transmission. It's borderline, and the owner could probably squeeze 2,000 to 3,000 more miles out of it. It should be replaced at the next oil change interval. The filter on the right shows how much light passes through a new filter.

1 FOLLOW the black plastic duct to the air filter box. Unscrew or unsnap the latches. Remove the filter. Note that the screen always faces the engine. The pleats face the incoming air.

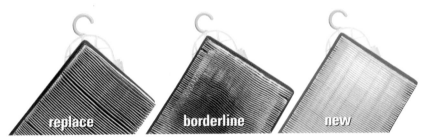
replace   borderline   new

2 Hold the filter over a shop light and compare it with the photos above. Reinstall or replace.

THE PCV STORY

The PCV (positive crankcase ventilation) valve is a one-way valve that recycles crankcase gases back into the engine to burn. A plugged PCV valve can result in a rough idle and poor mileage. Worse, it can cause costly oil leaks. Always follow your manufacturer's replacement recommendations. And never replace a PCV valve simply because it "looks dirty." All used PCV valves look dirty. Photos 1 and 2 show two ways to check its real condition.

1 REMOVE the PCV valve from its grommet. With the engine off, shake the valve. If it's good, you'll hear a solid clicking sound.

2 Or, CHECK it in place with the engine running. Pull the PCV valve from its housing and place your thumb over the PCV valve opening. You should feel it click. If the click sounds or feels mushy, replace the valve.

AUTO & GARAGE

AutoCare

CHANGE YOUR OWN
SERPENTINE BELT

It's easier than you think—if you have the right tools

If you're old enough to remember the good old days when you changed your own fan belts, then you can also remember the bruised knuckles and cursing that went along with it. And to make matters worse, there were often two or three belts to change.

Now, instead of separate belts for each component, most cars today use a single wider, multigrooved "serpentine" belt, named for the way it snakes around multiple pulleys.

Serpentine belts are easy to change because today's automatic belt tensioners eliminate the need to loosen bolts or pry components into position for retensioning. Just rotate the tensioner, remove the old belt and install a new one. When the belt ribs are seated into the pulley grooves, release the tensioner and you're done.

Start with a premium belt

You can buy an economy serpentine belt for as little as $15. But you shouldn't. The serpentine belt drives your generator, power steering, air conditioning and water pump. In other words, a belt failure can leave you stranded. The towing charges will cost far more than $30, the typical price of a premium belt. Here's how you can tell the difference between premium and economy belts:

1. **Cogs.** The manufacturers of premium belts mold cogs into the ribs of their belts. The cogs allow the belt to flex more easily, reducing heat buildup.
2. **Fabric backing.** Fabric adds stability and durability to the belt, resulting in better performance and longer life. The economy belt has no fabric backing.
3. **Compounding.** Premium rubber compounding isn't something you can see, but higher-quality compounds are more resistant to oil and coolant leaks and heat. They're also quieter.

Most economy and original equipment belts have a life of 30,000 to 40,000 miles (follow the manufacturer's schedule for belt replacement). Premium belts have almost double that life. The longer life easily justifies the slight additional expense.

Back Side
The premium belt has an embedded fabric backing and higher-quality rubber compounds that resist oil, coolant and heat. The economy belt has no fabric and is made from lower-quality materials.

Front Side
The premium belt has cogs molded into the ribs. The economy belt has none. Cogs increase belt flexibility, reduce heat buildup and dramatically increase belt life.

The right tools make it a do-it-yourself project

You can replace a serpentine belt with ordinary hand tools. But we don't recommend it. The spaces are often tight and the belt-driven devices difficult to reach. Using the Lisle serpentine belt tool and the Schley (or OTC) belt placement tool ($12), we completed the entire job in less than 15 minutes, without breaking a sweat (or a knuckle). The Lisle tool ($41) comes with an assortment of sockets, making it the perfect choice for all the cars in your family. The two extension bars can be configured to reach the tensioner at the proper angle, and the extra-long handle provides maximum leverage so you can release the pressure easily. The OTC belt placement tool allowed us to remove and properly place the new belt without reaching down into the pulley area. **Note:** If your car requires the removal of an engine mount in order to remove the serpentine belt, or the belt's just nearly impossible to get at, we recommend you leave the job to a professional.

The dealer quoted us $107 for the job shown here. Our total cost for the tools and a premium belt was about $86,

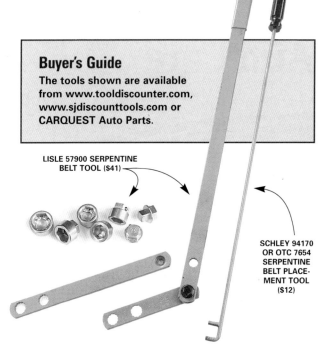

Buyer's Guide
The tools shown are available from www.tooldiscounter.com, www.sjdiscounttools.com or CARQUEST Auto Parts.

LISLE 57900 SERPENTINE BELT TOOL ($41)

SCHLEY 94170 OR OTC 7654 SERPENTINE BELT PLACEMENT TOOL ($12)

for a first-time savings of $21. Perform the job on your second family car and pocket a $77 savings ($107 minus $30, the cost of a premium belt).

BELT ROUTING DIAGRAM

1 EXAMINE the decal that shows the belt routing. If yours doesn't have one, draw one before you start the job.

TENSIONER

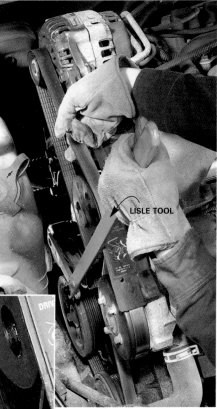

LISLE TOOL

2 USING the Lisle tool, rotate the tensioner to remove belt tension. Remove the old belt. Slowly release the tensioner.

OTC BELT PLACEMENT TOOL

3 USING the OTC belt placement tool, route the new belt around the belt path. Rotate the tensioner again while you load the belt around it. Double-check to make sure the belt is aligned with all the pulleys and that it follows the correct path. Slowly release the tensioner.

ARE YOUR **HOOD LIFTS** TOO POOPED TO PROP?

Don't jury-rig it. You can replace the lifts in less than 30 minutes

Think a snow brush makes a handy hood prop rod? Think again. Because if your makeshift prop breaks or you accidentally knock it out of place, you'll feel the full "impact" of your decision. Replacement lifts are inexpensive and easy to install, so why risk injury? Here's what you need to know to do the job yourself.

Hood and rear hatch lifts are available at any auto parts store. They cost $16 to $25 each. Since both the left and the right lifts receive the same amount of wear, you should always replace them in pairs. Right- and left-side lifts often differ only in very subtle ways, so before you leave the parts store, ask the clerk to label them. Labeling will save you time and frustration when you get home.

Every service manual says that hood/hatch lift replacement is a two-person job: One person holds the hood/hatch while the other performs the replacement. We agree with that procedure. However, Lisle Tool Co. makes a handy lift support clamp (see the Buyer's Guide) that allows you to do the job alone. The Lisle tool shown in **Photo 1** is what many professional mechanics use when they work on a car with weak hood lifts. Simply clamp it onto one hood lift (also known as a hood strut) while you work on the opposite lift.

If your car is too old to justify the cost of new hood/hatch lifts, you can also use the Lisle tool as an inexpensive and safer alternative to a makeshift prop rod.

Car makers use three different styles of lift connectors. The most popular is the "ball and socket" design, shown here on a 2000 Jeep Grand Cherokee. The ball is attached to the vehicle, and a circular spring clip secures the "socket" end of the lift onto the ball. To release the spring clip, slide a small flat-blade screwdriver into the recess on the back of the lift connector and pry the spring clip out slightly (**Photo 2**). Then pull the lift off the ball stud. Use the same procedure to install the new lift. Pry the clip out slightly, slip

PRESCRIPTION FOR DISASTER. DON'T DO THIS!

BROKEN LIFT

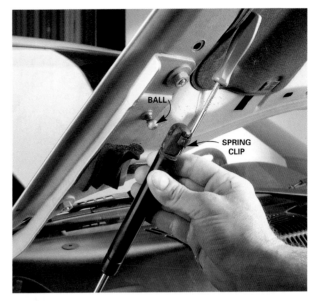

1 ATTACH a special lift support clamp to the lift shaft to hold the hood open. Have a helper temporarily hold the hood while you screw the lift support clamp into place.

2 SLIDE a small flat-blade screwdriver into the recess on the back of the ball and socket connector. Pry out the circular spring clip and pull the lift off the ball stud.

3 PRY OUT the circular spring clip on the new lift and slide the socket onto the ball stud. Use the same procedure at both ends.

4 A variation on the ball and socket has plastic fingers that snap around the ball. To release the tension on the fingers, pry off the four-legged friction cap and pull the lift off the ball stud.

the socket over the ball and push the clip back in. Another type of socket has integral plastic fingers that snap around the ball. To remove these lifts, first pry off the friction cap (**Photo 4**). Removing the cap releases tension on the fingers. Then pull the lift off the ball.

A second design uses a removable shaft held in place with "E" rings. If your car has this design, remove the E-ring with the corner of a small flat-blade screwdriver. Cover the end of the lift with a cloth to catch the E-clip when it releases. Remove the shaft and the lift. Reverse the procedure to reinstall.

A third design uses a lift that is permanently mounted

to a flange. To replace these lifts, you simply unbolt the flange from the car. Most flanges are secured with hex head bolts. However, newer vehicles may use star-shaped Torx fasteners. Check your vehicle before you go to the auto parts store. If you have the flange design and it uses Torx fasteners, you may need to buy an inexpensive set of Torx sockets or drivers.

AUTO & GARAGE

ORGANIZE YOUR **GARAGE** IN **ONE** MORNING

A plywood base plus baskets, shelves and hooks provides maximum storage in minimal space—for less than $200

by **Gary Wentz**

There are lots of ways to create more storage space in your garage, but you won't find another system that's as simple, inexpensive or versatile as this one. It begins with a layer of plywood fastened over drywall or bare studs. Then you just screw on a variety of hooks, hangers, shelves and baskets to suit your needs. That's it. The plywood base lets you quickly mount any kind of storage hardware in any spot—no searching for studs. And because you can place hardware wherever you want (not only at studs), you can arrange items close together to make the most of your wall space. As your needs change, you'll appreciate the versatility of this storage wall too; just unscrew shelves or hooks to rearrange the whole system.

We used three types of storage hardware: wire shelves, wire baskets, and a variety of hooks, hangers and brackets (see below). Selecting and arranging these items to suit your stuff can be the most time-consuming part of this project. To simplify that task, outline the dimensions of your plywood wall on the garage floor with masking tape. Then gather all the stuff you want to store and lay it out on

your outline. Arrange and rearrange items to make the most of your wall space. Then make a list of the hardware you need before you head off to the hardware store or home center.

Money, materials and planning

The total materials bill for the 6 x 16-ft. section of wall shown here was about $200. Everything you need is available at home centers. We used 3/4-in.-thick "BC" grade plywood, which has one side sanded smooth ($27 per

4 x 8-ft. sheet). You could save a few bucks by using 3/4-in. OSB "chip board" (oriented strand board; $16 per sheet) or MDF (medium-density fiberboard; $23 per sheet). But don't use particleboard; it doesn't hold screws well enough for this job. Aside from standard hand tools, all you need to complete this project is a drill to drive screws and a circular saw to cut plywood. You may also need a helper when handling plywood—full sheets are awkward and heavy.

This project doesn't require much planning; just decide how much of the wall you want to cover with plywood. You

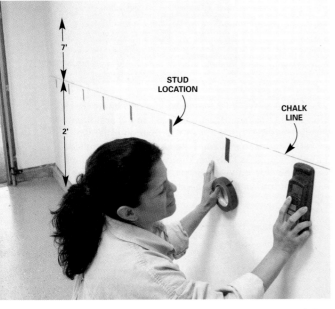

1 SNAP a level chalk line to mark the bottom edge of the plywood. Locate studs and mark them with masking tape.

2 SCREW temporary blocks to studs at the chalk line. Start a few screws in the plywood. Rest the plywood on the blocks and screw it to studs.

3 SET the upper course of plywood in place and screw it to studs. Stagger the vertical joints between the upper and lower courses.

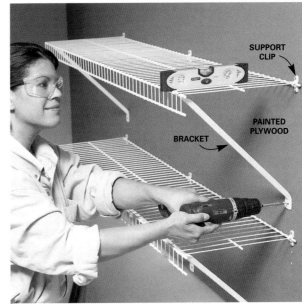

4 FASTEN the back edge of shelves with plastic clips. Set a level on the shelf and install the end brackets. Then add center brackets every 2 ft.

AUTO & GARAGE

Storage supplies for every need

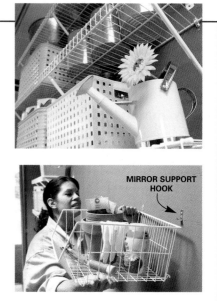

WIRE CLOSET SHELVES are sturdy and inexpensive, and they don't collect dust like solid shelving. They come in lengths up to 12 ft. and you can cut them to any length using a hacksaw or bolt cutters. Standard depths are 12, 16 and 20 in. A 12-in. x 12-ft. shelf costs about $10. You'll get more shelving for your money by cutting up long sections than by buying shorter sections. Brackets and mounting clips (Photo 4) are usually sold separately.

MIRROR SUPPORT HOOK

WIRE BASKETS are perfect for items that won't stay put on shelves (like balls and other toys) and for bags of charcoal or fertilizer that tend to tip and spill. They're also convenient because they're mobile; hang them on hooks and you can lift them off to tote all your tools or toys to the garden or sandbox. You'll find baskets in a variety of shapes and sizes at home centers and discount stores. The large baskets we used cost about $10 each. You can use just about any type of hook to hang baskets. Heavy-duty mirror supports fit our baskets perfectly.

HOOKS, HANGERS AND BRACKETS handle all the odd items that don't fit on shelves or in baskets. Basic hooks ($1 to $4) are often labeled for a specific purpose, but you can use them in other ways. Big "ladder brackets," for example, can hold several long-handled tools. "Ceiling hooks" for bikes also work on walls. Don't write off the wall area below the plywood—it's prime space for items that don't protrude far from the wall. We drove hooks into studs to hang an extension ladder.

can cover an entire wall floor-to-ceiling or cover any section of a wall. We left the lower 3 ft. of wall and upper 18 in. uncovered, since those high and low areas are best used for other types of storage. To make the most of our plywood, we combined a course of full-width sheets with a course of sheets cut in half. If your ceiling height is 9 ft. or less, a single 4-ft.-wide course of plywood may suit your needs.

Cover the wall with plywood

When you've determined the starting height of the plywood, measure up from the floor at one end of the wall and drive a nail. Then measure down to the nail from the ceiling and use that measurement to make a pencil mark at the other end of the wall. (Don't measure up from the floor, since

Sports

Beach

Lawn

Auto

Garden

5 ACRYLIC photo frames make great label holders. Just slip in your labels and hot glue the frames to wire baskets. Frames cost about $2 each at office supply and discount stores.

Handy Hooks

When you're out shopping, you might find elaborate hangers designed to hold specific toys and tools. These specialty hooks are neat, but you don't have to spend $10 or more just to hang a bike or garden tools. With a little ingenuity, you can hang just about anything on simple screw-in hooks that typically cost about $1. You can place hooks anywhere on your plywood wall. If you don't put them on the plywood, be sure to locate them at studs.

DRILL A HOLE AT A 45-DEGREE ANGLE AND TURN IN A SCREW HOOK TO HANG A BICYCLE BY THE FRONT WHEEL.

HANG LADDERS ON HOOKS BELOW THE PLYWOOD FOR EASY ACCESS.

garage floors often slope.) Hook your chalk line on the nail, stretch it to the pencil mark and snap a line (**Photo 1**).

Cut the first sheet of plywood to length so it ends at the center of a stud. Place the end you cut in the corner. That way the factory-cut edge will form a tight joint with the factory edge of the next sheet. Be sure to place the rough side of the plywood against the wall. Fasten the plywood with 10d finish nails or screws that are at least 2-1/4 in. long (**Photo 2**). We used trim screws, which have small heads that are easy to cover with a dab of spackling compound. Drive screws or nails every 12 in. into each stud. If you add a second course of plywood above the first as we did (**Photo 3**), you'll have to cut the plywood to width. You can use a circular saw, but a table saw gives you faster, straighter cuts. Some home centers and lumberyards cut plywood for free or for a small charge.

With all the plywood in place, you could go ahead and mount your hardware. But we took a few extra steps to dress up our wall: First, we added 3/4-in. cove molding along the lower edge of the plywood. This gave us a neater look and covered up the chalk line and screw holes left by the support blocks. We also framed the window trim with doorstop molding to hide small gaps between the trim and the plywood. Then we caulked gaps between the sheets of plywood and filled screw holes. Finally, we primed the plywood, lightly sanded it with 100-grit sandpaper and painted it. 🏠

Editor's Note:
Now's the time to add outlets

If your garage has bare stud walls, adding outlets is easy. But if your walls are covered, our plywood storage wall makes adding outlets or extra circuits easier because you can cut big holes in the drywall to run wire and cover up the damage with the plywood. No patching needed. (Exception: To meet fire code, if the wall adjoins living space, the hole must be patched.) Since the plywood itself will be covered with shelves and hangers, place new outlets below it for easier access. If you have an existing outlet that will be covered with plywood, cut a hole in the plywood about 1/8 in. larger than the junction box and add a box extender (see photo). All garage outlets must be either GFCI outlets or connected to a circuit that's GFCI-protected, so you may need to replace your existing outlet with a GFCI version.
— Gary

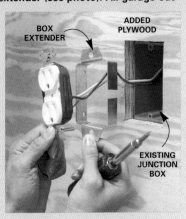

ADDED PLYWOOD

BOX EXTENDER

EXISTING JUNCTION BOX

AUTO & GARAGE

GreatGoofs®

Cut the lights

When I built my house, I wanted a tall garage opening to accommodate our full-size trucks. That meant I had to mount the garage door track just a few inches from the ceiling. The installation went without a hitch. The first time I hit the garage door button, the door opened perfectly, rolled smoothly along the rails—and sheared off my ceiling lights!

Ramped-up romance

My college girlfriend and I were on the skids. So when her new car was ready for its first oil change, I saw my chance to show that I was both a gentleman and a handyman. I brought my car ramps over to her place and inched up the ramps carefully. But not carefully enough. Clunk! The wheels rolled right off the ends of the ramps and the car was stuck there like a beached whale. Needless to say, this did not rekindle our romance.

GARAGE DOOR TUNE-UP

Quit fighting it! Tips for a quieter, safer, smoother-operating door

by **Bob Nelson**

When you hear the words "tune-up" and "garage" in the same sentence, you probably think of your car, motorcycle or lawn mower. But there's a different type of tune-up, one that's simple to perform and can extend the life of the "equipment" by up to five years: a garage door tune-up.

Squeaking and grinding noises, rough operation and poorly reacting safety mechanisms are sure signs your door needs attention. This article will show you how to maintain and inspect your garage door to ensure it will work smoothly and safely. The garage door in our example is a 16-ft.-wide steel door with an overhead torsion spring and automatic opener. Your door might be slightly different, but most of the maintenance steps described here will be the same.

Safety First

We won't show you how to deal with problems involving a high-tension torsion spring—the type mounted on a rod over your door that acts as a counterbalance and determines how much effort it takes you to raise and lower the door. These springs are dangerous. Some manufacturers, such as Clopay and Wayne Dalton, now have do-it-yourself–friendly systems that can be adjusted with a power drill. Unless you have this type of system (like the one shown on p. 267), and the instruction manual, hire a professional. Adjusting or replacing extension springs—the type mounted on each side of your door by the tracks—or the cables connected to them can also be dangerous and should be left to trained professionals.

You can adjust safety systems yourself, particularly the automatic reversal mechanism, but leave repairs to pros. Don't take chances when it comes to safety.

TORSION SPRING

TIGHTEN BOLTS ON GARAGE DOOR AND GARAGE TRACK BRACKETS

RIGHT FOR TIGHT

Tighten the bolts that connect the hinges to the door and those that secure the mounting brackets to the garage framework. Bolts on steel doors (like the one shown) rarely loosen; those on wood doors tend to loosen and should be examined and tightened regularly.

EMERGENCY RELEASE HANDLE

CHECK THE DOOR FOR BALANCE

With the garage door in the closed position, disengage the door from the automatic opener by pulling down on the emergency release handle. Manually open the door halfway and let go. If the door is balanced properly, it should stay in the halfway position or creep down slowly.

If the door closes quickly or if you have to pull it down hard from the halfway position, it isn't properly balanced and will overstress the automatic opener. Hire a garage door professional to adjust the spring tension.

Tip

Manually operated doors have brackets and locking tongues (one on each side) that are operated by cables connected to the exterior handle (inset). If your door has an automatic opener, remove the brackets; if these locks are accidentally engaged while the opener is trying to open the door, you could damage the door or opener.

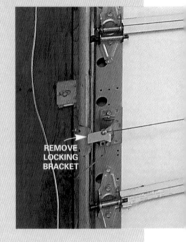

REMOVE LOCKING BRACKET

REPLACE WORN WEATHER SEALS

The elements, age and rodents (who rarely use the automatic opener) can all take their toll on the weatherstripping around the door, particularly the weather seal along the bottom. If you can see gaps at the bottom of the door when it's closed, replace the seal.

Most metal doors have two channels along the lower edge that the weather seal slides into. To replace the seal, first use a screwdriver to open the channels on their ends (they've usually been pinched to secure the existing seals in place) and slide the old seal out. Wipe the channels clean, lubricate them with dish soap or silicone spray, then slide the new seal into place. This process is much easier if you have a helper.

CHANNELS

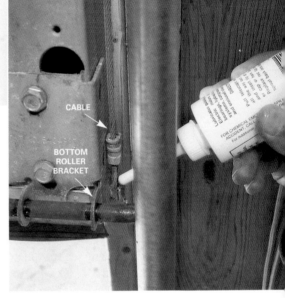

TORSION SPRING

CABLE

BOTTOM ROLLER BRACKET

LUBRICATE THE CABLE CONNECTIONS AND SPRINGS

While you shouldn't attempt to replace or adjust cables or springs, you should lubricate them:

- Apply one or two drops where the two cables connect to the bottom roller mount brackets. This is also a good time to check the cable for wear (**see below**).
- Run a bead of oil along the top of the torsion spring. The oil will eventually work its way down, coating the spring and preventing corrosion.

CHECK CABLES AND CABLE CONNECTION POINTS FOR WEAR

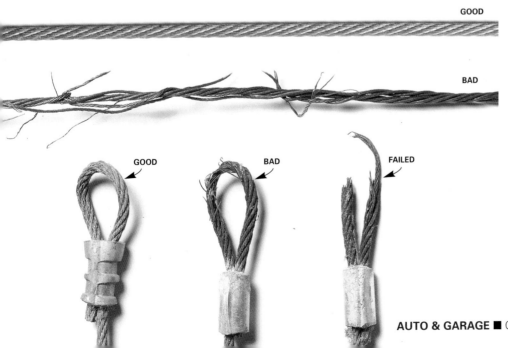

GOOD

BAD

GOOD   BAD   FAILED

Cables can fray and break in two places: along their length and at the ends where they connect to the roller brackets and spring mechanism. Inspect your cables; hire a professional to replace frayed cables immediately.

SAFETY
REVERSING
SENSORS

CHECK THE SAFETY
REVERSAL FEATURES

Today's garage doors and automatic openers include several safety features. To check the safety reversal system, set a 2x4 flat on the ground centered in the opening as shown. Close the door using the automatic opener. When the door contacts the 2x4, it should reverse itself and open.

To check the safety reversal sensors, start closing the door with the automatic opener, then wave your hand between the safety reversal sensors (**photo above**). The door should reverse and reopen.

If your door fails either test, read the opener owner's manual for adjustment guidelines. If your adjustments don't fix the problems, consult a trained professional to repair or replace the opener. If your opener lacks these safety features altogether, replace it.

2x4 CENTERED
IN OPENING

LUBRICATE THE HINGES,
ROLLERS AND TRACKS

Oiling the moving parts on your door will help it operate more smoothly and more quietly. Make sure to:

- Apply two drops of regular household oil (such as 3-in-One) in each seam of every hinge. Apply the oil on top so it can work its way down and lubricate the entire seam.
- Apply two drops in each seam of each roller mount bracket on the door, and a drop or two on the ends of each roller pin.
- Apply six drops of oil on the roller track. To ensure that all the rollers come in contact with the lubricated section, apply the oil about 1 ft. from the curve in the track. Note: Do NOT oil the track if your door has nylon rollers; certain oils can soften, gum up and ruin nylon rollers. After you've oiled all the parts, use the automatic opener to raise and lower the door a few times to help distribute the oil. 🏠

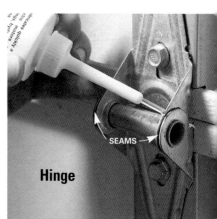

SEAMS

Hinge

Roller bracket and pin

SEAMS

ROLLER PIN

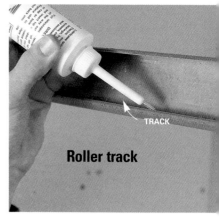

TRACK

Roller track

Tip Wipe away any grease buildup on the rollers and roller pins before lubricating the door. Grease combines with sand and grit to form a sludge that acts as an abrasive and eats away at the rollers.

WordlessWorkshop™

by **Roy Doty**

PULL-DOWN STORAGE BINS

GREAT NEW PRODUCTS FOR YOUR GARAGE

PARK ON A MAT TO CONTAIN A MESS

It's one thing to get dirt on your garage floor, but when your vehicle drips motor oil, transmission fluid, rain and melting snow, you can end up with a real mess and an ugly stain. It's even worse when you get it on your shoes and track it into the house. The solution? Park your vehicle on a giant mat.

The Clean Park Garage Mat ($110 to $240) is made with 20- or 50-mil vinyl, similar to a pool liner, to protect garage floors from tire tracks and dripping fluids. The raised 1-in. snap-on bracket edges contain water and slush. Buy it online.

Allmats, (866) 411-6287. www.allmats.com

VINYL MAT

SNAP-ON BRACKETS

HEAVYWEIGHT STORAGE

You'll be impressed with Loft-It—a motorized lift system capable of raising and storing 1,200 lbs. You can't beat it for storing ATVs and riding lawn mowers.

Loft-It uses a key-controlled switch (plugged into a standard outlet), so once you lift something, only your key can get it back down. No-fall drop protection makes it safe and secure. Get it online for $2,500 to $3,300.

Tivan, (800) 409-1350. www.loft-it.com

STORAGE PLATFORM

KEY SWITCH

TIVAN

MEDIUM-WEIGHT CEILING LIFT

Tired of shoving the stuff in your garage from one side to the other without gaining any floor space? Then try raising it to the ceiling. With the 4 x 4-ft. HeavyLift platform from Racor, you can load, lift and store up to 250 lbs.—keeping things off the floor.

A hand crank raises and lowers the platform (no ladder needed). The system ($200) can be mounted to ceilings up to 12 ft. high. It's perfect for seasonal items that you don't want to hassle with year round. Find retailers on the company's Web site or order online.

Racor, (800) 783-7725. www.racorinc.com

CEILING STORAGE FOR AWKWARD ITEMS

Lifting and storing large, odd-shaped items can be challenging, even if they're lightweight. But Harken's hoist systems make it easy for items up to 200 lbs. Two straps slide under or onto the item, then a single rope raises or lowers the load evenly. It'll lift the item right off a floor or vehicle, eliminating any manual lifting. A safety cleat automatically locks the load when you let go of the rope. Harken offers several types of hoist systems ($35 to $170) for everything from bikes to kayaks to pickup toppers. Look for these hoist systems at GarageTek stores (other retailers are listed at the Web address below).

Harken, (262) 691-3320. www.hoister.com

BIKE RACK

BIKE HOLDER

FOUR-BIKE RACK

There are a lot of bike stands on the market today, but we liked SportRack's telescoping storage rack. It maximizes space to hold up to four bikes and is easy to set up and take down. The "telescoping" pole adjusts to fit the span between the floor and a ceiling up to 10 ft. The rack costs $110 with holders for two bikes. Extra holders to store two more bikes run $52. Find it at The Complete Garage, www.completegarage.com, (866) 892-0200.

SportRack, (800) 561-0716. www.sportrack.com

TIGHTER-FITTING GARAGE DOOR

Warped garage doors and uneven concrete floors can leave gaps between the closed door and the floor. That's all it takes for leaves, water, blowing snow or critters to gain entrance.

The StormShield Garage Door Threshold provides a tight seal. Installation is quick and easy—cut it to length and glue it to the floor (adhesive included). A 10-ft. length costs about $60. Larger sizes are available. Call or go online to find a dealer near you.

Action Industries, (800) 321-1130. www.action-ind.com

WEATHERSTRIPPING

PARKING MAT

GARAGE PARKING GUIDE

If you want to know when to stop your vehicle in the garage, put this $20 polyethylene mat on the floor where your front wheel sits. You'll feel a bump when you drive over it, letting you know when to stop. The mats, like this one from Racor, can be used for all types of cars and trucks. Find retailers on the company's Web site or order online.

Racor, (800) 783-7725. www.racorinc.com

AUTO & GARAGE

HANDYMAN
DISASTERS

Avoid these common mistakes—and save
yourself big headaches and big money

RUSHING A CONCRETE POUR

Concrete pours are exciting. When the truck comes, you have to work fast and hard to place the heavy stuff carefully and finish it off before it hardens. They're risky, too. Many things can go wrong, and a mistake can mean tons of useless rock.

I witnessed that kind of disaster a few years ago when I helped a friend pour his driveway. It was a fairly ambitious project, about 4 yards of concrete, but we were experienced and he had enough helpers. Although the weather forecast included possible rainstorms, we thought we could knock it off in about two hours in the morning.

That morning the clouds darkened, but my friend wanted to go ahead anyway. We had completed about three-quarters of the pour when the deluge came. There was nothing we could do. Water poured into the forms and ruined the concrete. A few days later it had to be jackhammered out and hauled away.

When you're pouring concrete, consider:

- Are the forms solid? Once a form bows or dips under the weight of the concrete, it's almost impossible to straighten it. Avoid last-minute form building. Complete them before the truck arrives.
- Do you have enough tools and help? Placing and smoothing have to go well so the concrete doesn't harden too soon.
- How far can the truck back up? A loaded concrete truck can break driveways, walks and septic systems. It's better to wheelbarrow the concrete a little farther than to take a chance.
- Did you check the weather? Rain will ruin concrete that hasn't set (concrete usually sets in a few hours). After concrete has set, however, rain will actually help it cure (harden). Avoid pours in hot weather (above 90 degrees F), because the concrete will harden too fast.
- Did you order enough? Double-check the form dimensions and the order. Coming up short can ruin the pour.

BUILDING TOO CLOSE TO THE PROPERTY LINE

Property lines can be a sensitive issue when you're building close or right up to them. You have to deal with the neighbors and satisfy local code requirements. Recently a building inspector told me a tale about a homeowner who had decided to build his own garage in the back corner of his lot facing the alley. The city approved the plan and then gave the homeowner a sheet of paper with all the rules and restrictions such as property line setbacks and building heights.

The homeowner poured the slab and started framing.

While framing the roof, he decided to change the plan and extend the overhang to direct the water away from the foundation. When the job was finished, he called for the final inspection.

When the inspector showed up, he noticed that the eaves extended over the property line and told the homeowner he'd have to trim that side of the roof to comply. As you can imagine, nobody was happy about the extra work and expense. And the garage looks bad too.

The inspector's words of wisdom:

"Stick to your plan, and check your local building requirements whenever your project affects setbacks."

■ **Garages.** Double-check setback requirements before you pour the slab. Roof overhangs may also have to meet similar rules. Also check size and height limitations.

■ **Sheds.** These often have size and height limitations in addition to setback requirements. They may have design restrictions as well.

■ **Front porches. Surprise!** Front porches, like the main house structure, often must meet setback requirements from the street.

■ **Fences.** Check specific fence setback rules. Observe height restrictions. Most rules require the nicest side of the fence to face outward. Fences are a common source of neighborhood irritation.

■ **Decks.** Setbacks for decks may be the same as for the house. Always call the planning office with questions before you start your project or you too could be in for a costly but completely avoidable mistake.

SKIMPING ON FLOOR PREP

Home centers now have a spectacular array of floor coverings to choose from—oak, maple and exotic species of hardwood; a variety of ceramic and stone tile; handsome styles of sheet vinyl and vinyl tile; and durable laminates—most of which you can install yourself. But there's one big trap that can ruin all your efforts: inadequate subfloor preparation. All floors are just looking for an excuse to squeak, creak and groan, and that's exactly what yours will do unless you take pains to get the subfloor right.

A cabinetmaker friend of mine learned that the hard way when he recently installed 12 x 12-in. glue-down composite tiles in his kitchen. He partially scraped off the old vinyl tiles but gave up after a while because it was tough going. He then screwed thin plywood over the entire floor to create a smooth base and laid his new tile. But soon he noticed a crackling sound whenever he walked across the new floor. He finally concluded that patches of old adhesive were grabbing the new plywood underlayment as it flexed underfoot. Unfortunately, there's no fix except to tear everything out and start over.

When you're about to lay a new floor, you have the perfect opportunity to upgrade your subfloor to make it solid and squeak-free. While the specifics might vary a bit depending on your new flooring material, consider these issues:

- **Deflection/stiffness.** If you find soft spots in your floor or areas that "give" as you walk across them, stiffen them by adding framing from below or more underlayment on top. Ceramic tile floors require extra stiffness to keep grout lines from cracking.
- **Bounce.** If the dinner plates rattle every time you walk across your kitchen floor, you're getting too much vibration or bounce. Corrections must be made from below.
- **Flatness.** Now's the time to level off high spots and fill low areas so your new floor runs true.
- **Squeaks.** Drive screws through the subfloor into joists to eliminate the wood movement that causes squeaks. Use adhesive as well as screws to fasten new underlayment down.
- **Surface flaws.** Some flooring, like vinyl, linoleum and carpeting, requires perfectly smooth subfloors or underlayments. Otherwise, every flaw underneath will be telegraphed to the surface.
- **Moisture in concrete.** Always check the moisture level in concrete before laying flooring over it. Trapped moisture will ruin the floor and encourage mold.
- **Asbestos.** Asbestos, a proven carcinogen, was used in many types of flooring and adhesives. While old flooring isn't hazardous if left undisturbed, don't rip it out unless you know it's asbestos-free. Call your local health department for instructions about how to collect a sample and have it tested for asbestos.

"All floors are looking for an excuse to squeak, creak and groan—that's why there's no such thing as too much prep work when installing one."

CREAK! CREAK! CREAK! CREAK!

CALLING IN A BIG CREW FOR A CHALLENGING PROJECT

Assembling a large crew seems like the perfect solution when you're tackling a big job. But a large crew of inexperienced helpers can be a hazard to quality results. Like the 12 guys who helped my neighbor roof his house. He coached them on shingle layout and trimming techniques, but he couldn't supervise them all. A few hours later, after a flurry of hammering from every corner of the roof, he ended up with wavy rows of shingles, rows that didn't meet above gables and forgotten flashing at a dormer. He corrected the worst problems and the roof doesn't leak. But the job still looks bad and would cost thousands to redo.

Managing a big group is tough. On one hand, you want everyone to be engaged in the work, but it's not always obvious what task is best suited to each person's skills. And you can't be everywhere at once to supervise. And of course, you run the risk of hurt feelings and other "interpersonal complexities."

In planning for a big crew:

- Avoid complex projects like roofing, taping drywall, putting up siding and insulating. All require attention to detail, and mistakes are often difficult to correct.
- Focus on simple projects that require mostly unskilled labor, like painting, digging and backfilling (moving dirt!), demolition and cleanup, and hauling lumber and drywall.
- Select the helpers you need for more skilled projects like roofing, setting fence posts, hanging drywall and installing siding. Don't assume that friends and family understand the scope of the job just because they own a hammer or a tool belt.
- Invite only as many as you can manage and coach to meet your standards. They should understand your exact goals and expectations and be enthusiastic about meeting them. There is great satisfaction in a job well done.

CHANGING A FLOOR WITHOUT CONSIDERING THE HEIGHT

A flooring height change is one of the most complex issues a homeowner can face. It can affect thresholds, doors, stairs, cabinets and a myriad of other things with dire consequences. For example, a friend decided to install a new prefinished maple laminate floor right over the old vinyl flooring in his kitchen. He removed the range, the refrigerator and the dishwasher and got right to work.

Everything went fine until it came time to fit the dishwasher back under the countertop. It was 1/2 in. too tall even with the foot adjusters screwed all the way in. Eventually he had to remove the countertops, raise them and then rework the entire tile backsplash—two full days of extra work. And it could have been much worse. ⌂

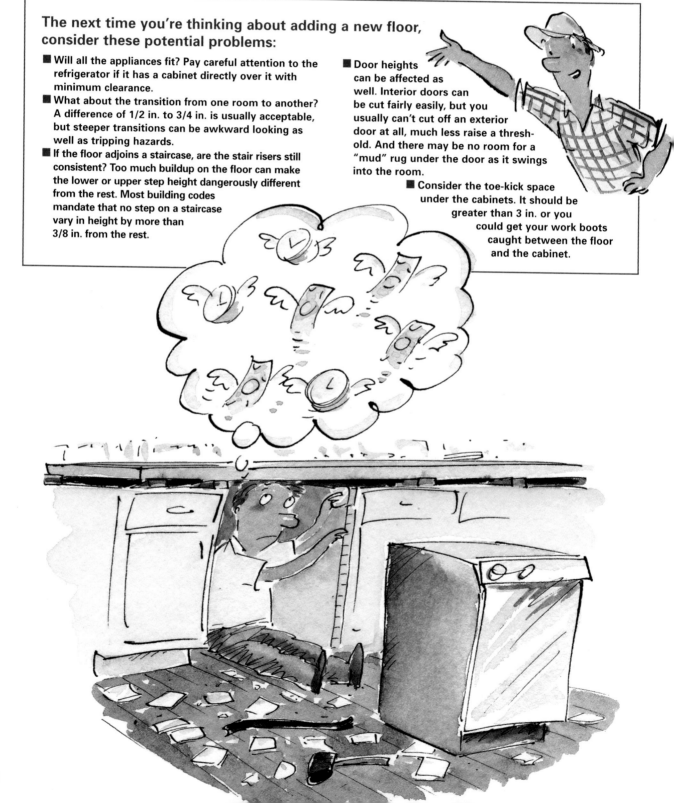

The next time you're thinking about adding a new floor, consider these potential problems:

- Will all the appliances fit? Pay careful attention to the refrigerator if it has a cabinet directly over it with minimum clearance.
- What about the transition from one room to another? A difference of 1/2 in. to 3/4 in. is usually acceptable, but steeper transitions can be awkward looking as well as tripping hazards.
- If the floor adjoins a staircase, are the stair risers still consistent? Too much buildup on the floor can make the lower or upper step height dangerously different from the rest. Most building codes mandate that no step on a staircase vary in height by more than 3/8 in. from the rest.

- Door heights can be affected as well. Interior doors can be cut fairly easily, but you usually can't cut off an exterior door at all, much less raise a threshold. And there may be no room for a "mud" rug under the door as it swings into the room.
- Consider the toe-kick space under the cabinets. It should be greater than 3 in. or you could get your work boots caught between the floor and the cabinet.

PREVENT HOUSEHOLD DISASTERS

Be a home hero! These 11 simple, low-cost tips could save you thousands!

MAIN WATER SHUTOFF

TURN OFF THE WATER SUPPLY BEFORE GOING ON VACATION

Water damage from undetected plumbing leaks will quickly ruin floors and walls, leading to repair bills in the thousands. This is especially true if you're away on vacation. Yes, such a leak is unlikely, but insurance companies report hundreds of these incidents every year. Look for the main valve near the water meter and turn it clockwise to close it. If it's stuck, leaks or doesn't turn on again, hire a plumber to replace it. The ice maker in your refrigerator may freeze up while you're gone, so shut it off too or thaw it with a hair dryer when you return.

USE METAL TUBING RATHER THAN PLASTIC FOR ICE MAKER SUPPLY LINES

If you've had mice in your home, use a copper (type L) or braided stainless steel line rather than a plastic supply line for the ice maker in your refrigerator. Mice like to hang out behind refrigerators and occasionally chew holes in plastic lines, causing a leak that can ruin floors and ceilings before you detect it. Plastic tubes also can harden over time and crack. Find metal ice maker lines at home centers and wherever appliances are sold.

SPECIAL BONUS SECTION

TEST YOUR SUMP PUMP BEFORE THE BEGINNING OF THE RAINY SEASON

The most common time for a sump pump to fail is the first heavy rainfall after months of not being used. The submerged or partially submerged portions of cast iron pumps may rust and seize. And they'll burn out when they switch on. Don't get caught with your pump down and the water rising. After a long dry (unused) spell, take a few moments to pour a bucket or two of water into the sump to make sure the pump kicks on.

MONITOR FOUNDATION OR WALL CRACKS AND CHECK MONTHLY TO DETECT MOVEMENT

Hairline cracks in a concrete foundation are normal, but cracks that continue to widen spell trouble. They'll eventually cause shifting and cracking in the walls above, tilt floors and rack doors and windows so they won't open and close. The movement is glacially slow. To help you spot it, measure and record the gap size. Check it every few months. If the cracks widen, call in a foundation specialist ("Foundation Contractors" in the yellow pages) to assess the foundation. Solutions can cost hundreds of dollars, but the cost of ignoring the problem is greater. A major foundation fix can cost thousands.

TRIM TREES AROUND THE HOUSE SO DEAD BRANCHES WON'T CRASH DOWN ON THE ROOF

Insurance companies get a flood of tree-related claims after major storms. You can't prevent all of these incidents, but many you can, if you trim out overhanging branches and dying trees just waiting to fall. Tree trimming is dangerous and not a do-it-yourself project. Call in a tree service to trim all tall trees around your home every few years. Don't procrastinate. Spending a few hundred dollars now could save you several thousands in roof and rain damage later.

PUT SPLASH PANS UNDER WASHERS AND WATER HEATERS TO CATCH LEAKS

Once upon a time, water heaters and clothes washers always sat on concrete floors near drains, where spills and leaks wouldn't hurt anything. Now they often sit on framed wood floors, sometimes on the second floor, where spills, overflows, broken hoses or slow drips can cause stains, rot and other potentially expensive water damage. For about $20, you can buy special pans at home centers and appliance dealers that catch slow leaks and mild overflows. Some have drain holes where you can connect a tube that leads to a floor drain. They won't stop burst water lines or massive overflows, but they're cheap insurance against water damage caused by minor spills and leaks.

BUY NO-BURST HOSES FOR YOUR CLOTHES WASHER

If your current hoses are more than five years old, replace them with no-burst hoses. The supply hoses to your clothes washer are always under pressure, just like the supply pipes in your water system. However, eventually the rubber will harden, crack and leak. If undetected, the leak can cause extensive water damage. An inexpensive solution is to buy no-burst hoses. These high-quality hoses are less likely to leak and they'll keep any leak from becoming a torrent. They cost less than $20 a pair at home centers, hardware stores and appliance stores.

ADD 6-FT.-LONG DOWNSPOUT EXTENSIONS

A 1-in. rainfall drops about 650 gallons of water on an average roof. And your downspouts concentrate all that water in only a few spots. If dumped too close to the house, the water will undermine your foundation, causing it to leak, shift or crack. Very expensive fix. Downspout extensions will prevent most major problems, including wet basements, cracked foundation walls, and termite and carpenter ant infestations.

ONCE A YEAR, INSPECT YOUR FOUNDATION FOR TERMITE TUNNELS

Pull out your flashlight and walk around your home, examining the foundation, both inside and out, to inspect for termite tunnels. Much of the damage termites do is invisible, inside walls and floors. Take the time to look for telltale sawdust and tunnels, because termites can do major damage before you even know they're there. If you spot signs of termites, call in a professional exterminator.

STRAP YOUR WATER HEATER IF YOU LIVE IN AN EARTHQUAKE-PRONE REGION

Earth tremors can tip water heaters and break the gas lines that lead to them, causing either water damage, or worse, an explosion and fire. Water heater straps can prevent this disaster. (They're required in California and other regions.) In earthquake-prone regions, you can find them at home centers and hardware stores for less than $15. Otherwise, order them over the Internet. One source is Earthquakestore.com, (888) 442-2220. On the home page, click on "disaster accessories."

WATER HEATER STRAP

INSTALL SURGE PROTECTORS TO PROTECT YOUR MICROPROCESSORS AND PREVENT DATA LOSS

Computer chips are sensitive and highly vulnerable to momentary power surges, especially powerful ones induced by lightning. Losing a $1,000 computer is bad enough, but losing photos, music and other irreplaceable stuff on your hard drive is often much worse. Insulate your valuable microprocessors from this danger by plugging them into a surge protector. Better surge protectors ($40 and up) will have the following ratings printed somewhere on the box: meets UL 1449 or IEEE 587; clamps at 330 volts or lower; can absorb at least 100 joules of energy or more; and handles telephone lines and video cables as well.

SURGE PROTECTOR

Have you ever trimmed the bottom off a door so it wouldn't drag on the new carpet—only to discover you trimmed the top by mistake? Or accidentally screwed a towel bar firmly in place—to a copper pipe? Or successfully hung an entire roomful of wallpaper—upside down?

If so, welcome to the Great Goofs Club, an organization to which most do-it-yourselfers automatically qualify in spite of their best efforts.

Since we started the Great Goofs department nine years ago, we've seen some doozies. Here are the best of the worst.

The best "clogged-drain" goof

1 "I did what you said, Dad"

My bathroom sink stopped up and I had to take off the trap to pull out a clog of gunk. I removed the trap and caught the water in a bucket—scummy, soapy, toothpaste goobery, hairy water. I then positioned myself under the pipe to look up and make sure that all the gunk was out of the drain. I handed the bucket of water up to my 4-year-old son and asked him to get rid of it. He did what seemed perfectly natural to him—he poured it down the sink! All of the slimy water came right back in my face with a vengeance.

2 Super Glue follies

In the middle of a bathroom repair, I left a bottle of Super Glue uncapped while I answered the phone. My husband went into the bathroom and disrobed for a shower—but first, he sat on the toilet. An inveterate bathroom reader, he picked up the glue bottle and started to read it. A few minutes later, I heard this muffled cry for help. I hung up and went to investigate. My husband had somehow glued his chest to his thighs. I got him backed out of the bathroom and onto the bed and tried to pull his legs free. We couldn't get him unstuck! I decided he must be rushed to the emergency room, but he refused to go naked. I mean, how do you get pants on a naked man glued to himself? I brought in a plastic lawn bag to wrap him in, but he refused to go like that. I called a nurse friend, who, after laughing uncontrollably, suggested I dribble nail polish remover onto his chest and work it into the glued area with cotton swabs. It worked, but to this day, any mention of Super Glue brings a look of terror to my husband's face.

3 Floor sander stampede

After giving our living room a fresh coat of paint, I decided to try my hand at refinishing the hardwood floors. So I rented a floor sander, an 80-lb. beast of a machine with a large rotating drum that sands the floor while you walk behind. I loaded a coarse-grit sandpaper, as recommended, and plugged in the machine. After sanding a few feet, the machine stopped. I noticed that the heavy plug had partially slipped out, so I walked over and wiggled it back into the outlet.

I quickly discovered that the sander's switch was still on. The thing started up and shot across the room like the rabbit at a dog race, with me chasing it. It crashed through the wall I had just painted, leaving a hole about the size of...well, a floor sander. Even worse, my wife and daughter had been watching. They quietly left the room. I also left the room...to get my drywall tools.

4 Doggone it!

I was building a doghouse for my son-in-law's dog in my compact 8 x 12-ft. workshop. Everything went fine until it was time to take it outside and paint it. I tried to get it out the door front-to-back, then side-to-side, then flipped it top-to-bottom, but it was still a couple of inches too wide. After all this work, I wasn't about to dismantle this fabulous project. Two hours later, I finally got it outside—after I had removed the trim, the door and the door frame!

5 Big porcelain doorstop

A friend of mine decided to replace his toilet with a great-looking new one. We pulled out the old one with confidence and hooked up the new toilet in no time. After finishing, we decided to relax and watch the game on TV. About a half hour later, we heard laughter coming from the bathroom. We rushed over and found his wife unable to close the bathroom door. The new toilet protruded a few inches farther, blocking the door from closing.

6 The copper stud

My wife wanted a slide-out tray in one of our kitchen cabinets, and this required a cleat screwed to the studs. I got out my electronic stud finder and it showed a stud in exactly the right spot. I screwed on the cleat and the tray, but when I put my tools away in the basement, I saw water dripping. The "stud" was actually the water pipe to our bathroom, now with two new drywall screws in it.

7 Super Bowl blackout

One mild Sunday morning this last winter, I decided to start digging up the ground for my new garden. The area was about 40 yards from the house, so I figured there were no underground electrical wires to worry about. What I didn't think about was cable TV. Well, you guessed it, I cut right through a cable line, which just happened to be the main feed for our entire neighborhood. No one had TV reception for the rest of the day. Talk about upset neighbors—it was Super Bowl Sunday!

8 Fillet o' boat

The best "I cut through it by mistake" goof

A friend of mine rounded up a group to make much-needed repairs on his storage shed. We each picked out tasks and got to work. The sawhorses were in use, so I suggested we do our cutting on the flat bottom of his 16-ft. johnboat. We had only sawed a few boards when we discovered a long saw cut through the bottom of the boat. Needless to say, our fishing trip that summer was canceled. I wonder if he'll call me for future projects.

9 Whoopsy daisies

The best "I hung it upside down" goof

On the weekend we were going to wall-paper our kitchen in a new floral pattern, I decided to let my wife sleep in a little and get started on my own. I'd been working for over an hour when my wife came down. I asked how she liked the wallpaper. She said she liked it a lot but felt it would look even better if the flowers were growing up, not toward the floor!

The best "I had to go to the emergency room" goof

10 Wrenching experience

I was using an older electric impact wrench to bolt the 2x4 plate to the foundation on an addition to my sister's house. When one of the 5/8-in. nuts got jammed in the socket, I used a finger to try to wiggle it loose. But I accidentally squeezed the trigger, and the wrench drove the nut to the second knuckle on my middle finger. In the emergency room, the doctor whispered to a nurse and handed her his car keys. She soon returned with a toolbox, and we all laughed when he pulled out an adjustable wrench. In a matter of minutes, he "unscrewed" the nut, but it took weeks for the thread marks to disappear.

INDEX

Visit www.familyhandyman.com to search five years of article archives.

ACKNOWLEDGMENTS

FOR THE FAMILY HANDYMAN

Editor in Chief	Ken Collier
Editor	Duane Johnson
Executive Editor	Spike Carlsen
Associate Editors	Jeff Gorton
	Travis Larson
	Eric Smith
	Gary Wentz
Assistant Editor	Brett Martin
Senior Copy Editor	Donna Bierbach
Design Director	Sara Koehler
Senior Art Director	Bob Ungar
Art Directors	Becky Pfluger
	Marcia Wright Roepke
Office Administrative Manager	Alice Garrett
Financial Assistant	Steven Charbonneau
Technical Manager	Keith Kostman
Reader Service Specialist	Roxie Filipkowski
Office Administrative Assistant	Shelly Jacobsen
Production Manager	Judy Rodriguez
Production Artist	Lisa Pahl

CONTRIBUTING EDITORS

Jeff Timm	Bruce Wiebe

CONTRIBUTING ART DIRECTORS

Kristi Anderson	David Simpson
Evangeline Ekberg	

PHOTOGRAPHERS

Mike Krivit, Krivit Photography
Shawn Nielsen, Nielsen Photography
Ramon Moreno
Tate Carlson
Bill Zuehlke

ILLUSTRATORS

Steve Björkman	John Hartman
Gabe De Matteis	Bruce Kieffer
Roy Doty	Don Mannes
Mario Ferro	Frank Rohrbach III

OTHER CONSULTANTS

Charles Avoles, plumbing
Al Hildenbrand, electrical
Kathryn Hillbrand, interior design
Jon Jensen, carpentry
Bob Lacivita, automotive
Dave MacDonald, structural engineer
Mary Jane Pappas, kitchen and bath design
Ron Pearson, environmental issues
Tom Schultz, drywall
Costas Stavrou, appliance repair
John Williamson, electrical
Butch Zang, painting and wallpapering
Ron Zeien, appliance repair
Les Zell, plumbing